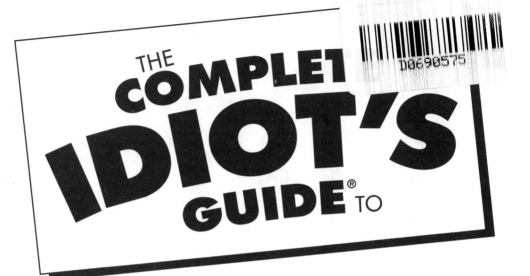

THE
COMPLETE
IDIOT'S
GUIDE® TO

Java 2

by Michael Morrison

A Division of Macmillan Computer Publishing
201 W. 103rd Street, Indianapolis, IN 46290

Trademarks

Warning and Disclaimer

Executive Editor
Tim Ryan

Development Editor
Melanie Palaisa

Managing Editor
Patrick Kanouse

Project Editors
Carol Bowers
Rebecca Mounts

Copy Editor
Molly Schaller

Indexer
Heather Goens

Proofreaders
Kim Cofer
Gene Redding

Technical Editor
Billy Barrons

Interior Design
Nathan Clement

Cover Design
Michael Freeland

Layout Technicians
Tim Osborn
Staci Somers
Mark Walchle

Contents at a Glance

Contents

About the Author

Michael Morrison is a skateboarder, cyclist, toy inventor, and the author of a variety of Java-related books including *Java 1.1 Unleashed* (Sams), *Presenting JavaBeans* (Sams), and *Sams Teach Yourself Internet Game Programming with Java in 21 Days* (Sams). When not glued to his computer, risking life and limb on his skateboard, or watching movies with his wife, Mahsheed, Michael enjoys hanging out by his koi pond and having stimulating conversations with his fish.

Dedication

To my brother Steve, the undisputed king of trashcan bicycle jumping, who taught me at an early age how much fun being a daredevil can be.

Acknowledgments

Thanks to Chris Van Buren at Waterside Productions, who has been a valuable source of guidance, not to mention opening the doors for many new opportunities. Also thanks to everyone at Que, especially Tim Ryan, for their patience and desire to make this an informative, yet entertaining book. Finally, I would like to thank my wife, Mahsheed, for being such a bright spot in my life.

Tell Us What You Think!

As the reader of this book, *you* are our most important critic and commentator. We value your opinion and want to know what we're doing right, what we could do better, what areas you'd like to see us publish in, and any other words of wisdom you're willing to pass our way.

As the Executive Editor for the Java team at Macmillan Computer Publishing, I welcome your comments. You can fax, email, or write me directly to let me know what you did or didn't like about this book—as well as what we can do to make our books stronger.

Please note that unfortunately I won't have time to help you with your Java projects, and that due to the high volume of mail I receive, I might not be able to reply to every message.

When you write, please be sure to include this book's title and author as well as your name and phone or fax number. I will carefully review your comments and share them with the author and editors who worked on the book.

Fax: 317-581-4663

Email: consumer@mcp.com

Mail: Greg Wiegand, Associate Publisher
          Macmillan Computer Publishing
          201 West 103rd Street
          Indianapolis, IN 46290 USA

Introduction

Fire, the inclined plane, the wheel, the transistor, the solar-powered nose hair clipper. These things are all discoveries and inventions that we, in our modern age, couldn't make it through the day without. Java should be added to the list somewhere between the transistor and the nose hair clipper. Well, maybe I'm getting a little ahead of myself. Java isn't exactly something we can't make it through the day with-out...yet.

Java is perhaps the most exciting computer technology to hit the street since the Internet, and it will no doubt play a role in the future of the online world—and more than likely, the world beyond computers. You see, Java isn't just a programming language coveted by techie insiders and gearhead computer book authors like myself. Java is a technology slated to touch our lives in ways you might not expect. How many times have you dreamed of being able to program your vacuum so that it could communicate with your electric blanket? Java will make this kind of communication commonplace.

All jokes aside, Java really is being integrated into a surprising number of devices that you don't typically associate with traditional programming languages. For example, cellular phones, video games, and hand-held computers are already being designed with Java in mind. That sounds great, but you were probably thinking more about Java's relationship to the Web when you picked up this book. Not a problem!

It's no surprise that Java's initial impact on the computing world was through the Web. Java is in fact still the primary technology used to add interactivity to Web pages. Consequently, the main focus of this book is on exploring different ways you can use Java to add excitement to your own Web pages.

To help reinforce the Java skills you learn throughout the book, I lead you through the development of a variety of different Java applets that you can use in your own Web page. These applets are available for download from the Macmillan Computer Publishing Web site at http://www.mcp.com/info. To navigate to the applets, click the link called **Downloadable Code, Examples, and Info for book "Companion Sites."** In the space provided under the Book Information section, enter **0-7897-1804-9**, which is the 10-digit ISBN for this book. Then click the **Search** button and you're there!

Why Do You Need This Book?

With literally hundreds of Java books to choose from, what possible reason could I give you for needing this book? Well, as if my cute analogies and pithy insights aren't enough, this book teaches you Java under the assumption that you are ready to put Java to use. In other words, if you're looking for an academic treatise on the philoso-phy of Java as it relates to third-world economics, you've come to the wrong place.

However, if you want to learn the fundamentals of the Java technology, along with how to build some applied examples that you can use in your own Web pages, then by all means read on!

All you really need to follow along in this book is a Ph.D. in mathematics, ten years of experience programming embedded space shuttle hardware, and a correspondence degree in TV/VCR repair. Just kidding. You really only need some experience with the Web and a desire to be creative and learn new things. It wouldn't hurt to know a little HTML and maybe have even tinkered a little with programming, but that's not essential.

How Do I Use This Book?

Although I won't stop you from reading this book on a family vacation, I'm not responsible for the glares you'll receive from family members. Actually, I encourage you to read the book with a computer nearby so that you can follow along with the programming examples. You don't necessarily have to type in all the code, but it is important to build and test the example programs if you really want to gain experience with Java. I also encourage you to try to read the book sequentially—that is, from front to back, in order. Most of the material builds on earlier material, so you might get into trouble if you jump around too much.

If you should forget an earlier topic or somehow get stuck, use the Table of Contents or the Index to find more information. You should be able to refer back to a section of the book for a quick refresher. Also, if you get confused about a term I'm using, feel free to refer to the "Speak Like a Geek" Glossary, which has definitions for all of the latest hip Java lingo. I always define new terms the first time I mention them, so you'll hopefully only need the Glossary as a refresher.

Also sprinkled throughout the book are special boxed notes that will help you learn more about Java and Java-related concepts:

These boxes contain helpful hints and supplemental information about a given Java topic.

These boxes contain technical information that provides a little more depth to a given Java topic.

Part 1

Getting a Handle on the Java Craze

So the hype finally got the best of your curiosity and you're ready to explore this exciting technology called Java! You don't understand exactly what it is, but based on what you've heard, you have a feeling it will make you a better person. Okay, so I'm exaggerating a little, but you have to admit Java has seen its fair share of limelight in the past couple of years.

Even if you decide that Java won't make you smarter, more attractive, or able to dunk a basketball, I think you'll agree that it is changing the way software is developed and used. Perhaps more importantly to you, Java serves as a great way to bring interactivity to your Web pages. Let's explore how Java makes this happen.

Chapter 1

What's the Buzz?

In This Chapter

➤ The Origins of Java

➤ How Java Changed the Web

➤ Java Can Make a Programmer Out of Anyone (Almost)

➤ Java and the Next Millennium

What *Is* Java?

Unless you've been living under a rock for the last two or three years, you've no doubt at least heard of Java. Even if you have lived under a rock, you probably are familiar with one of the non-nerd uses of the term Java. Fortunately, this book doesn't care if you are a rock dweller or not, or whether your notion of Java involves coffee or an Indonesian island.

Java is a programming language used to write programs called applets that can be run from within Web pages. Java programs can also be designed as standalone applications, in which case they run on their own, independent of Web pages. Much of the excitement surrounding Java stems from the fact that it is platform-independent, which means that a Java program can be run on just about any computer. Java promises a future where Macintosh users no longer have to lament over the tiny shelf devoted to Mac software versus the rest of the store devoted to Windows. It's a good thing too, because the Web doesn't particularly care about what kind of computer or operating system you are using.

Once Upon a Time on an Indonesian Island Far, Far Away

The origin of Java the programming language is rich with excitement and adventure. Legend has it that a team of Sun Microsystems engineers were on an expedition deep in the jungles of the Indonesian island of Java when one of them spilled a cup of hot coffee on his lap. The coffee left a stain on his shorts in the shape of a curly bracket "{", and the Java programming language was born. And if you believe any of that, email me for some exciting new cash-based investment opportunities. Seriously, Java's history is not terribly glamorous, but it is interesting because Java originally had nothing to do with the Web or the Internet.

Java started out as a project for studying how to put computers into everyday household items. It's not entirely clear what the benefits of a computerized garlic press would be, but the Sun engineers pressed on undaunted. A big part of this project, code named Green, was to have these computerized devices communicate with each other. Like humans, electronic devices require a language to communicate with each other—in this case, a programming language that would later shake up the online world. The original programming language was named Oak, after a tree that could be seen from the window of a prominent Sun engineer; this engineer, James Gosling, actually designed the Oak programming language.

To make a long story slightly shorter, the Oak programming language never made it to market as the standard programming language for toasters and alarm clocks. In fact, this market is still largely wide open, although no one appears to really be too concerned about having a programmable toaster.

More Java Puns Than You Can Twirl a Trackball At

The name Java provides all kinds of possibilities for cute technology puns, such as JavaBeans, which is in fact a very important technology based on Java. There is also a Java development environment named Café, another one named Roaster, and a Java tool named Mocha. The list goes on and on, but I'll spare you.

But, at about the same time that the Oak/Green project was coming to a screeching halt, the Web phenomenon hit, and the face of computing changed forever. Sun thought about their technology and realized that computers connected to the Web really aren't much different than a network of toasters, so they spun Oak into the programming language for the Web. Their marketing department decided that Java was a much cooler name than Oak. Besides that, Oak was already a registered trademark, which would make it pretty tough for Sun to promote and market its new technology.

The Best Friend the Web Ever Had

Our story left off with Java becoming the "programming language for the Web." Although no organized body (except maybe Sun) has ever endorsed such a phrase, the statement is true for all practical purposes. Let's examine why.

In its original incarnation, the Web was a big bunch of documents, or pages that pointed to each other. Imagine going into a library and seeing every book tied with pieces of string to other books. When you encounter a piece of string while reading one book, you could follow the string and find another book with (hopefully) a related piece of information. The strings serve as links that logically connect the books together. This is roughly how the Web works. The problem is that books are static, meaning that nothing in them changes. More importantly, books don't allow interaction with the reader, and neither did early Web pages. Enter Java.

Early Web pioneers realized that computers aren't static machines, and therefore Web pages shouldn't be either. Why turn a computer into an electronic librarian when it is capable of doing so much more? Java happened to be in the right place at the right time. Java offered a relatively easy-to-understand programming language that could be used on any computer. Furthermore, due to its origins in small appliances, Java was designed to be extremely efficient. It didn't take long for Netscape Communications Corporation to realize the potential of Java and support an early version of it in their immensely popular Netscape Navigator Web browser. Now it was possible to have Web pages with full-blown programs embedded right there within the static text and images. Incidentally, the Netscape Navigator Web browser eventually evolved into Netscape Communicator, as it is now known.

A Beastly Approach to Interactivity

Technically, there were interactive Web pages prior to Java, but they required special programs that had to be installed on Web servers. That in and of itself is not a problem because many server-side applications are still in use today. However, early interactive Web pages were forced to push client-side processing onto server programs. For example, the processing involved with image maps was carried out on the server. This type of task, which is closely associated with user input, should be carried out in the client Web browser. There was no standard means of injecting client-side interactivity into Web pages until Java came along.

What's the big deal with having programs embedded in Web pages? Well, for one thing, you can develop fully interactive Web pages where the user interacts with the page and manipulates information dynamically. For example, you could use a Java applet to customize and buy a new car. You could pick and choose the components via a Java applet and then have the car assembled and priced out on a Web page. This is such a good idea that Saab has just such a Java applet, as shown in the following figure.

Java and HTML: Different Solutions to Different Problems

A question I hear a lot is how does Java relate to HTML? A lot of people new to Java mistake it for some kind of replacement for HTML. Java and HTML actually work together to solve two different problems. HTML, which stands for Hypertext Markup Language, is used to determine the physical layout of a Web page much like a document in a word processor determines the layout of your camp letters home to mom. Java, on the other hand, is used to develop programs (applets) that run within Web pages. You use HTML to place a Java applet within a Web page, but the applet runs because of Java. In this way, HTML and Java work hand in hand to provide the structure and dynamics of modern Web pages.

So, if you wanted to create a Web-based version of the not-so-popular Hunt the Wumpus game, you would use HTML to layout the Web page, including a title image, instructional text, and a reference to the Java applet. The Java applet would be the game itself, which is programmed in Java and then referenced via HTML from the Web page.

Another usage of Java applets I find interesting is that of news and information tickers. The Web is a place rife with up-to-the-minute information, and there's no reason why you shouldn't have it delivered directly to your monitor. Instead of having someone update a Web page every minute, why not just have a Java applet crank out news items non-stop? As you might have guessed, this has already been done as well. The next figure shows the Quantum Banner by Quantum Leap Communications, which maintains a constant stream of MSNBC news headlines. Clicking a headline takes you straight to the complete story. "Information at your fingertips" is starting to make much more sense!

To close the sale and convince you that Java can make Web pages do things previously unimaginable, take a look at the figure that follows.

The figure shows a chat taking place in ChatPoint, a very innovative Java applet that enables users to chat with each other within the context of a Web page. You enter your name, decide what you want to look like, and then choose a location; in this case the location is a train station. Your friends, who can be physically located anywhere, simply login the same way and begin chatting with you. Granted, there is no audio and you have to type your conversation in on the keyboard, but this approach sure is more cost effective than long distance telephone calls!

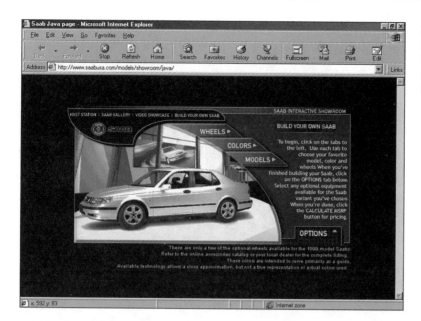

Saab's Interactive Showroom Web site, which makes use of a car customization Java applet.

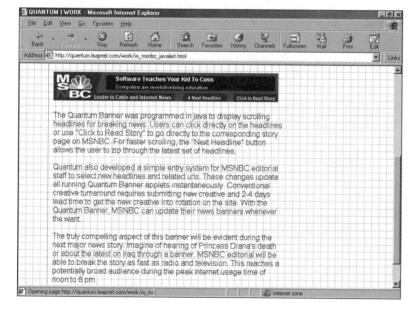

Quantum Leap Communications' Quantum Banner, which uses a Java applet to display up-to-the-minute MSNBC news headlines.

ChatPoint's Web site, which uses a Java applet as the basis for a cartoon chat room.

Java: A Programmer's Kwan

In the movie *Jerry Maguire*, the football player character played by Cuba Gooding, Jr., Rod Tidwell, referred to the complete package he needed as "the kwan." To him "the kwan" meant the love, respect, community, and money that goes along with being a sports superstar. Although I can't promise any of these things will come to you by simply reading this book, I will argue that Java is a programmer's kwan of sorts. Seriously, more so than any other programming language to date, Java makes the bridge from human concept to computer reality much easier and with a lower learning curve. Let's quickly examine why this is so.

Before the era of modern programming languages, programmers had to fiddle with bits inside a computer to make the computer do anything useful. Trust me, I'm using the term "useful" pretty loosely here. It wasn't until the advent of modern programming languages such as BASIC, Fortran, Pascal, and C that we really started seeing some interesting things happen with computers because it was much easier for a human programmer to think in terms of "begin" and "end" as opposed to 01101001 and 11010011.

Similar to the languages mentioned above, Java enables programmers to think in very human terms to create programs that run on computers—which happen to "think" much differently than people. Java also frees programmers from having to worry about the specific types of computers on which their programs might later be run; with Java, it simply doesn't matter.

Another major benefit Java offers programmers is an extensive class library. A class library is a big bunch of Java code that performs useful operations such as accessing networks, compressing files, and providing slick looking buttons and user interface gadgets. Practically every programming language prior to Java required a third-party add-on to attain the functionality built in to Java. I could go on and on, but I think you are starting to get the picture. Java has lots to offer programmers, even if it doesn't quite measure up to Rod Tidwell's kwan.

Platform Independence

Just in case this seems like a minor benefit, think again! No programming language has ever truly made cross-platform computing a reality. Java still hasn't reached perfection in this regard, but it is well on its way.

Into the Future with Secret Java Decoder Rings

Okay, you understand where Java came from and how it changed the Web, and you even endured a random movie reference while I chattered on about the benefits of Java. But the question you really want to know is where is Java headed? I mean, you'd hate to waste your time learning Java only to have it replaced in a couple of years by Fiji, the hot new programming language from Microsoft. To quell your fears, let me run through some of the interesting areas that Java is headed into so you'll have the confidence to continue onward through the book. Incidentally, Microsoft has no programming language in the works called Fiji as far as I know, but it sure sounds scandalous doesn't it?

Java owes a great debt to the Web, because Java would probably have never attained fame and fortune without it. However, now that the Web has made Java part of pop culture, the time has come for Java to expand elsewhere. Not surprisingly, the "programming language for the Web" is now very rapidly becoming "the programming language, period." Seriously, Java is aiming for no less than a complete takeover of Pascal, Basic, and more importantly C and C++. If you aren't too familiar with any of these programming languages, just think of it as some hot new building product replacing stone, brick, and plywood. It's that sweeping, trust me.

If that analogy sounds a little far-fetched, then consider the fact that practically every vendor of software development tools has felt compelled to rush a Java product to market. Development tools, albeit part of the ever-changing world of software, aren't traditionally very fickle in terms of new technologies. A whole-hearted embrace of Java by the development tool community is a sure sign of Java becoming a long-term fixture in the programming landscape.

What does this mean to you? Well, for one thing it means having more job opportunities as more companies search for employees with Java experience. It also means that you'll have a chance to be a part of carving out the future of software as we know it. Honestly, I'm not getting melodramatic here—we are living in an era in which software development technology is evolving as fast as the software it is used to create. I strongly feel that Java is a significant milestone in the evolution of software development technologies.

You might be surprised to learn that Java is coming full circle by heading back to its roots. That's right, we might end up seeing Java-powered toasters after all. Sun has expanded the focus of Java beyond traditional computer applications to include appliances and hand-held electronic devices. Expect to see Java popping up in digital phones, mobile hand-held computers, Web television boxes, and possibly even appliances such as dishwashers.

As an example of how far out Java applications might become, consider this example of a real Java device that was introduced at the 1998 JavaOne Conference in San Francisco. All conference attendees received a Java Ring, which is a ring worn on your finger with a microchip embedded as a sort of jewel. The microchip ran a Java applet that allowed attendees to enter information about their favorite kind of coffee. Upon snapping the ring into a special coffee maker, personalized coffee was served. Now that's what I call innovative technology! Maybe knuckle-top computing will be the rage of the future. Only time will tell.

The Least You Need to Know

Well, you didn't really get your feet wet using Java just yet, but you did learn some interesting things about Java. More specifically, you learned:

➤ How Java began as an experimental project that almost died.

➤ How Java permanently changed the perception and usefulness of the Web.

➤ Java and HTML work together to make the Web a loving, more interactive place for us all.

➤ Java really has nothing to do with the movie *Jerry Maguire*, but I nonetheless tried to relate the two.

➤ Java is still in the process of realizing its full potential.

Java: The Web's Darling

Making the Java-HTML Connection

Although I touched on it in the preceding chapter, I want to take a moment to clarify the relationship between Java and HTML because it is critical to understanding how Java applets work. If you are already an HTML wizard, then please bear with me for a moment while I establish some HTML ground rules.

HTML stands for Hypertext Markup Language and is essentially a language used to define the layout and structure of Web pages. HTML is not a programming language because it isn't possible to write HTML programs. Instead you create pages, which are documents much like you would create in a word processor or desktop publishing program. In the case of HTML, however, the documents are intended for the Web instead of print. HTML documents certainly can be printed, but they typically aren't designed with printing in mind.

HTML documents are stored as simple text files with an .html or .htm file extension. You can open them up in any text editor, which has traditionally been a good way to learn the intricacies of HTML because you can easily study the usage of HTML in existing Web pages. As an example, try visiting a Web page and selecting the **View Source** command in your Web browser. This command is usually found under the **View** menu. The following figure shows the Frequently Asked Questions (FAQ) page of an urban folklore Web site, which has lots of interesting information. I highly recommend perusing this site if you need a breather from this book.

The alt.folklore.urban *newsgroup's Urban Folklore Web site's Frequently Asked Questions (FAQ) page.*

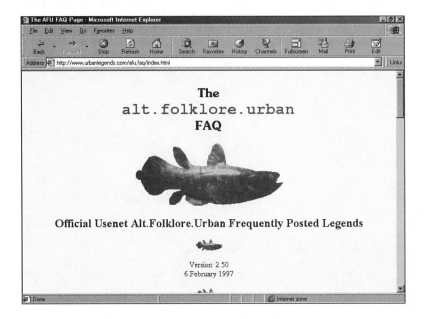

Selecting the **View Source** command from your Web browser results in a text editor opening and displaying the HTML source code that defines the Web page, as shown in the next figure.

You should be able to quickly study the HTML source code displayed for a Web page and understand exactly what is going on in the page. Just kidding. HTML can actually get pretty messy, as you can no doubt tell from the figure. My intention isn't to intimidate you by showing you a big scary HTML document. Actually, the point I'm trying to make is that all Web pages ultimately boil down to HTML text documents that define the layout and structure of the pages.

Unlike HTML documents, Java applets are stored in binary form and therefore cannot be viewed as text. This is because Java applets are compiled, which means that a text Java source code file is run through a special program that translates it into instructions understood only by the Web browser. This special program is called a Java compiler, and is required to create any Java program, including Java applets. When a Web page references a Java applet, it actually references the compiled executable Java program, which is stored in a file with a .class file extension. You can see how a Java applet's .class file fits into a typical Web page in the following figure.

```
index.html - Notepad
File  Edit  Search  Help
<HTML>

<HEAD>
<TITLE>The AFU FAQ Page</TITLE>
<base href=http://www.urbanlegends.com/afu.faq/>
</HEAD>

<BODY
  bgcolor="#fffdfa"
  text="#000000"
  link="#d00000"
  vlink="#0000d0"
  alink="#00ff00"
>

<img vspace=10 src="img/dot_clear.gif" alt=""><br>

<div align="center">
<center> <!-- for those still using Netscape 1.1 -->
<a href="http://c.gp.cs.cmu.edu:5103/prog/webster?the">
  <img
  align="bottom" src="img/the-t.gif" height=22 width=44 alt="The " border=0></a><br>

<img vspace=5 src="img/dot_clear.gif" alt=""><br>
<a href="news:alt.folklore.urban">
  <img width=357 height=24 align="bottom" src="img/afu-t.gif" alt="alt.folklore.urban"
  border=0></a><br>

<img vspace=5 src="img/dot_clear.gif" alt=""><br>

<a href="http://curia.ucc.ie/cgi-bin/acronym?FAQ">
  <img width=53 height=22 align="bottom" src="img/faq-t.gif" alt=" FAQ" border=0></a><br>

<img vspace="10" src="img/dot_clear.gif" alt=""><br>

<a
href="http://www.Sun.COM/smi/ssoftpress/books/vanderLinden/vanderLinden.html"
```

The HTML source code for the Urban Folklore Web site's Frequently Asked Questions (FAQ) page.

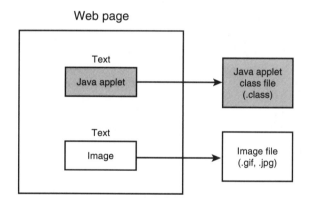

A Java applet's .class file referenced from a Web page.

Notice in the figure that both Java applets and images are referenced as external files. This is necessary because Java applets and images are stored as binary files, and therefore aren't suited to be included directly into a text HTML file. I think it's safe to say now that the dead horse relating Java and HTML has been successfully beaten! Let's move on.

Just Enough HTML to Get You into Trouble

Before you learn how to incorporate Java applets into Web pages, it's necessary to understand a few things about the structure of Web pages in general. As you just learned, Web pages consist of HTML code stored in a text file with an .html or .htm

15

A Glimpse at Java's Underpinnings

Java programs are stored in files with a .class file extension because Java programs are comprised of classes. Ah, but what is a class? A class is an object-oriented programming construct that attempts to make the modeling of real world objects in software much more intuitive. At the risk of jumping way too far ahead of the current discussion, allow me to provide a quick example. Let's say you are creating a Java shoot'em-up space game applet that is going to appear in your Web arcade. Your game would no doubt involve aliens, space ships, and lasers; no self-respecting space shoot'em-up would dare miss out on these elements! Anyway, you would create a Java class to model the data and behaviors associated with each of these objects; hence the term "object-oriented programming." Granted, aliens and space ships aren't the best examples of "real world" objects, but you get the idea. Classes and objects rear their ugly heads in much more detail in Chapter 5, "Let's Try and Be Objective."

file extension. That's fine, but how does HTML code actually define a Web page? I was just about to get to that.

Bare Bones HTML

The HTML language is comprised of tags, which are used to identify different parts of HTML documents, along with specifying formatting attributes for text, images, and so on. All HTML tags are enclosed in angle brackets <> and typically come in pairs. For example, text is made bold by enclosing it within the <B> and </B> tags, like so:

```
<B>This is a very bold statement!</B>
```

Following is somewhat of a skeletal HTML page, which demonstrates some of the most commonly used tags:

```
<HTML>
<HEAD>
<TITLE>Skeletal HTML</TITLE>
</HEAD>
<BODY>
<H1>This is a large heading.</H1>
This is a paragraph of text. This is another
sentence in the paragraph. This sentence has a
word in <I>italics</I> and a word in
<B>bold</B>.
<H2>This is a smaller heading.</H2>
</BODY>
</HTML>
```

The next figure shows the preceding HTML document as viewed in a Web browser.

As you can see in the figure, the HTML tags used in the document do not appear on the Web page. This confirms the fact that they are used solely as a means of defining page attributes. You might notice that the text "Skeletal HTML" doesn't appear on the Web page. That's because the title of a page, as denoted by the <TITLE> and </TITLE> tags, appears instead in the title bar of the Web browser. Closer inspection of the Web browser title bar in the figure reveals this to be true.

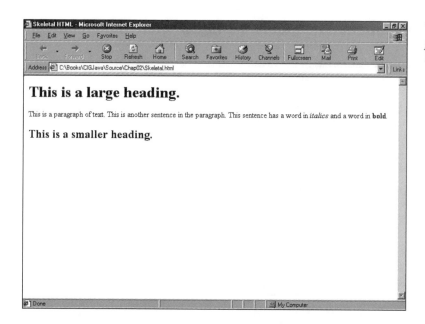

The <H1> and </H1> tags are used to identify headings. This touches on an important point: HTML is a little more generic than a full-blown word processor document, for example. In HTML you typically aren't allowed to use specific fonts or point sizes because Web pages are viewed on such a wide range of computers. Instead, you describe a general font style using HTML tags such as <H1> and </H1>. Smaller headings are identified with smaller numbers, resulting in tags such as <H2>, <H3>, and so on.

HTML Imagery

Placing images in an HTML document is pretty straightforward—you just use a special tag. More specifically, you use the <IMG> tag, which requires an image filename specified in the SRC attribute:

```
<IMG SRC="Skate.jpg" ALT="Skateboarding picture">
```

This line of HTML code indicates that an image stored in the file Skate.jpg is to be displayed. However, if for some reason the image can't be displayed, the ALT attribute identifies text that is displayed instead, which in this case is the phrase "Skateboarding picture." The following table lists the attributes supported by the <IMG> tag.

Table 2.1 Attributes That Can Be Used with the `<IMG>` Tag

Attribute	Purpose
SRC	Identifies the image filename for the image
ALT	Identifies text to be displayed if the browser can't display the image
ALIGN	Aligns the image with the text it appears next to (TOP, MIDDLE, or BOTTOM)
WIDTH	Sets the horizontal image dimension
HEIGHT	Sets the vertical image dimension
HSPACE	Adds extra space to the left and right of the image
VSPACE	Adds extra space to the top and bottom of the image
BORDER	Sets the width of the border surrounding the image (0 results in no border)

The following example demonstrates how to include an image in an HTML document:

```
<HTML>
<HEAD>
<TITLE>Skateboarding Image Example</TITLE>
</HEAD>
<BODY>
<H1>Skateboarding Picture</H1>
<HR>
<IMG SRC="Skate.jpg" ALT="Skateboarding picture" BORDER=2
➥ALIGN=MIDDLE>
To the left is a picture of a frontside invert, which is also known as
➥a handplant.
</BODY>
</HTML>
```

Nothing shocking here, except to note that the image border is set to 2 and the image is set to align with the middle of the line of text next to it. The following figure shows the somewhat predictable results.

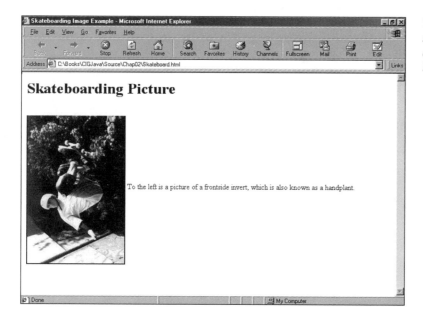

The Skateboarding Image sample HTML Web page as viewed in a Web browser.

Linking the World

A whirlwind tour of HTML wouldn't be complete without learning how to link Web pages together. Geez, without hyperlinks none of this stuff would really matter too much because the Web wouldn't be a web! Hyperlinks are established using the <A> and </A> tags. The only requirement for a link, or anchor as they are sometimes called, is the address of the Web site to which you are linking. This address is identified in the HREF attribute of the <A> tag. Keep in mind that links involve text, meaning that a word or phrase is always associated with a link. For example, the following snippet of HTML code provides a link to the ever-popular Yahoo search engine:

```
<P>
To search the Web for a given topic, click <A
HREF=http://www.yahoo.com><B>here</B></A>.
</P>
```

In this example, the word "here" serves as a link to the Yahoo Web site at http://www.yahoo.com; when the word is clicked, the Web browser will navigate to the Yahoo Web site. The word is made bold using the <B> and </B> tags to make it a little more obvious. However, keep in mind that linked words and phrases are typically colored and underlined automatically to distinguish them from the rest of the text on a page. One other thing worth noticing in this example is the usage of the <P> and </P> tags, which are used to delimit paragraphs of text.

Just in case you think text hyperlinks are a little too boring, HTML allows you to use images as links. All you have to do is insert an `<IMG>` tag in place of the text that typically is sandwiched between the `<A>` and `</A>` anchor tags. The following example demonstrates:

```
<HTML>
<HEAD>
<TITLE>Skateboarding Image Example 2</TITLE>
</HEAD>
<BODY>
<H1>Skateboarding Picture</H1>
<HR>
<A HREF="http://www.skateboarding.com"><IMG SRC="Skate.jpg"
ALT="Skateboarding picture" BORDER=2></A>
<P>
Above is a picture of a frontside invert, which is a skateboarding
trick of the handplant variety. Click on the image to navigate to an
interesting skateboarding Web site, or just click <A
HREF="http://www.skateboarding.com">here</A>.
</P>
</BODY>
</HTML>
```

This sample page uses an image link and a text link to provide alternate links to a Web site. The `<P>` and `</P>` paragraph tags are also used to move the paragraph of text below the image.

Making a Space for Applets

I know you could have sworn this book was supposed to be about Java, but trust me, the HTML stuff is about to come full circle. Unfortunately, you simply can't be a Java applet programmer without having some understanding of HTML. The good news? You're now ready to officially learn how to embed Java applets in Web pages. And it all begins with the `<APPLET>` tag. Not surprisingly, the `<APPLET>` tag denotes a Java applet in HTML.

The `<APPLET>` tag requires three attributes: `CODE`, `WIDTH`, and `HEIGHT`. The `CODE` attribute specifies the name of the Java applet's .class file. The `WIDTH` and `HEIGHT` attributes specify the horizontal and vertical dimensions of the applet on the Web page. Following is a simple example of how to use the `<APPLET>` tag:

```
<HTML>
<HEAD>
<TITLE>Clock Applet Example</TITLE>
</HEAD>
<BODY>
```

```
<H1>Clock Applet</H1>
<HR>
<APPLET CODE="Clock2.class" WIDTH=170 HEIGHT=150></APPLET>
<P>
Above is the Java Clock applet, which displays the current time and
date.
</P>
</BODY>
</HTML>
```

In this example, the compiled Java applet stored in the file Clock2.class is embedded in a region of the Web page that is 170×150 pixels in size. Changing this size might or might not change the display of the Java applet, depending on how the applet is designed. In the case of the Clock applet, it displays the same size clock regardless of how much room you allow for it on the page. In the next figure, you see the Clock applet example at work as it would look on the Web.

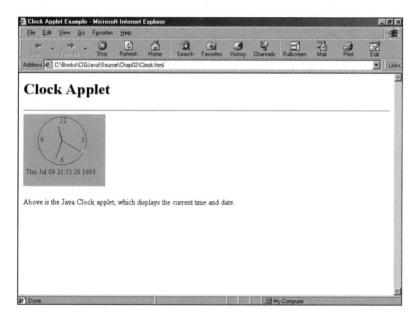

The Clock applet sample HTML Web page as viewed in a Web browser.

The <APPLET> tag supports some additional attributes beyond the three (CODE, WIDTH, and HEIGHT) that you've learned about thus far. The following table lists these attributes and their meanings.

It's All Just a Bunch of Pixels

The width and height of a Java applet referred to in the <APPLET> tag is specified in screen pixels, which are tiny rectangular blocks on the screen. Everything you see on a computer screen is actually just a bunch of pixels of varying colors that are arranged next to each other. You've no doubt heard people talk about the resolution of computer monitors. The resolution simply refers to the number of pixels currently being displayed. So, a monitor running at 800×600 resolution is actually displaying 800 pixels across and 600 pixels down, for a total of 480,000 pixels. Likewise, the standard resolution of 640×480 consists of 640 pixels across and 480 pixels down, for a total of 307,200 pixels.

Table 2.2   Attributes That Can Be Used with the <APPLET> Tag

Attribute	Purpose
CODE	Identifies the Java applet class name for the applet
ALT	Identifies text to be displayed if the browser can't run the applet
ALIGN	Aligns the applet with the text it appears next to (TOP, MIDDLE, or BOTTOM)
WIDTH	Sets the horizontal applet dimension
HEIGHT	Sets the vertical applet dimension
HSPACE	Adds extra space to the left and right of the applet
VSPACE	Adds extra space to the top and bottom of the applet
BORDER	Sets the width of the border surrounding the applet (0 results in no border)

Hey, the stuff in the table looks awfully familiar! In fact, with the exception of the CODE attribute replacing the SRC attribute, the <APPLET> tag attributes are the same as the <IMG> tag attributes. This actually shouldn't come as too big of a surprise considering the fact that an applet appears to a Web page as not much more than an image that draws itself. This is admittedly a gross oversimplification of what an applet really is, but it has some validity when you look at an applet purely from the perspective of a Web page; applets and images both require a rectangular section of space on a page.

Some applets have properties that enable them to be customized when incorporated into a Web page. These applet properties are called parameters, and you assign them values when you embed an applet via the <APPLET> tag. Applet parameters are entirely applet-specific, meaning that the name and usage of parameters depend on the specific applet in question. Following is an example of embedding an applet named NervousText that has a property that enables you to specify a line of text to be displayed:

```
<APPLET CODE="NervousText.class" WIDTH=300 HEIGHT=50>
  <PARAM NAME=text VALUE="I sure am nervous."></APPLET>
```

As the example demonstrates, applet parameters are specified with the <PARAM> tag and require you to provide the name of the parameter and its value. The parameter name is assigned to the NAME attribute, and the value is assigned to the VALUE attribute. No tricks there! An applet is capable of having multiple parameters, in which case you would have an individual <PARAM> tag for each parameter. It's important that the <PARAM> tags appear between the <APPLET> and </APPLET> tags.

In the NervousText applet example, the applet parameter name is text, and its value is set to the text "I sure am nervous.". When the applet is run, it queries the Web page for this property value and then displays it accordingly (see the next figure).

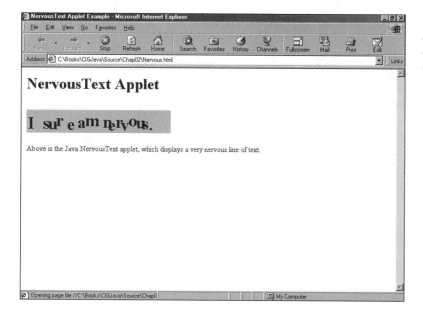

The NervousText applet sample HTML Web page as viewed in a Web browser.

Insecurity or Sensitive Applets?

Now that you have some practical knowledge and usage of Java applets under your belt, let's take a moment to address a very important subject, applet security. It doesn't take long for someone new to Java to realize that being able to run full-blown programs inside a Web page creates some potentially dangerous security scenarios. Acquiring and running software in a vastly networked environment like the Internet certainly could be dangerous. Could a misguided or downright malicious applet take your hard drive for a spin or corrupt memory and send your whole system down in flames? Fortunately, the answer to this question is a resounding no!

Of the many different aspects of Java that were thoroughly examined in its development stages, security had to be at the top of the list. For this reason, applets have an extremely stringent security code by which they live. It's pretty simple really: hands off! Under normal circumstances Java applets have absolutely no access to your hard

A Plethora of Applets to Get You Started

Both of the applets you just learned about, Clock and NervousText, are provided as sample applets with the Java Development Kit, or JDK. The JDK is the standard set of Java development tools freely available from Sun Microsystems. You learn much more about the JDK and how it is used to build applets in the next chapter. For now, however, you can think of it as a free source of ready-to-use Java applets you can incorporate into your own Web pages!

A Safe Place for Applets to Play

Sun has described the security restrictions imposed on Java applets as a "sandbox." Like a child playing in a real sandbox, a Java applet is considered secure so long as it doesn't venture outside of its virtual security sandbox. Unlike children, applets are completely relegated to staying within the confines of their sandbox, so there is no risk of them leaving and causing problems.

drive, for reading or writing. Applets also are limited in how they access networks; they may only request information from the computer from which they came, which is typically the Web server computer that is serving up the page containing the applet.

If that's not enough, consider the fact that every Java program is analyzed line by line before it is run to make sure there is nothing fishy about the program. This keeps hackers from developing malicious applets that do tricky things with memory, for example.

The Least You Need to Know

HTML isn't too much of a brain bender, but it still takes some getting used to. The good news is that it doesn't take much work to put applets to good use with HTML. In this chapter, you learned:

➤ HTML documents are stored as text files, but Java applets are stored as binary class files.

➤ Images and Java applets are referenced externally from a Web page; they reside in different files.

➤ The HTML language is comprised of tags, which are used to identify different parts of HTML documents.

➤ How to link Web pages together using text and images.

➤ How to embed applets in Web pages and supply them with custom parameters.

Tooling Around with Java

Tools for the Modern Nerd

Just as a carpenter or electrician requires a special set of tools suited to their trade, so does the Java programmer. In fact, Java programmers have many more options than carpenters or electricians when it comes to selecting their development tools. Fortunately, there is a standard suite of Java development tools that serves as a good starting point for new Java developers, and you're unlikely to hammer your thumb or shock yourself using them! I'm referring to the Java Development Kit, or JDK, which is freely distributed by Sun Microsystems, the maker of Java.

The JDK includes all of the tools, utilities, and related resources necessary to build Java applets and applications. As you might recall, Java applets run in Web pages, and Java applications run by themselves like traditional computer programs. Aside from being freely available, a really important aspect of the JDK is that it is the official standard development environment for Java. This means that Java programs developed with the JDK are guaranteed to be compliant with the version of Java supported by the JDK. In practice, most third-party development environments are really reliable in terms of maintaining Java compliance, but using the JDK is guaranteed to produce compliant Java programs.

Are You Java Compliant?

When I refer to Java compliance, I'm basically talking about programs conforming to the Java standards set forth by Sun Microsystems. If you use the JDK to build your Java programs, they are guaranteed to be Java compliant. In general, it is also safe to use third-party development environments as long as they are certified as being 100% Java compliant. This is usually prominently displayed on the packaging, so there isn't too much mystery in determining if a development tool is safe to use. The primary reason compliance is such an important issue is because Java is constantly changing, which means development tools must keep pace and correctly support new features and enhancements.

Another more obvious consideration regarding Java compliance is the computing platform you are using to develop Java programs. Currently, the JDK is only available for Windows and UNIX. However, there are third-party Java development tools for other platforms such as Apple Macintosh; Roaster Technologies' Roaster and Metrowerks CodeWarrior come to mind.

Before you get started learning about the JDK, it's important for you to have the latest version. Java and the JDK are constantly changing with enhancements, bug fixes, and other updates, so make sure you take the time to get the latest version. The JDK is freely available from Sun's Java Web site at http://java.sun.com (see the next figure). This Web site contains late-breaking news and information about Java, along with the latest release of the JDK and a wealth of other Java resources. I can't stress enough how rapidly the Java technology is changing, so I encourage you to visit this site often to keep tabs on Java and where it is headed (see the following figure). For information about how to install the JDK, please refer to Appendix A, "Installing the Java Development Kit (JDK)."

The JDK consists of a variety of tools, utilities, and resources, but for now I'll focus on those that are most useful for creating Java applets and applications. Following is a list of the most important JDK components you will use as a beginning Java developer:

➤ The Java Compiler

➤ The Java AppletViewer

➤ The Java Runtime Interpreter

➤ Demo Java Applets

These tools and resources are covered in more detail throughout the rest of this chapter. It's important to know that all of the tools in the JDK are command-line tools, which means that you have to launch them from a command line such as a Windows MS-DOS prompt. This might seem like a hassle, but the JDK is designed to be a very simple, yet effective suite of tools. Consequently, Sun has avoided adding too many frills.

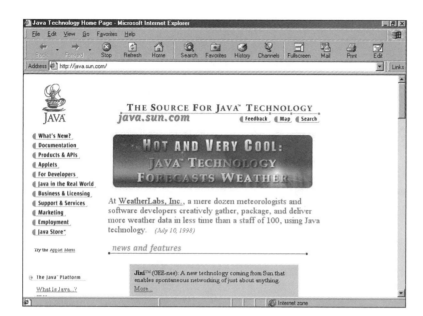

Sun's Java Web site.

The Java Compiler

The Java compiler is the tool used to compile Java source code into executable Java programs. This is by far the most important tool in the JDK because it is responsible for the actual creation of Java programs. Before I get into the details of the tool itself, let's take a moment to examine the compilation process.

A Java program begins as one or more source code files that are stored as normal, run-of-the-mill text files. In other words, you can open Java source code files in any text editor and view or edit the source code as text. If you are familiar with another programming language such as BASIC or Pascal, this probably doesn't come as too much of a shock. If not, then suffice it to say that as far as your computer is concerned, Java source code looks no different than an email message. The distinction between the two arises from how they are used. Email messages are sent through an email program to someone who reads them as text. Java source code is fed to the Java compiler, which reads the text and spits out executable program code (see the next figure).

Frilly Java Development Tools

Although the JDK is very functional, I'll admit that it is lacking when it comes to having the look and feel of modern development environments. You have to move over to third-party development tools for more advanced features like graphical source code editors and browsers. Appendix B, "Java Tools & Technologies," contains information about some of the more popular third-party Java development tools.

The Java compiler compiles Java source code into executable program code.

| Java Source Code (Text) | → | Java Compiler | → | Java Executable Program (Bytecode) |

The executable program code created by the Java compiler is called bytecode, which is something unique to Java. Compilers for most other programming languages generate native executable code, which is code that is created to run on a specific type of computer platform. As an example, if I compile a C program on my Windows computer, it will only run on other Windows computers. The Java compiler is very different in this regard because the bytecode it generates is generic, meaning that it can be executed on any platform that supports Java. This is a large part of the reason why Java programs often run slower than programs written in other programming languages, but it also explains why practically anyone can run Java applets on the Web.

The .class file extension

Java programs, whether they are applets or applications, always begin as source code files. A single program can, and often does, consist of multiple source code files. These files are compiled using the Java compiler, with the results stored in executable bytecode files with a .class file extension. If you recall from the preceding chapter, the .class file extension is a result of the fact that Java is an object–oriented programming language. You learn much more about this aspect of Java in Chapter 5, "Let's Try and Be Objective."

Taking the Java Compiler for a Spin

Getting back to the Java compiler, you'll be glad to know that it's very easy to use. The Java compiler, javac, is part of the JDK. If you don't yet have the JDK installed, please refer to Appendix A. Because the Java compiler is a command-line tool, there are command-line options you can set when compiling Java source code. These options aren't terribly important right now because you won't try anything tricky with the Java compiler just yet. You'll learn about the different options throughout the book, as their usage becomes necessary. For now, let's take the compiler for a spin without using any options.

Before you can use the Java compiler, you must obtain a command-line prompt. In Windows this is accomplished by starting an MS-DOS session. To do this, click the Start button, select the **Programs** menu, and then select **MS-DOS Prompt**. You will be presented with a window containing a command-line DOS prompt that can be used to enter commands such as running the Java compiler.

The file TicTacToe.java that ships with the JDK contains the source code for a demonstration Java applet that enables you to play Tic-Tac-Toe against the computer. To compile this source code file into an executable applet with the Java compiler, you would issue the following command at a command-line prompt:

```
javac TicTacToe.java
```

As you might have guessed, javac is the name of the Java compiler and TicTacToe.java is the source code file to be compiled. Upon issuing the preceding command, the file TicTacToe.class will be created, which is the executable applet class file that is suitable for being embedded in a Web page. The Web page TicTacToe.html contains the embedded applet, and must be opened in a Web browser in order to run the applet. This is accomplished by selecting **Open** from the **File** menu in your Web browser and navigating to the file. The following figure shows the TicTacToe applet running within a Web page.

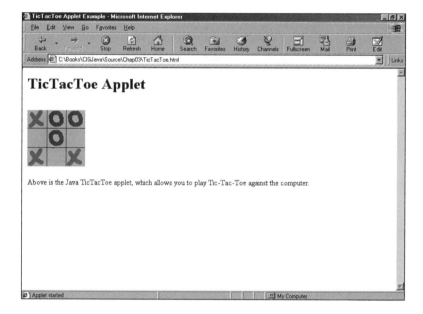

The TicTacToe Java applet running from within a Web page.

An Applet with a View

After you've compiled a Java applet, you no doubt want to test it and see it run. Although you could run it in a Web browser as we just did, there is another option; you can use the AppletViewer. The AppletViewer is like a pared down Web browser that just runs applets. This might not seem like a big deal because Web browsers these days fully support Java, but you have to consider the fact that Web browsers do a whole lot more than run Java programs. In other words, you are incurring a lot of unnecessary overhead by using a Web browser just to test an applet. Trust me, next to the Java compiler, the AppletViewer is the tool you will be using the most heavily as a Java applet developer.

Another major benefit of using the AppletViewer is that it is guaranteed to support the version of the JDK you are using. Again, this might not seem like a big deal, but you have to factor in the lag time between a Java feature appearing in the JDK and its

Finding the Book's Applet and Java Application Examples on the Web

To find the applets and Java application examples provided in this book, enter the address `http://www.mcp.com/info` in the location box. Click the link called **Downloadable Code, Examples, and Info for book "Companion Sites."** In the space provided under the Book Information section, enter **0-7897-1804-9**, which is the 10-digit ISBN for this book. Click the **Search** button.

Applets Galore

Like the applets you learned about in the preceding chapter, the TicTacToe applet is provided with the JDK as a demonstration applet. These demonstration applets come with complete source code so you can study them and learn how they work. Some of the applets can be put to good use in making Web pages more interesting. For example, there is an applet called Animator that animates a series of images and will even play a soundtrack to go along with the animation.

being incorporated into the major Web browsers. Sometimes this lag time is substantial, in which case you wouldn't have any way of testing an applet without the AppletViewer. This has happened to me numerous times, and I have always relied on the AppletViewer.

Okay, so I've convinced you that the Java AppletViewer is a good thing, but exactly how does it work? Well, because it effectively emulates the Java part of a Web browser, the AppletViewer expects you to provide it with a Web page that contains an embedded Java applet, which is designated by inserting the <APPLET> tag in the HTML source file for the Web page. The AppletViewer ignores everything but the <APPLET> tag and displays a window containing the executing applet. The applet appears in this window just as it would in a Web browser, excluding of course any HTML elements surrounding the applet.

Running the AppletViewer is a simple matter of executing a command at the command line and providing the appropriate Web page name. Following is an example of running the TicTacToe applet within the AppletViewer:

```
appletviewer TicTacToe.html
```

As you can see, the actual name of the AppletViewer program is `appletviewer`. The name of the Web page containing the TicTacToe applet, `TicTacToe.html`, is provided as the only argument to the AppletViewer. Similar to the Java compiler, the AppletViewer has options associated with it that affect the manner in which applets are executed. These options are rarely used, so I won't muddy the water with them right now. The following figure shows the TicTacToe applet running in the AppletViewer.

The figure clearly demonstrates the manner in which the AppletViewer simulates an applet running within a Web page. If you compare the applet running in the AppletViewer with the previous figure that shows it running in a Web browser, you'll see that there really is no difference between the two. That's the whole idea behind the AppletViewer, and is ultimately why it is so useful.

The TicTacToe Java applet running from within the Java AppletViewer.

Can I Get an Interpreter?

Although applets are certainly what caused the initial popularity of Java, they don't tell the whole Java story. Java is in fact gaining ground as a programming language useful for creating standalone applications. Java applications have no ties to a Web page or a Web browser, which is why they are referred to as "stand-alone" applications. There is a small hitch when it comes to running Java applications, however, which takes us back to the generic Java bytecode created by the Java compiler.

As you recall from earlier in this chapter, Java programs are actually created as generic byte-code. There is no magic behind this platform-independence, but it does require that each platform have a suitable Java interpreter.

The Bottom Line

The bottom line with the AppletViewer is that it provides a simple, efficient way to test Java applets. Of course, at some point you should always test your applets with a real Web browser just to be safe, but the AppletViewer often plays a vital role during the applet development cycle.

What's a Java interpreter? Well, a Java interpreter is a program responsible for translating Java bytecode into native code that can execute on a given platform. So, on a UNIX Solaris computer, for example, there is a Java interpreter that takes a byte-code Java program and translates each piece of bytecode into native code as it runs the program.

To make sure you get this interpreter stuff straight, let's pretend that you only speak Spanish and that you have a word processor that only understands Spanish. Let's also assume that someone has written you a letter in English, which for our purposes is considered a generic "standard" language. To read the English letter, your word processor would need an English interpreter. This interpreter would translate English words into Spanish words and present you with a Spanish letter that you can read. In this analogy, Spanish is equivalent to the native code of your computer and English is akin to generic Java bytecodes. The Java interpreter literally works like this human language interpreter because it takes Java bytecode and translates it into a form understood by different computing platforms, as shown in the figure that follows.

A Java interpreter translates executable Java bytecode into native code specific to a given computing platform.

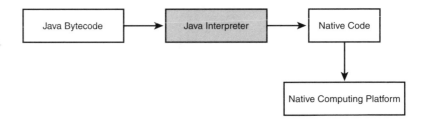

What this all boils down to is that you must have a Java interpreter to run a standalone Java application. I suppose that makes it not quite so "standalone," but you get the idea. Fortunately, the JDK comes standard with a Java interpreter that you can use to run Java applications. The Java interpreter is called java and is executed like this:

```
java Memory
```

In this example, the Java interpreter is executing the Java application named Memory, which is stored in the executable program file named Memory.class. This application reports how much free memory is available in the Java interpreter along with the amount of total memory to which the Java interpreter has access. Following are the results reported by the application when I ran it on my computer:

```
Free memory : 901KB
Total memory : 1023KB
```

Of course, the free memory and total memory reported by the Memory application will vary largely across different computers. But enough about memory, let's get back to the Java interpreter!

It's important to understand that the Java interpreter is very different from the Java AppletViewer in that it doesn't provide any graphical support such as a window for a program to execute within. Consequently, many Java applications don't utilize graphics in any way; instead, they rely on the standard text-based input and output provided by the command line. Java applications can certainly utilize graphics if they are designed to do so, but it requires a little more work on the programming end than creating an applet.

For the purposes of this book, you'll only use the Java interpreter to run command-line Java applications that illustrate a particular aspect of the Java language. All graphical programs will be developed as applets because you no doubt want to use Java primarily as a means of jazzing up Web pages.

The Least You Need to Know

As an aspiring Java developer, you now know something about the tools of the trade. The Java compiler, AppletViewer, and interpreter are the hammer, chisel, and saw of Java programming. Your ability to wield these tools will largely determine how fast

you progress as a Java programmer.
Fortunately, they are easy to master and much
safer to use than their carpentry counterparts.
In this chapter, you learned:

➤ The Java Development Kit (JDK) is the
standard development tool suite for Java.

➤ The Java compiler is used to compile Java
source code into executable Java bytecode.

➤ The Java AppletViewer is used to run
applets outside the context of a Web
browser.

➤ The Java interpreter is used to run standalone Java applications.

➤ The Java AppletViewer and Web browsers
contain a built-in Java interpreter.

Interpreted Applets?

Although I made a big distinction
between the Java AppletViewer and
Java interpreter, they both actually
perform very similar functions in
that they execute Java programs.
However, the Java interpreter stops
short at only interpreting Java bytecode. The AppletViewer goes a step
further by providing a graphical
framework for applets to run in.
You can think of the AppletViewer
as a special Java interpreter with
some extra stuff that is used to support the graphical requirements of
applets.

If the AppletViewer is a type of Java
interpreter, where does that put
Web browsers that are capable of
running applets? Like the
AppletViewer, Web browsers also
have Java interpreters built in to
them that are used to execute Java
applets. Web browsers are also
responsible for providing graphical
support to applets, just like the
AppletViewer. However, neither the
AppletViewer nor Java-supported
Web browsers are capable of running standalone Java applications.

Constructing Applets of Your Own

A Little GUI Never Hurt Anyone

Java applets are graphical programs, which means that they display information and allow you to interact with them through the use of graphics. As a comparison, the Memory application you ran in the preceding chapter is not graphical because it displayed information as text at a command-line prompt. Graphical Java applets can still display text, but they have the capability of using different font styles, font sizes, and other graphical text attributes.

Java applets are graphical because they make use of a graphical user interface. This is a fancy way of stating that you can use a mouse to point and click and interact with a program graphically. Or to state things more literally, a user interacts with a program by communicating through a graphical interface. A graphical user interface consists of the buttons, check boxes, scrollbars, and other gadgets that have become so prevalent in modern software applications. The term graphical user interface is often shortened to GUI, which is pronounced "gooey." Please try not to get sidetracked repeating this acronym over and over; it's happened to many an aspiring GUI programmer.

GUI's Aren't All Created Equal

Because Java applets are capable of running on a variety of different computing platforms, their graphical user interfaces function similarly across these platforms. Applet GUIs do function similarly across different platforms, but every different computing platform has its own native GUI that addresses the problems inherent in making a computing environment graphical. Because these native GUIs were all developed independently, there is some variance in specific GUI features.

Java has to average the GUI variances across platforms and provide a standard GUI, but the standard Java GUI can't directly support every nuance associated with the different native GUIs. For example, Macintosh computers don't have right mouse buttons, so the Mac GUI doesn't support right-click mouse operations. The Java GUI takes a generic approach and leaves out direct right mouse button support.

Java 2 includes an updated GUI that attempts to imitate the native GUI on the underlying computing platform. You learn more about this aspect of Java in Chapter 14, "Making a Great First Impression."

Other than just wanting to teach you a cool acronym, I presented the GUI discussion here because I want you to think about the consequences of a Java applet being entirely graphical. Any input you receive from the user must be obtained in a graphical manner. Likewise, all output displayed by the program must be graphical as well. If you regularly use a Windows, Macintosh, or UNIX operating system such as Solaris, you are no doubt already familiar with GUI applications. Fortunately, Java is chock-full of features to make it relatively easy to support GUI input and output in Java applets. Let's learn about some of them!

A Java API Primer

Unlike most other programming languages, Java comes standard with a wide range of features that enable you to do everything from playing a sound to encrypting an email message. Technically speaking, these features aren't part of the actual Java language, but instead are part of the standard Java API, or Application Programming Interface. An API is a group of support programs that are geared toward performing specific functions such as playing sounds and encrypting messages. By the way, unlike the acronym GUI, you pronounce API as the individual letters A-P-I.

The Java API is very large and is broken down into different functional parts called packages. The following table contains a list of some of the more important Java API packages, along with the types of features they support.

Table 4.1 Commonly Used Packages in the Java API

API Package	Supports
java.applet	General applet features
java.awt	Windowing and GUI features
java.io	Data input and output
java.lang	Core language features

API Package	Supports
java.math	Math routines
java.net	Networking
java.security	Security
java.text	Text handling features
java.util	Miscellaneous utility features

One of these packages is specifically devoted to providing features useful for creating applets. This package is named java.applet, and contains everything you need to create Java applets. The primary thing it contains is the Applet class, which is a class that serves as the basis for all applets. I know you aren't too familiar with classes at this point, so for now just think of them as blueprints for programs. The Applet class provides the general support features required for all applets. Applets that you create will rely on the Applet class to perform general applet functions; your own code will take on the chore of performing functions specific to your applet.

As an example, consider an applet named DateTime that displays the current date and time. The applet would determine the current date, format it appropriately, and draw it to the applet window as text. How does the applet know the size of the applet window? How does it create the applet window? The Applet class handles these types of lower level applet considerations. The DateTime applet therefore relies on the Applet class to create its applet window and size it according to the WIDTH and HEIGHT <APPLET> tag attributes. In object-oriented terminology, the DateTime class "derives" these features from the Applet class. You learn much more about object-oriented programming and how it affects Java in the next chapter.

Shaking the API Tree

The Java API is organized into a tree-like structure, which is evident by the names of the packages. For example, the java.awt package contains the sub-packages java.awt.datatransfer, java.awt.event, and java.awt.image.

All standard Java API package names begin with "java.", which makes them easily distinguishable from other user-created packages. For this reason, you aren't allowed to name your own package beginning with "java". You learn all about packages and how to create your own in Chapter 10, "Why Classes Appeal to the Architect in All of Us."

Perusing the Packages

For more information on the packages that comprise the standard Java API, please refer to the JDK documentation. Incidentally, I'm not trying to skirt responsibility here—you'll learn a great deal about the Java API and its packages throughout the remainder of the book. However, I thought you might be curious and want to take a peek at the API documentation now. The Java API documentation is actually installed separately from the JDK, but it is installed into the same directory with the JDK. Check out the file `index.html` in the docs directory beneath your JDK installation for more information.

Building Your First Applet

The main thrust of this chapter is to get you comfortable creating applets of your own. Granted, this is a little tough because you haven't been exposed to the inner workings of the Java language yet, but I know you probably want to put Java to work for you as quickly as possible. So, I'm going to proceed and lead you through the development of a fully functioning Java applet that you can use in your own Web pages. It really isn't terribly important if you don't grasp every detailed element of the applet's code; at this stage it's more important for you to get a grasp on a bigger picture.

Before getting into any specifics about the applet, you need to think about how it will be used. Let's briefly discuss some general applet development guidelines. The very fact that an applet resides on a Web page presents some interesting development concerns:

➤ How much physical space does the applet take up on the page?

➤ Does the applet accept user input or does it just display information?

➤ Does the applet need to read/write files?

➤ Does the applet make use of images?

➤ Does the applet make use of sounds?

➤ If so, how long will it take to load them?

➤ Will the sounds potentially annoy some users?

This is by no means a complete list of concerns to be addressed for every applet, but it gets you thinking about the challenges associated with developing applets. The good news is that these questions are easily answered for most applets.

In addition to these questions, you should consider how customizable you want an applet to be. If you recall from Chapter 2, "Java: The Web's Darling," applets accept parameters that can be customized when an applet is embedded in a Web page. For example, the background color of an applet can be set based on a parameter value. Of course, applets should always have default parameter values in the event that any parameters aren't assigned customized values.

After you have addressed the initial concerns regarding the construction of your applet, you are ready to begin constructing the applet. It is important at this stage to know which development tools you are going to use throughout the development process. For the purposes of this book, I recommend you stick with the JDK as the comprehensive tool suite for programming Java applets and applications. More specifically, for applet development you will need to be familiar with the Java compiler and Java applet viewer. You will also need a suitable text editor such as Windows Notepad for Windows users.

Applet: DateTime

A little earlier in the chapter I used a DateTime applet as an example when discussing the `Applet` class. Surprise, this is the applet you are now going to build as your first foray into Java applet development!

As fun as it would be to just throw the source code at you and see what happens, I think you'll be better served by seeing the applet in action first. The following figure shows the DateTime applet running within a Web page. Just keep in mind that the process usually works in reverse; if you find a programming language that allows you to see the finished product before you start programming, please let me know!

The DateTime applet running within a Web page.

As you can see in the figure, the DateTime applet displays the current date and time. Okay, this might not seem like all that big of a deal, but try to accomplish the same goal with HTML alone. Even the relatively simple task of displaying the current date and time is impossible using straight HTML code.

Globetrotting with Java

You might be surprised to learn that the DateTime applet is a global Java program, which means that it displays the date and time according to the international standards of the computer on which it is running. For example, a Portuguese speaking user in Brazil would see the date and time formatted differently than a French user in Canada. This support for internationalization is an automatic feature of Java of which the DateTime applet takes advantage.

Finding the Book's Applet and Java Application Examples on the Web

To find the applets and Java application examples provided in this book, enter the address `http://www.mcp.com/info` in the location box. Click the link called **Downloadable Code, Examples, and Info for book "Companion Sites."** In the space provided under the Book Information section, enter **0–7897–1804–9**, which is the 10-digit ISBN for this book. Click the **Search** button.

Speaking of code, it's time to bite the bullet and look at the Java code that makes this applet tick, so to speak. Following is the source code for the DateTime applet, which is stored in the file `DateTime.java`:

```
import java.applet.*;
import java.text.*;
import java.util.*;
import java.awt.*;

public class DateTime extends Applet {
  public void paint(Graphics g) {
    // Format the current date/time
    DateFormat df =
DateFormat.getDateTimeInstance
➥(DateFormat.LONG,
      DateFormat.SHORT);
    String str = df.format(new Date());

    // Draw the date/time
    FontMetrics fm = g.getFontMetrics();
    g.drawString(str, (getSize().width -
    ➥fm.stringWidth(str)) / 2,
      ((getSize().height - fm.getHeight()) /
      ➥2) + fm.getAscent());
  }
}
```

Hey, I know this code probably looks very foreign to you; if it didn't, you wouldn't be reading my book. Let's tackle it a section at a time to try and digest its meaning. It's not terribly important that it all make perfect sense right now. You have the rest of the book to learn the nuances of the Java programming language and API. The idea here is to get your feet wet by showing you what it takes to create a real Java applet.

As you now know, the Java API provides lots of neat features that Java programs, such as applets, are likely to use. To use a feature in a given API package, a Java program must import the package by using the `import` statement. The first four lines of the DateTime applet result in the applet having access to the features in the packages `java.applet`, `java.text`, `java.util`, and `java.awt`:

```
import java.applet.*;
import java.text.*;
import java.util.*;
import java.awt.*;
```

If you recall from the earlier table, these packages provide general applet features, text handling features, miscellaneous utility features, and window and GUI features, respectively.

The next line of importance is the line that defines the applet class, `DateTime`, and indicates that it is derived from the `Applet` class:

```
public class DateTime extends Applet {
```

The `DateTime` class derives from (extends) the `Applet` class because the `Applet` class provides a great deal of applet overhead such as the management of the applet's window. Notice that the line ends in an open curly brace ({). This indicates the start of the code for the `DateTime` class. Everything appearing between this curly brace and the closing curly brace (}) at the end of program is considered part of the `DateTime` class.

Next on the agenda is the line that defines the `paint()` method:

```
public void paint(Graphics g) {
```

Methods are isolated sections of Java code that perform a given function such as painting graphics. The `paint()` method is responsible for painting the date and time to the DateTime applet's window. Similar to the `DateTime` class definition, the `paint()` method definition includes a pair of curly braces. To give you an idea of how the curly braces work, following is the complete `paint()` method:

```
public void paint(Graphics g) {
  // Format the current date/time
  DateFormat df = DateFormat.getDateTimeInstance(DateFormat.LONG,
    DateFormat.SHORT);
  String str = df.format(new Date());

  // Draw the date/time
  FontMetrics fm = g.getFontMetrics();
  g.drawString(str, (getSize().width - fm.stringWidth(str)) / 2,
    ((getSize().height - fm.getHeight()) / 2) + fm.getAscent());
  }
```

The `paint()` method consists of two functional parts: formatting the current date and time and drawing the formatted date and time. These two sections are highlighted by comments that begin with the comment characters (//). These comment characters (//) indicate that the remainder of the line on which they appear is to be ignored by the Java compiler.

Painting on Demand

The paint() method is very important because it largely determines
the appearance of applets. The
paint() method is called anytime
an applet's appearance needs to be
updated. This would happen if you
minimized a Web browser and then
restored it. As the browser redraws
the Web page, any applets on the
page would call their paint()
methods to redraw themselves. For
this reason, you typically place all of
the graphical output code for an
applet in the paint() method. You
learn the ins and outs of the
paint() method in Chapter 11,
"Java as an Artist's Canvas."

The code that formats the date and time relies on
special date-handling classes to format the date and
time and store it as text. This text is then measured
and drawn centered in the applet window, again
using special drawing classes. You learn about these
classes in due time.

To compile the DateTime applet using the JDK Java
compiler, enter the following command at the command line:

```
javac DateTime.java
```

When the Java compiler finishes, it will leave behind
a file named DateTime.class, which is the executable bytecode file for the applet. This is the file
you will reference in the <APPLET> tag from HTML
code. Following is the HTML code for the
DateTime.html Web page containing the DateTime
applet:

```
<HTML>
<HEAD>
<TITLE>DateTime Applet Example</TITLE>
</HEAD>
<BODY>
<H1>DateTime Applet</H1>
<HR>
<APPLET CODE="DateTime.class" WIDTH=200 HEIGHT=50></APPLET>
<P>
Above is the Java DateTime applet, which displays the current date and
time.
</P>
</BODY>
</HTML>
```

This code should look pretty familiar to you because you already have some experience with embedding applets in Web pages. Just to recap, the <APPLET> tag references
the DateTime applet class (DateTime.class) using the CODE attribute. Additionally, the
width and height of the applet are set to 200 and 50, respectively, using the WIDTH
and HEIGHT attributes.

Before leaving you with the DateTime applet, I wanted to suggest trying out the
applet in the Java applet viewer. The following command runs the applet viewer with
the DateTime applet:

```
appletviewer DateTime.html
```

The following figure shows the applet running within the applet viewer.

The DateTime applet running within the applet viewer.

That pretty much wraps up the DateTime applet. Now you have an applet you can incorporate into your own Web pages to display the current date and time!

The Least You Need to Know

It's official, you can no longer proudly claim ignorance to Java. That's right, as of this chapter, you moved beyond the theory and straight into the practical guts of what it takes to put Java to use in a real applet. Granted, it was a somewhat spoon-fed approach to building a Java applet, but you built it nonetheless. Let's recap what you learned in this chapter:

➤ GUI stands for Graphical User Interface and is pronounced "gooey."

➤ Java provides a standardized GUI that is consistent across different computing platforms.

Cracking the Case

It's very important to point out that Java is a case-sensitive programming language, which means that there is a distinction between the name `count` and `COUNT`. This especially applies to the Java API, which consists of classes, methods, and variables that are all given case-sensitive names. Even the names of applets are case sensitive, which means the name of the applet in the source code (`DateTime`) must match the name of the source code file (`DateTime.java`).

➤ The Java API (Application Programming Interface) consists of a bunch of support programs bundled into packages.

➤ Java is a case-sensitive programming language, which means the name `shwing` is very different from `SHWING` or even `Shwing`.

➤ It isn't too hard to build an applet that displays the current date and time, provided someone gives you the source code.

Let's Try and Be Objective

The Land Before Objects

Once upon a time the word "object" was not a part of the programmer's vocabulary. Sure, the vocabulary of a programmer was still pretty colorful with words like "struct" and "goto," but you never heard the word "object." If Java is your first programming language, this might not seem like a big deal. Let me assure you that it *is* a big deal because object-oriented programming represents the most sweeping change in programming in recent years. Java is an object-oriented programming language, which is why I'm devoting a chapter to getting you up to speed with objects.

To understand object-oriented programming, you have to understand what programming was like without it. Programming languages originally were procedural, which means that everything revolved around chunks of programming code known as procedures. A program stored its data in one place and its procedures in another. To change the data in some way, you would call a procedure. There was no logical or organizational connection between the data and procedures, however, which is the primary shortcoming of procedural programming. The following figure shows the relationship between procedures and data in a procedural program.

The relationship between procedures and data in a procedural program.

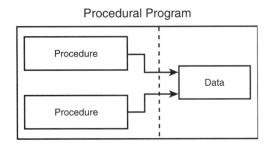

The procedural world I've just described worked relatively well in terms of giving programmers the flexibility to build small- to medium-sized applications. However, large projects proved to be exceedingly complicated to develop and maintain because it became difficult to manage hundreds of procedures acting on hundreds of pieces of data. The procedures and data didn't directly tie in together, so there was always a logical distance between the two.

Human Brain, Meet Computer Brain

As the procedural programming model started to break down, a few folks got to working on a better approach. This takes us back to the whole premise behind programming languages. The idea of a programming language is to bridge the gap between the human brain and the computer brain. A computer program simply tells the computer to do things, but it does so in human terminology. Well, sort of. You and I probably wouldn't have a casual conversation that consisted of "while (x < 5) x++;" but that's not exactly my point. My point is that programming languages attempt to make it easier for humans to craft instructions for computers.

To better understand this, consider for a moment the absolute ideal programming language for humans. English! That's right, the ideal programming language, at least in terms of feeling natural, would be English. It is the most commonly spoken language worldwide. Imagine how simple programming would be if a program consisted of the phrase "analyze this data and graph the results." A program like this would truly bridge human thought to computer thought, but it would be unbelievably difficult to construct a compiler intelligent enough to make the conversion to computer code. What specific data do you want to analyze? Exactly what type of analysis do you have in mind? And what kind of graph do you want?

Human languages are too subjective and have too many shades of gray to scale well to computers. So we settle on programming languages that combine words familiar to humans and symbols familiar to computers to bridge the gap between human brains and computer processors.

Thinking in Objects

Getting back to our history of programming languages, the successor to procedural programming is known as object-oriented programming. If you've been anywhere near the computer section of a bookstore in the last five years, you've certainly seen the hype surrounding object-oriented programming, or OOP (rhymes with hoop) for short. The advent of Java has only served to elevate the excitement surrounding OOP. OOP attempts to do a much better job of bridging the gap between problems in the real world and solutions in the computer world.

In the real world, people tend to think in terms of "things." Where pre-OOP programming languages forced people to think in terms of blocks of code (procedures) and the data they manipulate, OOP promotes a way of programming that enables programmers to think in terms of objects, or things. Maybe it should be called thing-oriented programming, or TOP for short? OOP sounds a little more interesting I suppose. Anyway, the OOP approach to programming is a very natural and logical extension of the way people already think.

The OOP approach to programming revolves around a few major concepts:

➤ Objects
➤ Classes
➤ Messages
➤ Inheritance

Objects

At the heart of OOP is encapsulation, which is the packaging of data together with procedures. Encapsulation leads to objects, which are bundles of data and the procedures that act on that data. The procedures in an object are known as methods. The merger of data and methods provides a means of more accurately representing real-world objects. The following figure shows the relationship between methods and data in an object-oriented program.

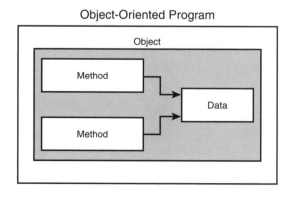

The relationship between methods and data in an object-oriented program.

To better understand the benefit of objects, think about the common characteristics of real-world objects. Lions, cars, calculators, and boulders all share two common characteristics: state and behavior. The state of an object is the condition that the object is in, as defined by its attributes. The behavior of an object is the collection of actions that the object can take.

As an example, the state of a lion might include color, weight, and whether the lion is tired or hungry. Lions also have certain behaviors such as roaring, sleeping, hunting, and eating. A car also has a state and behavior. The state of a car includes the current speed, the type of transmission, whether it is two-wheel drive or four-wheel drive, whether the lights are on, and the current gear, among other things. The behaviors for a car include turning, braking, and accelerating.

Like real-world objects, software objects under OOP possess two common characteristics: state and behavior. The state of an object is determined by its data, and the behavior of an object is determined by its methods. Paralleling the characteristics between real-world objects and software objects makes it much easier to develop programs that deal with real-world issues and problems. You could use the lion object to represent a real lion in an interactive software zoo. Similarly, car objects would be very useful in a racing game or an interactive educational Web site for mechanics.

Classes

You've encountered classes a few times throughout the book thus far but I've put off discussing them. Well, the time has come to step up and deal with classes head on! A class is a template, or specification, that defines a type of object. A class is to an object what a blueprint is to a house. Many houses can be built from a single blueprint; the blueprint outlines the structure and makeup of the houses. Classes work exactly the same way, except that they outline the makeup of objects.

In the real world, there are often many objects of the same kind. Using the house analogy, there are neighborhoods with lots of different houses, but as houses they share common characteristics. In object-oriented terms, you would say that your house is a specific instance of the class of objects known as houses. An instance of a class is an object that has been created in memory using the class as a template (blueprint). Instances are also sometimes referred to as instantiated objects.

Going back to the example of the car object, you might create a car class as part of a racing game. You could create multiple car objects from this class and even give them different attributes. For example, some of them could be two-wheel drive, some four-wheel drive, etc. However, all of the car objects would have the same types of data and methods defined in the car class. The car objects in the game would be considered individual instances of the car class.

Messages

An object acting alone is rarely very useful; most objects require other objects to do anything meaningful. For example, the car object is pretty useless by itself with no other interaction. Add a driver object and a stretch of road, however, and things get much more interesting! Knowing this, it stands to reason that objects need some kind of communication mechanism in order to interact with each other.

Software objects interact with each other via messages. When the driver object wants the car object to accelerate, it sends a message to the car object. The following figure shows how the driver object would send a message to the car object informing the car to accelerate.

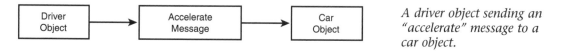

A driver object sending an "accelerate" message to a car object.

If you want to think of messages more literally, then consider two people objects. If one person wants the other person to come closer, they might say to the other person, "come here, please." In this case, the phrase "come here, please" is the message sent to the other person. This is a very literal message. Software messages are a little different in form, but not in theory; they simply tell an object what to do. In Java, the act of sending a message to an object consists of calling one of the object's methods. The following figure shows a more accurate representation of the driver object sending an "accelerate" message to the car object by calling its `accelerate()` method.

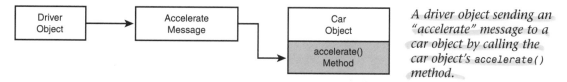

A driver object sending an "accelerate" message to a car object by calling the car object's `accelerate()` method.

Many times, the object receiving a message needs more information so that it can know exactly what to do. When the driver tells the car to accelerate, the car needs to know by how much. This information is passed along with the message as message parameters.

To summarize, a message consists of three things:

➤ The object to receive the message (car)

➤ The action to perform (accelerate)

➤ Any parameters required for the action (+15 mph)

Just so you don't get confused, understand that "message passing" is another way of saying "method calling." When an object sends another object a message, it is really just calling a method of that object. The message parameters are actually the parameters to the method. In Java OOP parlance, messages and methods are synonymous.

Inheritance

The last important OOP topic you need to understand is inheritance, which you have actually already seen at work. Inheritance is the process of creating a new class with the characteristics of an existing class, along with additional characteristics unique to the new class. Remember the `DateTime` applet class in the preceding chapter? The `DateTime` applet class inherited features from the standard `Applet` class, but also provided its own unique `paint()` method. This is a perfect example of inheritance at work.

Inheritance provides a means of creating classes based on other classes. When a class is based on another class, it inherits all of the properties of that class, including the data and methods for the class. The class doing the inheriting is referred to as the child class (subclass), and the class providing the information to inherit is referred to as the parent class (superclass). Inherited classes form a hierarchical relationship with each other that closely resembles a family tree.

Using the car example once more, you might derive gas-powered cars and electric cars from the car class. Both new car classes share common car characteristics, but they also add a few unique characteristics of their own. The gas car would have a fuel tank and gas cap, while the electric car might have an additional battery and a plug for recharging. The following figure shows the car inheritance tree, which reflects the relationship between the car parent class and the gas and electric car child classes.

The car inheritance tree, which reflects the relationship between inherited car classes.

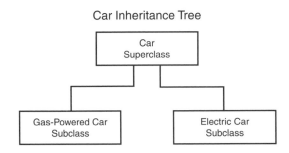

The real power of inheritance is the ability to inherit properties and add new ones; child classes can have variables and methods in addition to the ones they inherit from the parent class. Remember, the electric car has an additional battery and a recharging plug. Subclasses also have the capability of overriding inherited methods and providing their own versions. For example, the gas car would probably be capable of going much faster than the electric car. The `accelerate` method for the gas car could reflect this difference.

What's This Have to Do with Java?

I promise my theoretical OOP tirade is now over! So, what does it all have to do with Java? As I mentioned earlier, Java is an object-oriented programming language, which means you must understand OOP to understand Java. Granted, you can do some things in Java without fully understanding OOP, but at some point it will catch up with you. So, I decided to go ahead and establish some OOP ground rules so you'll have a better understanding of Java as you encounter OOP constructs throughout the book.

Java programs are extremely object oriented in nature. Java applets are objects, which is evident by the fact that the DateTime executable applet is compiled into a file named `DateTime.class`. When you run the applet in the Java applet viewer or within a Web page, an object of type `DateTime` is created based on the `DateTime` class. This applet object is what you see running as the DateTime applet.

The OOP nature of Java also reveals itself in the Java API. You learned in the preceding chapter that the Java API is a large group of packages containing special Java programs that perform different functions. These special Java programs are actually classes, which is why the Java API is sometimes referred to as a class library. As an example, the `java.awt` package contains a class named `Image`, which represents a graphical image. Applets need only use the `Image` class to manipulate and draw images as if they were real-world objects.

Another good example of how OOP makes Java easier to understand and use is the `Color` class, which is also located in the `java.awt` package. Not surprisingly, the `Color` class represents a color such as red, yellow, or orange. After you create a `Color` object from the `Color` class, you can work with the color as if it were a physical object in the real world. Java also provides standard `Color` objects for common colors. Following are a few of these standard `Color` objects:

➤ `Color.red`

➤ `Color.yellow`

➤ `Color.orange`

➤ `Color.green`

➤ `Color.blue`

➤ `Color.gray`

I presented this list of `Color` objects because I wanted to show you how they come into use in a practical scenario. If you want an applet to have a colored background, you can call the `setBackground()` method on the `Applet` class and pass in a suitable `Color` object:

```
setBackground(Color.blue);
```

This line of code would change the applet's background color attribute to blue, which results in the background being colored blue. Granted, the preceding line of code isn't quite as simple as saying "color the background blue," but it is pretty easy to understand, considering it is legal Java code. There aren't too many programming languages that provide a form and structure that is so easy to understand and use. This is largely due to the fact that Java is an object-oriented programming language.

The Least You Need to Know

I sincerely apologize for taking such a theoretical detour in this chapter, but I think you'll appreciate it later. OOP is an incredibly important part of the Java programming language and is therefore an integral part of learning how to develop Java programs. You'll revisit and learn more about these OOP concepts as they reveal themselves throughout the remainder of the book. This chapter taught you that:

➤ Procedural programming has weaknesses that reveal themselves as programs get large and complex.

➤ Programming languages enable people to communicate with computers and tell them what to do.

➤ OOP stands for object-oriented programming, and rhymes with hoop.

➤ The heart of OOP is encapsulation, which is the packaging of data together with procedures.

➤ Objects are bundles of data and the procedures, or methods, that act on that data.

➤ A class is a template, or specification, that defines a type of object.

➤ The Java API is sometimes referred to as a class library because it consists of a large set of classes organized into packages.

Part 2
This Is Your Brain on Java

The Java programming language provides the mortar and brick to build Java applets and applications. As a programming language, Java is very streamlined and easy to learn. That isn't to say that learning to be a Java programmer is a walk in the park; every programming language has its challenges. However, Java puts your brain under significantly less stress than its closest relative, C++.

You are about to dig into the fundamentals of the Java language, which are essential for writing meaningful Java programs. Don't worry, I'll try to keep things as interesting as possible by guiding you through some colorful example programs along the way. Let's get started!

Your First Peek Inside Java

Of Applications and Applets

When using Java, you have the option of creating one of two types of programs: applets or applications. As you already know, applets are graphical programs that run within the context of a Web page. Applications, on the other hand, can be graphical or command-line, and run on their own without any help from a Web page or Web browser. Java applications are akin to traditional programs developed in other programming languages such as BASIC or C++.

Like applets, applications are created as Java classes, but they are executed using the Java interpreter instead of a Web browser or the AppletViewer. Unlike applets, command-line Java applications don't have to be derived from any special class. This is because command-line applications really don't require any special overhead such as managing a frame window.

Java Is Popular Even Off the Web

Most of this book is devoted to the study and creation of applets, which are more than likely your main reason for learning Java. However, you shouldn't entirely push Java applications aside because Java is rapidly becoming a popular programming language.

Perhaps the biggest difference between applets and applications is security. Because applets are Web based and could potentially cause lots of trouble on a computer with little warning, they have stringent security limitations. Applications, on the other hand, presumably are manually installed by the user and are therefore considered secure by default. This security distinction between applets and applications makes for interesting gaps in what the two can functionally accomplish. For example, you could develop an application that searched the local hard drive for information, but an applet couldn't normally accomplish this task because of its security limitations.

Choosing Between Graphical and Command-Line Applications

Graphical Java applications look a lot like applets except that they create and manage their own frame window; a Web page provides the frame window for an applet. Graphical applications are even developed in much the same way as applets except for the extra code required to manage the frame window. Graphical applications are useful when you want to create a program with a graphical user interface that doesn't reside on the Web. For example, you might want to write a graphical application to inventory your personal CD collection, in which case it wouldn't necessarily need to have any connection with a Web page.

You'll more than likely create command-line Java applications to serve as simple utilities that perform tasks such as processing files or getting system information, because their overhead is so minimal. For this reason, I've provided several command-line applications throughout the book to demonstrate some non-graphical aspects of Java programming.

Additionally, command-line Java applications can be very useful for testing code that you don't feel like framing into an applet. For example, suppose you want to develop a subroutine that sorts a list of text names into alphabetical order. It really isn't necessary to perform this sort in a graphical application when all you care about seeing are the names displayed in order.

A command-line application also might come in handy if you were building a pond behind your house and you wanted to determine the volume of the pond based on the dimensions and depth of the hole. This isn't such an off-the-wall example as you might think. I recently built a koi pond and wrote just such a command-line Java application to calculate the volume so that I could determine the appropriate size of pump and filter. You see this application in action a little later in the chapter.

The Main Event

Command-line Java applications are pretty simple in structure and don't really require any special overhead such as a parent class. The one thing all Java applications do require, however, is the main() method. The main() method is the heart of a Java application and is called by the Java interpreter to actually run the application. When I refer to an application running in the Java interpreter, this really boils down to the interpreter calling the main() method and executing the code within it. The following figure shows how the main() method is called by the Java interpreter to execute an application.

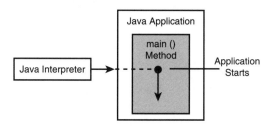

The Java interpreter calls the main() *method to execute a Java application.*

The following code shows a bare-bones command-line Java application, which should give you an idea as to how simple they can be:

```
class Skeleton {
  public static void main (String args[]) {
  }
}
```

This application doesn't do anything, which is evident by the empty main() method. When you execute this application in the Java interpreter, the main() method is called, but there is no code to execute. So, the method returns and the interpreter terminates the application. In this way, the main() method determines when an application is to finish executing. When the last line of code in the main() method is executed, the main() method finishes (returns) and the interpreter ends the application. The following figure shows how an application ends when the main() method finishes executing.

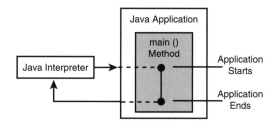

A Java application is terminated by the Java interpreter when the main() *method finishes executing.*

Applets with Security Clearance

Lest you think the security constraints of applets relegates them to only being useful for novel tasks like animations and financial calculators, let me assure you that there is a way for applets to bypass Java's strict security. No, this isn't some kind secret backdoor or weakness in Java's security model. Rather, it is a way to declare an applet safe for use so that users can feel comfortable giving the applet access to their system for performing useful functions.

Applets are allowed to run under more relaxed security by having a digital signature attached to them, which is a lot like a handwritten signature in function. A digital signature associated with an applet verifies that the applet came from a given source and that it hasn't been tampered with. If you trust the source and deem it reliable, then you can feel safe running the applet. Applets running in this type of scenario are called signed applets, and have limited or no security constraints.

Getting Confrontational with Command-Line Arguments

If you recall from Chapter 2, "Java: The Web's Darling," Java applets accept parameters that enable you to customize an applet when you embed it in a Web page. Java applications have a similar customization feature in the form of command-line arguments. Command-line arguments consist of information entered on the command-line when you execute an application using the Java interpreter.

A good example of a command-line application is an application I mentioned earlier called PondVolume, which calculates the volume of water for a pond based on the rectangular dimensions and depth of the pond. Granted, the calculation is simple enough to perform on a calculator, but I've got to use my expensive computer for something useful other than just writing computer books! Anyway, the following command demonstrates how to supply command-line arguments to the PondVolume application:

```
java PondVolume 7 12 2.5
```

As you can see, the command-line arguments are entered on the command line just after the application name. In this case, the arguments (from left to right) are the length, width, and depth of the pond. Following are the results of this command:

```
Pond length = 7.0 feet
Pond width  = 12.0 feet
Pond depth  = 2.5 feet
Pond volume = 1575.0 gallons
```

The PondVolume application displays the length, width, and depth that were provided as command-line arguments, along with the calculated pond volume. Pretty simple, right?

But what if I gave you the PondVolume application and didn't specify the meaning or order of the command-line arguments? You might struggle to figure out how to use the application. Or not. Most command-line applications that expect arguments will display usage information if you don't specify any arguments at all. For example, the following command executes the PondVolume application with no arguments:

```
java PondVolume
```

When the PondVolume application detects that no arguments were provided, it displays usage information to help the user in providing arguments:

```
Usage: java PondVolume Length Width
Depth
```

Pretty nifty! You can think of usage information as kind of a primitive help system for command-line applications. Fortunately, it's very easy to include usage information when building command-line applications, as you shall soon see.

The key to command-line arguments lies in the main() method. Let's take closer look at the definition for the main() method:

```
public static void main(String[]
args) {
```

Notice the word args inside the parentheses? This is a method parameter, which is information passed into a method that the method might need to use. In this case, the args parameter contains the list of command-line arguments provided by the user at the command line. The argument list is provided to the main() method as an array of strings, which is a fancy way of saying a "list of text." You learn

Does Michael Jordan Run or Execute?

I apologize if I've confused you by randomly interchanging the terms "run" and "execute" when referring to applets and applications. To set the record straight, the terms mean the same thing. In other words, running an application is no different than executing an application. It just so happens that sometimes one word sounds better than the other does in a given context.

Another way to think about this comparison is to consider professional sports. When watching the NBA Finals this year, all I heard from the announcers was how well the Bulls **executed** their offense. Well, when I used to play basketball we often **ran** plays, but I don't really know if we ever **executed** them. Was there really a difference? I'm not sure if I have the answer, but it might have something to do with why I'm not playing professional sports now.

about both arrays and strings in the next chapter, but for now just think of the args parameter as a container that holds the arguments passed into the application on the command line.

I could probably drone on for days about command-line arguments and how they might be used in different applications, but I think you would be better served to see how they work in real Java code. Following is the complete code for the PondVolume application:

Building Character with Strings

Simply put, a string is a series of characters stuck together. Anytime you work with text in a Java program, you do so by using strings. All of the following are examples of strings: "Hello," "123," "Ouch!," "$50.00," and "This is a sentence." Because strings consist of a series of characters, you can determine the length of a string, which is how many characters there are in the string. You can also reference individual characters within a string. You learn lots more about strings in the next chapter, but I couldn't resist giving you a little primer because strings are heavily involved in command-line arguments.

```java
public class PondVolume {
    public static void main(String[] args) {
        // Make sure we have the right number of
        args
        if (args.length != 3) {
            System.out.println("Usage: java
            PondVolume Length Width Depth");
            System.exit(0);
        }

        // Convert the args to floats
        float length =
        Float.valueOf(args[0]).floatValue();
        float width =
        Float.valueOf(args[1]).floatValue();
        float depth =
        Float.valueOf(args[2]).floatValue();
        float volume = length * width * depth *
        7.5f;

        // Display the pond size and volume
        System.out.println("Pond length = " +
        length + " feet");
        System.out.println("Pond width  = " +
        width + " feet");
        System.out.println("Pond depth  = " +
        depth + " feet");
        System.out.println("Pond volume = " +
        volume + " gallons");
    }
}
```

Please don't get intimidated by the amount of code involved in this application because it really is pretty simple, honest! Let's start with the beginning of the `main()` method, which is where the usage information is presented if no command-line arguments are provided:

```java
if (args.length != 3) {
    System.out.println("Usage: java PondVolume Length Width Depth");
    System.exit(0);
}
```

The user must provide three arguments for the application to function properly. So, if the length of the argument list, `args.length`, is unequal to three, then the application prints a message regarding its usage. The message is printed using the `System` object, which is a standard Java object used for performing command-line input and output. You learn more about the `System` object in a moment. Also notice that the

`System` object is used to exit the application after displaying the usage information message.

The remainder of the PondVolume application deals with converting the text arguments to numbers, calculating the pond volume, and displaying the results. The following lines of code convert the three text arguments into numbers that can be used to calculate the pond's volume:

```
float length = Float.valueOf(args[0]).floatValue();
float width = Float.valueOf(args[1]).floatValue();
float depth = Float.valueOf(args[2]).floatValue();
```

Text and numbers are treated very differently in Java, as they are in most programming languages. Therefore, it is necessary to perform a conversion if you want to manipulate a number stored in text as a mathematical number. The numbers in the PondVolume application happen to be floating point numbers, which means that they have a fractional part. For example, 3.0 and 3.14 are floating point numbers; 3 is not. After converting the three text arguments to floating point numbers, the application stores them in variables named `length`, `width`, and `depth`, respectively.

The actual pond volume is calculated with a single line of code:

```
float volume = length * width * depth * 7.5f;
```

This code creates a floating-point variable named `volume` and stores the calculated pond volume in it. The calculation is pretty simple to understand because it consists of multiplying the length times the width times the depth times 7.5. The last multiplication is necessary to convert cubic feet to gallons.

The last section of code in the application displays the results of the pond volume calculation by again using the `System` object:

```
System.out.println("Pond length = " + length + " feet");
System.out.println("Pond width  = " + width + " feet");
System.out.println("Pond depth  = " + depth + " feet");
System.out.println("Pond volume = " + volume + " gallons");
```

There is no longer any sense in trying to skirt the issue of what the `System` object is doing. Read on to learn how it works!

Standard I/O: No Frills Communication

Modern computers support lots of different devices that are capable of inputting and outputting information in a variety of different ways. For example, you can scan a picture, touch it up by viewing it on your monitor and guiding the mouse appropriately, and then print it back out using a color printer. All of these devices working in concert are what makes computers such powerful tools. And what do all of the devices have in common? They input and output information!

Tupperware for Information

My mom is somewhat obsessed with Tupperware and other types of plastic storage containers. Her pantry is a sea of meticulously labeled plastic storage containers with everything from cereal to brown sugar neatly sealed off from the harsh elements of the modern kitchen. Variables in Java programs act much like my mom's Tupperware, except they are used to store information instead of granola. Java variables are data containers that can hold text, numbers, and special true/false conditions known as Boolean values.

When you create a program that manipulates information, you typically place the information in variables for the duration of time you are working with it. You then have the option of later throwing the variables away or saving the information to disk for later retrieval. Variables are stored in your computer's memory alongside the Java program itself. You get a formal introduction to variables and the types of data they can hold in the next chapter.

It probably isn't a big surprise to you that inputting and outputting information is also a key part of any Java program. If your Java programs couldn't read data from devices or write it back out to them, the devices wouldn't be of much use, not to mention the Java programs!

There are varying degrees of complication associated with inputting and outputting information in Java. Not surprisingly, you're going to start by learning about the most simple way to input and output information. I'm referring to standard I/O, which is the most basic form of input and output available to a Java program. Incidentally, I/O stands for Input/Output, just in case that reference went over your head.

In Java, standard I/O operates under the premise of your computer having a standard input device and a standard output device. That's right, one of each. Examine your computer and make a guess as to which two devices are the most logical candidates for standard input and output. Give up? Well, the force-feedback bio-mechanical glove is the standard input device and the digital tie-dye silk-screening press is the standard output device. Just kidding. Actually, the keyboard and monitor are the respective standard input and output devices.

What does this mean to you and me? Well, it means that we can input information from the keyboard and output it to the monitor with relative ease using a couple of special Java objects. The objects I'm referring to are actually part of the `System` object, which you saw a little earlier in the chapter. More specifically, the objects you're interested in are the `in` and `out` objects, which are referred to programmatically as `System.in` and `System.out` because they belong to the `System` object. You can think of these two objects as logical information links to the keyboard and monitor.

First, the `System.out` Object

OK, standard I/O sounds interesting, but how does it work? The `System.in` and `System.out` objects contain methods you can call to input data from the keyboard or output it to the monitor. The `System.out` object is by far the one you'll use the most, so let's focus on it. Probably the most popular method it contains is `println()`, which enables you to print a line of text to the standard output device (monitor). Following is an example of using the `println()` method to print a simple text message:

```
System.out.println("Hi mom!");
```

This line of code would come in handy if you were ever busy writing a Java program at a major sporting event and the cameraman happened to pan over to you. Of course, I'd recommend leaving the laptop at home and just watching the game. Anyway, the `println()` method is extremely useful for outputting information to the monitor. You can also use it to print numbers, like this:

```
System.out.println("5280");
System.out.println(5280);
```

It's worth pointing out the difference between these two lines of code. The first line prints the text "5280," and the second line prints the actual number 5280. This might seem like a fine distinction, but it matters because there are actually different versions of the `println()` method for printing text and numbers. Incidentally, there are 5,280 feet in a mile. Just a little factoid I thought I might pass along!

The `System.out` object also has a `print()` method that is very similar to the `println()` method. The only difference between the two is that the `println()` method starts a new line after it is finished printing. The following code demonstrates the difference:

```
System.out.print("This is the first
➥half ");
System.out.println("of a
➥sentence.");
System.out.println("This is another
➥sentence.");
```

Are They Standard or Not?

So far I've painted the picture that the keyboard and monitor are always the standard input and output devices used in standard I/O. Although this holds true in the vast majority of situations, it is technically possible for a computer to rely on a different device for standard I/O. As an example, consider an embedded "computer" in an automobile or appliance that doesn't even have a monitor. In this case, a series of lights might serve as the only output device available to the computer. Or there might be a data capture computer that has no keyboard and receives all of its information from a live data feed.

Admittedly, both of these scenarios are a little out of the ordinary in terms of the types of Java programs you are likely to develop. However, Java is quickly making its way into embedded computers and other types of hardware such as cellular phones, and somebody has to program them!

Also, you can output information from an applet to the standard output device using standard I/O, which is a little tricky because applets are graphical, and standard I/O is inherently textual. In this case, the standard output "device" is a special window within a Web browser. More on this a little later in the chapter.

This code would result in the following output:

```
This is the first
half of a sentence.
This is another sentence.
```

Now, the `System.in` Object

The `System.in` object can be used to retrieve input from the keyboard in a command-line application. It isn't very useful in applets or graphical applications because you would use GUI widgets such as edit boxes and buttons to retrieve information from the user instead. For all practical purposes, you can ignore the `System.in` object when it comes to applets and graphical applications.

If that's not bad enough, let me add that the `System.in` object isn't entirely useful in command-line applications because data is often provided as command-line arguments. Most users prefer entering command-line arguments instead of the line-by-line entry afforded by the `System.in` object. I'm not saying the `System.in` object is totally useless, because I firmly believe a purpose will always rise up to meet even the most esoteric of inventions. However, its usefulness is limited enough that I don't want to waste your time learning any more about it.

Consolation for Applets

If you're feeling like the command-line nature of standard I/O leaves applets out in the dark, then take heed! Standard I/O can actually be put to very good use in applets thanks to a lesser-known feature in Web browsers known as the Java console window. The Java console window is a special window in Web browsers that serves as the standard output "device" for applets. Whenever an applet prints information to the `System.out` object, it appears in the console window.

The console window can be put to use as a primitive debugging tool for applets by strategically calling the `println()` method in the applet's code. Following is a revised version of the DateTime applet from Chapter 2 that contains strategically placed `println()` method calls to monitor the applet's progress:

```java
import java.applet.*;
import java.text.*;
import java.util.*;
import java.awt.*;

public class DateTime extends Applet {
  public void paint(Graphics g) {
    System.out.println("Start of paint() method");

    // Format the current date/time
    System.out.println("Formatting the date/time");
```

```
DateFormat df = DateFormat.getDateTimeInstance(DateFormat.LONG,
   DateFormat.SHORT);
String str = df.format(new Date());
System.out.println("The date/time is " + str);

// Draw the date/time
System.out.println("Drawing the data/time");
FontMetrics fm = g.getFontMetrics();
g.drawString(str, (getSize().width - fm.stringWidth(str)) / 2,
   ((getSize().height - fm.getHeight()) / 2) + fm.getAscent());

System.out.println("End of paint() method");
   }
}
```

This code is the same as the DateTime applet in Chapter 2, except for the addition of five calls to the System.out object's println() method. To see the results of these changes, try running the new DateTime applet in the applet viewer. The applet viewer will output the results of the println() method calls to the command-line prompt, like this:

```
Start of paint() method
Formatting the date/time
The date/time is July 23, 1998 3:17 PM
Drawing the data/time
End of paint() method
```

You can also view standard output information in a Web browser, in which case it appears in the browser's Java console window. You must first make sure the Java console window is enabled in the browser, however. In Microsoft Internet Explorer 4.0 this is accomplished by going to the Advanced tab within the Internet Options dialog box. After you are there, you'll find a Java VM section that contains a check box titled *Java console enabled*. Make sure this box is checked. If it isn't then check it, restart your computer, and start Internet Explorer again. The following figure shows the Java console enabled check box in the Internet Options dialog box.

With the Java console enabled, you're ready to try it out. Open the Web page DateTime.html in Internet Explorer to run the DateTime applet. Then select **Java console** from the **View** menu to display the Java console window. The following figure shows the Java console window displayed for the DateTime applet. Notice the first few lines of output and how they relate to the output code added to the applet.

The Java console window also supports a few commands, which are displayed in the preceding figure. The following figure shows the results of clearing the console window (pressing the **C** key on the keyboard) and then determining the Java interpreter's memory usage (pressing the **M** key).

The Java console option in Internet Explorer's Internet Options dialog box.

The Java console window being displayed for the DateTime applet.

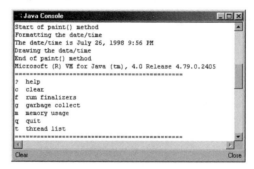

The Java console window after entering commands for clearing it and determining memory usage.

The Least You Need to Know

Although graphical Java applets certainly are the main emphasis throughout this book, it isn't wise to entirely write off command-line Java applications. Command-line applications can actually be quite useful for testing code or building utilities that are suited for being executed from a command line. The standard form of input and output typically associated with command-line applications also can have a surprisingly useful purpose in applets. Let's go over what you learned in this chapter:

➤ Graphical Java applications look like applets but they are responsible for creating and managing their own frame window.

➤ Applications are considered secure by default; applets are not.

➤ The `main()` method is the heart of all Java applications.

➤ Command-line applications are customized through the use of command-line arguments.

➤ The keyboard and monitor are the standard Java input and output devices, respectively.

➤ Standard Java output can be utilized in applets thanks to special Java console windows found in Web browsers.

Chapter 7

Jumping into Java

In This Chapter

➤ Tokens and the Java Compiler

➤ Types of Java Tokens

➤ Variables and Data Types

➤ Understanding Arrays

➤ Strings of Text

Tokens (No, These Can't Be Used in Video Games)

When the Java compiler compiles a program, it first breaks the program down into tokens. If you're like me and grew up in the golden age of video arcades, the word "token" conjures up memories of hours spent playing Donkey Kong and Zaxxon. Or maybe I just spent too much time in arcades! In terms of Java, a token is the smallest code element in a program that is meaningful to the compiler. For example, the following line of Java code contains five tokens:

```
int count = 10;
```

The tokens in this example are int, count, =, 10, and ;. Tokens describe the structure of the Java programming language and are therefore critical to your understanding of Java. Java tokens can be broken down into five categories:

➤ identifiers

➤ keywords

➤ literals

➤ operators

➤ separators

Things that aren't considered tokens include comments and white space (spaces, tabs, and end-of-lines), which are ignored by the Java compiler. The next few sections cover the five different types of tokens recognized by the Java compiler.

Identifiers

Identifiers are tokens that represent names. Anything in a program that has a name uses an identifier. Let's go back to the example from earlier:

```
int count = 10;
```

Can you guess which token is an identifier? The count token is an identifier because it "identifies" the name of the variable. Identifiers are extremely important in Java programs because they serve as the means of uniquely identifying parts of a program. Class names are also identifiers. Good examples include the Skeleton, PondVolume, and DateTime classes with which you worked in the previous chapter.

Although you can be creative in naming identifiers, there are a few limitations. All Java identifiers are case sensitive and must begin with a letter, an underscore (_), or a dollar sign ($). Letters include both uppercase and lowercase letters, which are differentiated from each other because Java is case sensitive. Subsequent identifier characters can include the numbers 0 to 9. The only other limitation to identifier names is that an identifier cannot share a name with a Java keyword, which you learn about in just a moment.

Before moving on, let's take a look at some identifier names:

➤ 4scoreand7

➤ jerky

➤ Gimme5

➤ check_ya

➤ Hi there

➤ Hithere!

➤ Howdy

Can you guess which of these are valid and which are invalid? 4scoreand7 is invalid because it begins with a number. jerky, Gimme5, and check_ya are all valid. Hi there isn't valid because it contains a space. Hithere! isn't valid because it contains an exclamation point. Finally, Howdy is a perfectly valid identifier, not to mention a powerfully warm greeting!

Keywords

Keywords are special identifiers that are set aside for use in the Java programming language. Following is a list of keywords reserved for use in Java:

abstract	float	return
boolean	for	short
break	goto	static
byte	if	strictfp
case	implements	super
catch	import	switch
char	instanceof	synchronized
class	int	this
const	interface	throws
continue	long	transient
default	native	true
do	new	try
double	null	void
else	package	volatile
extends	private	while
false	protected	widefp
final	public	

Hurry, memorize all of these because there's going to be a quiz at the end of the chapter! No, just kidding. Hopefully you recognize a few of the keywords listed, but it's not too critical that you have them memorized at this point. I mainly wanted to show them to you so you could start getting familiar with them. Just remember that every keyword has a reason for being included in Java. Some keywords perform a vital function and others are placeholders intended to keep you from using a particular word as an identifier. You learn the significance of most of these keywords throughout the book as you dig deeper into the Java language.

Literals

Literals are parts of a program that are constant, such as numbers and strings. Going back to the earlier example:

```
int count = 10;
```

In this example, 10 is a literal because it represents a constant number. The following code demonstrates a string literal:

```
String name = "mike";
```

In this case the constant string "mike" is a literal. Literals really don't get any more complicated than that!

Operators

Operators are used to specify an evaluation or computation. I know this description sounds kind of vague, so maybe an example is in order. Actually, let's revisit both examples you've seen thus far in this chapter:

```
int count = 10;
String name = "mike";
```

Any idea as to what the operators might be in these examples? Both examples rely on the same operator, =, which is the assignment operator. The assignment operator takes the value on the right and stores it (assigns it) to the variable on the left.

There are all kinds of operators in Java, so I won't get into all of the details right now. However, it's worth looking at a few more examples, just to get you more comfortable with the idea. I described operators as being used to specify an evaluation or computation. It shouldn't come as too much of a surprise that + and - are both operators. Following is an example:

```
int num1 = 7 + 4;
int num2 = num1 - 6;
```

Without resorting to a calculator, can you guess the value of num2 based on this code? Are you finished carrying the one? Seriously, the + and – operators act just like their counterparts on a calcuator. So, the first line of code results in a value of 11 being stored in num1. The second line then effectively performs the computaion 11 - 6, which results in a value of 5 being stored in num 2.

Separators

The last type of tocken you're going to learn about is separators. Separators are symbols used to inform the Java compiler of how things are grouped in the code. For example, items in a list are separated by commas, much like lists of words in a sentence. Following are the separators used in Java:

```
{   }     ;     ,     :
```

Data Types for Every Occasion

I alluded to variables in the previous chapter when I talked about storing information in a program. If you recall, variables are storage containers used to hold data of a given type. Java supports a variety of data types that dictate the type of information that can be stored in a variable. To create a variable in a Java program, you must declare it by providing the type of the variable as well as an identifier that uniquely identifies the variable. You've seen a few different variable declarations in this chapter already:

```
int count = 10;
String name = "mike";
int num1 = 7 + 4;
int num2 = num1 - 6;
```

The first line of code declares a variable named count whose data type is int, which is an integer (whole number) data type. The second line of code declares a variable named name whose data type is String, which holds text. The last two lines, like the first, also declare integer variables.

All of these declarations set aside memory in your computer for each variable. The data type determines the amount of memory set aside for a variable. You can declare multiple variables of the same type by separating them with commas:

```
float distance, rate, time;
```

No, I'm not going to use one of those painful word problems from Algebra I with this example code! Rather, I want you to see how three variables with the names distance, rate, and time are created on one line of code. These variables are all of type float, which is a floating-point data type. A floating-point number is a number with a fractional part, such as 1.5 or 3.14.

OK, so you get the idea about how variables hold data of a given type. But what different data types are available for storing data? Java data types can be broken down into two major types: simple and composite. A simple data type, also called a primitive data type, is a core data type that isn't derived from any other type and represents a single piece of information. Composite data types, on the other hand, are based on simple types and are used to represent more complex information. The next few sections cover the simple data types available in Java. A little later in the chapter you learn about strings, which are the most commonly used composite data type.

Elephants, Integers, and Light Switches

It is commonly accepted that elephants have extremely good memories, yet they have very small brains relative to their body size. How much memory is required of an elephant to keep up with integer numbers? A byte requires 8 bits of memory, which is roughly equivalent to 8 transistors in your computer's memory or 8 neurons in the elephant's brain. A short requires 16 bits, an int requires 32 bits, and a long requires 64 bits.

Are you starting to see a pattern here? Computer memory revolves around the number 2, meaning that everything happens in powers of two. A short is twice as big as a byte, an int is twice as big as a short, and so on. Most things in a computer are associated with the number two because computers are binary machines, which means they only think in terms of something being on or off.

Numbers in a computer are actually based on this on/off premise. An 8-bit byte in memory is very much like having 8 on/off light switches. The particular combination of the on/off states of the switches determines the number being stored.

Integer Numbers

Integer numbers, which are whole numbers without fractional parts, are represented by a few different simple data types: byte, short, int, and long. The significance between these different integer data types is the amount of memory each requires. This in turn determines how large (or small) a number each can store. For example, the byte data type requires the least memory but can only store numbers in the range –128 to 127. On the other hand, the int data type requires four times as much memory as byte and can store numbers in the range –2,147,483,648 to 2,147,483,647. The long data type is even larger than int and can store numbers much larger than you and I are capable of comprehending. Realistically, the int type provides plenty of flexibility, in most cases, for dealing with a wide range of numbers.

Floating-Point Numbers

Floating-point numbers, which are numbers with fractional parts, are represented by two different data types: float and double. Like integer data types, the only difference between the two floating-point data types is the amount of memory each uses. The float type requires 32 bits of memory and the double type requires 64 bits of memory. Consequently, a double can store much larger (and smaller) numbers than a float. Even so, a float is sufficient for storing floating-point numbers in many programs.

Booleans

The boolean data type is used to store values with one of two possible states: true or false. You can think of the boolean type as representing a 1-bit integer value, because 1 bit can have only two possible values, 0 or 1. You could also think of the boolean type as the data type of choice if you were creating a Java program for issuing true/false tests for teaching purposes. Each question in a test has only two possible answers, true or false. This is a perfect situation for using a boolean variable. To declare a boolean variable, you use the boolean data type in a variable declaration like this:

```
boolean answer;
```

You set a boolean variable by using the true and false keywords. See, I told you earlier that keywords would slowly creep into your life! Following is an example of setting the answer variable to false:

```
answer = false;
```

Characters

The last of the simple data types is the char type, which is used to store characters. No, the char type isn't used to store cartoon characters, character actors, or even shady characters. Instead, it is used to store individual characters of text like A, B, C, and so on. You could liken a character to a letter, but characters extend beyond letters to include symbols like & and *, along with special control characters that aren't printable.

A string of text in Java can always be broken down into a series of characters. In fact, deep inside the inner workings of Java, strings are actually stored as a series of characters, but don't tell anyone I told you. As an example, consider the following string of text: GALT. This string of text is actually the four characters G, A, L, and T stuck together. It is important to understand the relationship between characters and strings because it is often necessary to manipulate a string based on its length, which is the number of characters it contains.

To declare a character variable, you use the char data type in a variable declaration like this:

```
char firstInitial;
```

You could also create two character variables by using a comma, like this:

```
char firstInitial, lastInitial;
```

One other thing worth mentioning in regard to characters is character literals. If you recall, a literal is a fixed value used in a program, such as 10, 8.72, false, and "help". These four examples include integer, floating-point, Boolean, and string literals, in that order. A character literal is a single fixed character used in a program, such as 'A', '$', and 'c'. Notice that the characters are all enclosed by single quotes (' '); this is required for character literals.

Following is an example of using character literals to set my first and last initials using the two variables declared earlier:

```
firstInitial = 'M';
lastInitial = 'M';
```

Arrays and Strings

Now that you have a pretty good understanding of variables and data types, it's time to press onward and tackle two very important and somewhat related topics, arrays and strings. Let's take them one at a time. An array is a special construct in Java that enables you to store a list of items of the same data type. You can think of an array as a series of variables of the same type. Unlike a series of variables, however, an array is actually a single variable. The different elements within an array are numbered and are accessed based on their number.

Array variables are declared with square brackets ([ ]). Following are a couple of examples of array declarations:

```
int[] score;
char[] alphabet;
```

The square brackets appearing after the variable type indicate that the variable is an array. The problem is, you haven't specified how many elements are in the array. This is accomplished with a little more code. In fact, I have to jump ahead a little to explain how an array is sized. To specify the size of an array, you must use the new operator and provide the number of elements the array is to hold, like this:

```
int[] score = new int[2];
char[] alphabet = new char[26];
```

As you can see, the new operator is used to create an int array containing two elements; the char array contains 26 elements. I know this code probably looks a little strange, but it is absolutely required of all arrays before you can use them. Otherwise, Java wouldn't know how big an array was, and you would get into trouble if you tried to use it. The new operator is actually used to allocate memory for an array, which is why you must perform this task before using an array.

The best way to understand the array creation process is to initially think of an array variable as a placeholder for an array. In this way, an array variable is like a label that you intend to place on a box to identify its contents. You don't actually get the array storage container until you use the new operator to create it. Or, using the box analogy, you don't actually get the box for your label until you use the new operator to create it. This explains why it doesn't make any sense to try and store something in an array prior to using the new operator; ever tried to stuff an old pair of shoes into a label without a box?

After you create an array, you access its individual elements using square brackets and an integer index, like this:

```
alphabet[0] = 'A';
alphabet[1] = 'B';
alphabet[25] = 'Z';
```

Each element in an array is associated with an integer index, which is used to access the element. Array indexes range from 0 to the length of the array minus 1. So, in the case of the alphabet array, its indexes range from 0 to 25 because the array is 26 characters long. Java arrays are known as zero-based arrays because their indexes always begin with zero.

A neat trick that makes arrays easier to create is array initialization. It is possible to create an array and fill it with values all in one line of code, like this:

```
char[] vowels = {'A', 'E', 'I', 'O',
'U'};
```

In this example, the vowels array is automatically created to hold five char values, and then it is filled with the values 'A', 'E', 'I', 'O', and 'U'. Notice that the new operator isn't required in this case, because the number of elements for the array is implicitly identified by the list of initialization values. It's important to also note the use of curly braces ({}) to enclose the array's initialization values.

Objectionable Arrays

The real reason you have to use the new operator to create an array is because arrays aren't simple data types. Arrays are composite data types, which actually means that they are objects. Java objects are always created using the new operator. It might seem strange that arrays are objects because they are often composed of a series of elements of a simple data type. However, the management of multiple pieces of information is beyond the realm of a simple data type, which is why Java arrays are objects. You don't really get the inside scoop on creating and working with objects until Chapter 10, "Why Classes Appeal to the Architect in All of Us."

Incidentally, you might be wondering if the following code is acceptable:

```
char[] name = "lurston";
```

I did allude earlier to the fact that a string could be thought of as an array of characters. Although this is often a useful way of thinking of strings, it doesn't hold true when it comes to Java code. An array of characters is not the same as a string. Character arrays and strings are similar in that they are both objects, but that's about as similar as they get. Speaking of strings, let's go ahead and learn how they work in Java.

In Java, strings of text are represented by a special class named `String`. The `String` class is the one Java class you will probably use more than any other Java class. Fortunately, it is extremely easy to use and offers many neat features for working with strings. Following is an example of creating a couple of `String` objects:

```
String message;
String name;
```

As you can see, creating strings is pretty simple. There is one small caveat to this example code, however. Remember the label and box analogy from before? The same thing applies here. This code only creates placeholders for strings; memory isn't actually allocated for the strings unless you use the `new` operator, like this:

```
String message = new String();
String name = new String();
```

The two `String` objects are now officially created and ready to use. But they don't hold any text yet. Assigning them values is extremely easy, as the following example code demonstrates:

```
message = "How are you?";
name = "Mortimer";
```

On the other hand, you can create a string simply by assigning it a string value and sidestep creating an empty string first. The following code demonstrates:

```
String message = "How are you?";
String name = "Mortimer";
```

Notice that the `new` operator isn't required in this example because you are providing enough information for the strings to be created without it. This brings up a subtle but important point regarding strings: String literals like `"Mortimer"` are actually objects themselves. This is important to understand because it explains why you can assign a string literal to a string variable that hasn't been created via the `new` operator.

Let me offer one more thought regarding string creation. The previous example that creates two strings by assigning them string literals could also have been coded like this:

```
String message = new String("How are you?");
String name = new String("Mortimer");
```

This code is a little more explicit and clearly shows what is taking place. You can use any of these approaches, but this latter approach is the most descriptive when it comes to showing how strings are created and initialized.

One really useful property of strings is how they are concatenated, or added together. You can use the + operator to add two strings together, which means the second string is appended to the end of the first. The following code demonstrates:

```
String s1 = "Would you tell me ";
String s2 = "what time it is?";
String s3 = s1 + s2;
```

In this example, the sentence fragments in the strings s1 and s2 are added together and stored in s3. The resulting string stored in s3 is the complete sentence "Would you tell me what time it is?".

Is your brain starting to swell? I know this chapter has been pretty technical thus far, so let's take a step back and put some of this newfound knowledge to use. The next section leads you through the development of an applet with a very practical and tasty purpose.

Applet: Recipe

I love to cook, and one of the first things I learned how to cook was fudge. My dad taught me the recipe, so I'm about to divulge a family secret by building an applet around my dad's fudge recipe. It's actually not really a family secret, but it is a very good recipe all the same. Anyway, let's get back to Java.

The Recipe applet displays a recipe that has been stored in an array of strings. An array of what? That's right, we've talked about arrays and we've talked about strings, but we haven't talked about arrays of strings. Arrays aren't limited to simple data types like integers and characters; they can also consist of composite data types like strings. Following is an example of creating and initializing an array of strings:

```
String[] colors = { "red",
                    "green",
                    "blue",
                    "purple",
                    "orange" };
```

Notice that the strings are enclosed by curly braces; this is important any time you are initializing an array. You might also be curious about the fact that the strings are all lined up perfectly. This is purely a style issue and doesn't affect the functionality of the code, but it does make it much easier to read.

Okay, back to the Recipe applet. The Recipe applet consists of two string arrays, one that holds the ingredients for the fudge recipe and another that holds the steps involved in preparing the recipe. Following is the code for these two string arrays:

```
String[] ingredients = { "2 cups sugar",
                         "1/4 cup cocoa",
                         "1/2 cup milk",
                         "1/2 stick margarine",
                         "1 tsp. vanilla" };
String[] steps = { "Mix all ingredients except vanilla.",
                   "Bring to boil over medium heat.",
                   "Stir while boiling for 3 minutes",
                   "Immediately place pan in cold water in sink.",
                   "Add vanilla and stir until it thickens.",
                   "Pour into a buttered dish and let cool.",
                   "Cut and enjoy!" };
```

All the applet must do is display each of these strings, one after the next. It is also visually appealing to include some separation between the ingredients and the steps. Following is the code required for drawing the strings:

```
FontMetrics fm = g.getFontMetrics();
g.drawString(ingredients[0], 0, fm.getAscent());
g.drawString(ingredients[1], 0, fm.getAscent() * 2);
g.drawString(ingredients[2], 0, fm.getAscent() * 3);
g.drawString(ingredients[3], 0, fm.getAscent() * 4);
g.drawString(ingredients[4], 0, fm.getAscent() * 5);
g.drawString(steps[0], 0, fm.getAscent() * 7);
g.drawString(steps[1], 0, fm.getAscent() * 8);
g.drawString(steps[2], 0, fm.getAscent() * 9);
g.drawString(steps[3], 0, fm.getAscent() * 10);
g.drawString(steps[4], 0, fm.getAscent() * 11);
g.drawString(steps[5], 0, fm.getAscent() * 12);
g.drawString(steps[6], 0, fm.getAscent() * 13);
```

This code should look vaguely similar to the drawing code in the DateTime applet from the previous chapter. The important thing to note in the code is the access of each array element using an appropriate index. The only tricky thing going on here is the vertical position of the strings, which increases for each string so that they are drawn below each other. The fm.getAscent() method call gets the height of a string using the current font, which gives you the height of a line of the recipe. Multiplying this value by an increasing number for each string solves the problem of drawing the strings in a vertical list. Easy as pie, or fudge in this case!

The following figure shows the Recipe applet running in the AppletViewer.

*The Recipe applet running
in the AppletViewer.*

Following is the complete code for the Recipe applet:

```java
import java.applet.*;
import java.awt.*;

public class Recipe extends Applet {
  public void paint(Graphics g) {
    // Create the recipe strings
    String[] ingredients = { "2 cups sugar",
                             "1/4 cup cocoa",
                             "1/2 cup milk",
                             "1/2 stick margarine",
                             "1 tsp. vanilla" };
    String[] steps = { "Mix all ingredients except vanilla.",
                       "Bring to boil over medium heat.",
                       "Stir while boiling for 3 minutes",
                       "Immediately place pan in cold water in sink.",
                       "Add vanilla and stir until fudge thickens.",
                       "Pour into a buttered dish and let cool.",
                       "Cut and enjoy!" };

    // Draw the recipe
    FontMetrics fm = g.getFontMetrics();
    g.drawString(ingredients[0], 0, fm.getAscent());
    g.drawString(ingredients[1], 0, fm.getAscent() * 2);
    g.drawString(ingredients[2], 0, fm.getAscent() * 3);
    g.drawString(ingredients[3], 0, fm.getAscent() * 4);
    g.drawString(ingredients[4], 0, fm.getAscent() * 5);
    g.drawString(steps[0], 0, fm.getAscent() * 7);
    g.drawString(steps[1], 0, fm.getAscent() * 8);
    g.drawString(steps[2], 0, fm.getAscent() * 9);
    g.drawString(steps[3], 0, fm.getAscent() * 10);
    g.drawString(steps[4], 0, fm.getAscent() * 11);
    g.drawString(steps[5], 0, fm.getAscent() * 12);
    g.drawString(steps[6], 0, fm.getAscent() * 13);
  }
}
```

81

The Least You Need to Know

You can't be a successful carpenter without learning about the different types of nails and wood at your disposal. Likewise, you can't be a successful Java programmer without learning the fundamental constructs of the Java programming language and how they are used. This chapter explored the basic structure of a Java program and the pieces and parts therein. There is still plenty more to learn, but hopefully you're leaving this chapter with a little more insight into the structure of Java code. Let's recap what you learned in this chapter:

➤ When the Java compiler compiles a program, it first breaks the program down into tokens.

➤ Identifiers are tokens that represent names such as `pokey` and `hitPoints`.

➤ Keywords are special identifiers such as `while` and `new` that are set aside for use in the Java programming language.

➤ Literals are constant parts of a program such as `6.22` and `"Shirley"`.

➤ Operators, which are usually symbols such as `+` and `-`, are used to specify an evaluation or computation.

➤ The `boolean` data type is used to store values with one of two possible states: `true` or `false`.

➤ Arrays enable you to store a list of items of the same data type.

➤ In Java, strings of text are represented by a special class named `String`.

Chapter 8

Expressing Yourself in Java

In This Chapter

➤ Java Expressions

➤ Fun with Operators

➤ Branching Program Flow

➤ A Name Guessing Application

Feeling Expressive

Whether it's a Mohawk hairdo, a tattoo on your forehead, or a hoop through your neck, these days everyone seems to be into expressing themselves. Java provides just the outlet for those of us who aren't quite as adventurous with self-expression. I'm referring to Java expressions, which form a fundamental part of the Java language. You've actually already seen a variety of different Java expressions, because it's tough for a program to do much without them.

An expression is somewhat of a programming equation, meaning that it usually involves an equal sign (=) and somehow manipulates one or more variables or values. More formally, an expression is a combination of operands and operators that produces a result. Following is a simple example of an expression:

```
x = 5 + 2;
```

No extra credit for guessing the value of x! In this expression, x is a variable, = is the assignment operator, 5 and 2 are integer literals, and + is the addition operator. This expression states that the number 2 is added to the number 5, and the result is assigned to the variable x. The process of performing the operations in an expression to get a result is referred to as "evaluating an expression." Pretty simple, right? Well, let's try a more complicated expression:

```
x = 3 * 4 + 18 / 9;
```

Before analyzing this expression, let me point out that the operators for multiplication and division are * and /, respectively. Okay, back to the expression. Any ideas on how it should be evaluated? Let me give you a hint: Expressions are always evaluated from left to right. However, there is a catch: Operators are not created equal, so you can't just run from left to right, performing the evaluation.

It just so happens that the multiplication and division operators have a higher precedence than the addition and subtraction operators do, which means that you always perform a multiplication or division before an addition or subtraction. Applying this rule, the equation resolves into:

```
x = 12 + 2;
```

Excusing Aunt Sally

Because Java expressions are similar in many ways to algebraic expressions, the popular phrase taught in high school algebra classes might come in handy here. The phrase "Please Excuse My Dear Aunt Sally" provides a quick way to remember operator precedence for mathematical equations. Taking the first letters of the phrase, you get P-E-M-D-A-S, which helps you remember: Parentheses, Exponents, Multiplication, Division, Addition, and Subtraction.

Unfortunately, Java doesn't exactly conform to this rule, because exponents have a lower precedence than the other operators do. So, we need to modify the phrase a little to fit Java. How about trying "Picture My Dear Aunt Sally in England." This phrase results in the letters P-M-D-A-S-E, which is the order that you evaluate the basic Java operators for Parentheses, Multiplication, Division, Addition, Subtraction, and Exponents. I'll leave it up to you to formulate a longer phrase that covers every operator in Java. Actually, it might end up being a paragraph!

Now you can go back to the left-to-right rule and simply add 12 and 2, which results in a value of 14 being stored in x. Operator precedence is extremely important and is responsible for countless bugs due to programmers not taking care to observe it. Now that I've practically already explained operators to you, let's take some time to learn more about them.

Smooth Operators

It's practically impossible to write a Java program without using operators, which is why you already have some experience with them. Java supports a variety of operators, but some are more commonly used than others. Following are the major types of Java operators:

> ➤ Numeric operators
> ➤ Boolean operators
> ➤ String operators
> ➤ Assignment operators

Not surprisingly, the types of operators mirror to some extent the types of data supported by Java. The next few sections examine each of these types of operators and provide examples of how they are used.

Numeric Operators

Quick, guess what numeric operators are used to manipulate? Don't strain too hard because the answer is right in front of you. Numeric operators are used to manipulate numbers! Numeric operators range from simple addition (+) and subtraction (-) operators to more advanced operators such as modulus (%). Actually, the modulus operator isn't really all that advanced; it just isn't as familiar as addition and subtraction. You learn about it in a moment.

Numeric operators are divided across three different types: those that operate on a single number, those that operate on two numbers, and those that compare two numbers. Let's start by looking at the first of these types.

Numeric operators that operate on a single number are called unary operators. The two most commonly used unary operators are ++ and --, which are used to increment or decrement a number by 1. Following is an example of using the unary operators:

```
int x = 5;
float y = 13.7;
x++;
y--;
```

Although these unary operators work with all numbers, there is a difference between using them with an integer and with a floating-point number. In the previous example, the integer variable x is incremented by 1, and the floating-point variable y is decremented by 1.0. The distinction is the increment or decrement of 1.0 instead of 1 for floating-point numbers.

To make things a little more interesting, you have the option of using the unary operators as either prefix or postfix operators. This applies when a unary operator is used within an expression. A prefix operator is applied before the expression is evaluated, and a postfix operator is applied after the expression is evaluated. Confused? Maybe an example will help clarify the difference:

```
int w = 7, x = 18, y, z;
y = w + x--;
z = w + --x;
```

The Lazy Man's Operators

The increment (++) and decrement (--) operators don't actually offer anything you can't accomplish with a combination of the addition (+) and assignment (=) operators. However, the increment and decrement operators require less code and, consequently, less work on your behalf. You can think of them as shortcut operators that simplify the code for incrementing and decrementing numbers.

When the first expression is evaluated, x is first added to w and assigned to y, and then decremented. The resulting value of y is 7 + 18, or 25. The second expression is very similar, but x is prefix decremented. In this expression x is decremented first and then added to w and assigned to z. Keep in mind that x was already decremented once after the first expression, so the resulting value of z is 7 + 16, or 23.

Numeric operators that operate on two numbers are called binary operators. Following is a list of the most commonly used binary operators:

➤ Addition (+)
➤ Subtraction (-)
➤ Multiplication (*)
➤ Division (/)
➤ Modulus (%)

You probably have a pretty good idea about how all of these operators work except for the last one. The modulus operator is associated with the division operator. To understand its purpose, let's take a quick trip back in time. Let's go back to the days before calculators—when everyone had to perform multiplication and division by hand. The one aspect of hand-division that isn't present in most calculators is the remainder. When a number doesn't perfectly divide into another number, the remainder is the number that is left over. The modulus operator effectively performs a division on two numbers and gives you the remainder. Let's try it out:

```
int x = 37 % 5;
```

The value of x in this example is 2 because the remainder of 37 divided by 5 is 2. Now consider the same expression with a division operator (/) instead of modulus:

```
int x = 37 / 5;
```

In this case, the value of x is 7 because 5 goes into 37 7 times with a remainder of 2. This demonstrates the relationship between the division and modulus operators.

The last type of numeric operator you need to know about is the relational operator, which compares two numbers. Relational operators perform a comparison on two numbers and return a Boolean (`true` or `false`) result. Following are the relational numeric operators available in Java:

➤ Less-than (<)

➤ Greater-than (>)

➤ Less-than-or-equal to (<=)

➤ Greater-than-or-equal-to (>=)

➤ Equal-to (==)

➤ Not-equal-to (!=)

Initialization Duplication

You might have noticed in the previous example that not only are multiple variables declared, but also two of them (w and x) are initialized in the declaration. This simply means that the w and x variables are assigned values upon creation. Initializing multiple variables is a standard Java feature and is really no different than initializing one variable; you just string out the variable initializations with commas between them. You can also mix in variable declarations that aren't initialized, as the example demonstrates. Regardless of whether any initialization is taking place, don't forget that multiply declared variables are all of the same data type.

These operators are invaluable in determining differences between numbers. Following is an example:

```
int x = 19, y = 14;
boolean b1 = x < y;
boolean b2 = x > y;
boolean b3 = (x == 19);
boolean b4 = (y != 11);
```

The first Boolean variable, b1, is set to `false` because x is not less than y. The second Boolean variable, b2, is set to `true` because x is greater than y. The third Boolean variable, b3, is set to `true` because x does equal 19. Finally, the last Boolean variable, b4, is set to `true` because y is not equal to 11.

Parenthetically Speaking

You might be wondering why I grouped the comparisons in the last two lines of the example code within parentheses. This isn't strictly necessary, but it helps distinguish the comparison from the assignment operator (=), because they both look somewhat alike. Java programmers often use parentheses like this to make things easier to understand—not for the computer, but for themselves!

Boolean Operators

Boolean operators are a lot like the relational numeric operators except they are used with Boolean values instead of numbers. Boolean operators are very useful because they allow you to perform logical comparisons. Remember, Boolean values are always in one of two states: `true` or `false`. Following are the most commonly used Boolean operators:

➤ AND (&&)

➤ OR (¦¦)

➤ Negation (!)

➤ Equal-to (==)

➤ Not-equal-to (!=)

The AND operator (&&) compares two values and only returns `true` if they are both `true`. The OR (¦¦) operator compares two values and returns `true` if either of the values is `true`. The negation operator (!) flips the state of a value; if a value is `true` it becomes `false`, and if it is `false` it becomes `true`. The equal-to (==) and not-equal-to (!=) operators work just like their numeric equivalents, except these deal with Boolean values.

String Operators

Moving right along, next on the operator agenda is string operators. Actually, I'm exaggerating a little because there is only one string operator, the concatenation operator (+). Concatenation is really just a fancy way of saying "stick two strings together." However, it could be a useful word to throw on your non-programming friends. How about "could you help me concatenate these two hose pipes?" They'll either be really impressed or really annoyed. I typically shoot for both, but that's the kind of guy I am.

Anyway, the concatenation operator is very simple to use. Let's take a look at an example:

```
String nickname = "oldtimer";
String message = "Hello there, " + nickname + "!";
```

I think you have an idea how this code will turn out when executed. The `nickname` variable is effectively placed in the middle of a sentence. This code is a little bit like a form letter in that you provide a fixed sentence and a fill-in-the-blank name to plug into it. And all of it thanks to the concatenation operator!

Assignment Operators

Rounding out this marathon discussion of operators are the assignment operators, one of which you already have considerable experience with. Assignment operators all perform some type of operation that results in a value being stored in a variable. Not surprisingly, all of the assignment operators have an equal sign (=) in them. Following are the most commonly used assignment operators:

➤ Simple assignment (=)

➤ Addition (+=)

➤ Subtraction (-=)

➤ Multiplication (*=)

➤ Division (/=)

➤ Modulus (%=)

➤ AND (&=)

➤ OR (¦=)

Beyond the simple assignment operator (=), which assigns a value to a variable, all of the other assignment operators can be considered shorthand versions of other operators combined with an assignment. For example, the addition assignment operator (+=) functions just like an addition operator used in conjunction with a simple assignment. Please allow me to demonstrate:

```
x += 17;
```

This code is functionally equivalent to the following code:

```
x = x + 17;
```

In both examples the value 17 is added to x and then assigned to x. Even though the function performed by assignment operators can be achieved with a combination of other operators, they still serve a vital purpose in simplifying code.

Conditional Branches

No, this section is not about the decisions all trees must make when they contemplate sprouting a new branch. Rather, it is about the ability of a Java program to alter the flow of execution and run one branch of code instead of another. I know this sounds kind of tricky, but I can assure you that it's not. To better understand the significance of branches, let's consider how a Java program flows without branches. Take a look at the following figure.

A Java program executing sequentially with no branches.

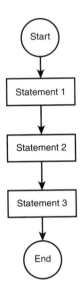

As the figure shows, a Java program without branches executes sequentially from start to end. Each statement in a program is executed from one to the next until the end of the program is reached. Incidentally, a statement is just a line of code in your program. When a program is executed, you can think of it as executing one statement at a time.

The problem with the previous figure is that there is no way for a program to take a different path of execution. This might not seem like a big deal, but it's actually very common for you to want a program to conditionally execute one section of code instead of another. The following figure shows how a branch gives the program more freedom.

By adding a branch to the program in the figure, you give the code two optional routes to take, based on the result of the conditional test. The concept of branches might seem trivial, but imagine if you were to take off in your car and never encounter a branch in the road—and I'm not just talking about forks in the road; I mean any type of turn-off that puts you on a different road. You would never be able to exit for food or drink or a restroom, not to mention the fact that you would run out of gas. Stranded on the side of the road, no one else would be able to help you because they would be in the same predicament as you. As you can clearly see, branches save lives!

Java supports two different kinds of branches, if-else and switch, which you learn about in the next couple of sections.

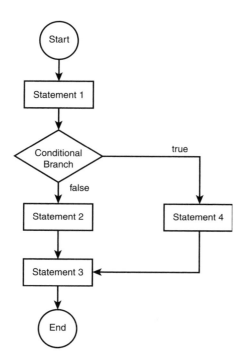

A Java program executing sequentially with a branch.

The *if-else* Branch

The if-else branch is the most commonly used branch in Java programming and is useful in situations where you need to conditionally execute one section of code or another. Following is the syntax for the if-else branch, which will help you understand how it works:

```
if (Condition)
   Statement1
else
   Statement2
```

If the Boolean Condition is true, Statement1 is executed; otherwise Statement2 is executed. Following is a simple example that should clear things up:

```
if (isHungry)
   timeToEat = true;
else
   timeToEat = false;
```

If the Boolean variable isHungry is true, the first statement is executed and timeToEat is set to true. Otherwise, the second statement is executed and timeToEat is set to false.

91

If you have only a single statement that you want to execute conditionally, you can leave off the else part of the if-else branch, like this:

```
if (isThirsty)
   pourADrink = true;
```

On the other hand, what happens if you have more than two branches you want to conditionally choose between? In situations like this you can string together a series of if-else branches to get the net effect of multiple branches. Check out the following code:

```
if (age < 13)
   type = "child";
else if (age < 18)
   type = "teenager";
else if (age < 65)
   type = "adult";
else
   type = "retiree";
```

This code can take one of a number of different branches based on the value of the age variable. Keep in mind that the conditional evaluations are performed in order, so if you arrive at the test age < 65, you already know that age is at least 18 or greater. Otherwise, the previous if conditional would have evaluated to true. Also, remember that only one of the branches is executed.

There is one other aspect of the if-else branch worth mentioning, and that is the issue of compound statements. A compound statement is a block of code surrounded by curly braces ({}). The significance of compound statements is that they appear to an if-else branch as a single statement. The following example code demonstrates:

```
if (needSysInfo) {
   processor = "Pentium II";
   speed = 400;  // Megahertz
   memory = 64;  // Megabytes
}
```

This example shows how multiple statements can be executed within a single if branch by enclosing them in curly braces. Placing the opening curly brace ({) at the end of the line with the if conditional is a pretty standard Java convention, along with placing the closing curly brace (}) on a new line following the compound statements.

I deliberately overlooked an operator in the earlier section of the chapter that covered operators. The reason is because there is an operator that functions very much like a shorthand if-else branch. The conditional operator (?:) evaluates a test expression and conditionally evaluates another expression based on the test. I know this doesn't really make much sense, so let's look at an example:

Commenting for Clarity

In addition to demonstrating the usefulness of compound statements, the previous example also shows how comments can be used to clarify the meaning of numbers. This is a good habit to develop when using numbers in situations where something about their meaning might not be totally apparent. It is beneficial if someone else ever needs to modify or reference your code or if you ever come back to the code and can't immediately remember all of the details.

```
boolean b1 = true;
int x = b1 ? 4 : 11;
```

When using the conditional operator, if the Boolean test is true, the expression to the left of the colon (:) is evaluated; otherwise, the expression to the right of the colon is evaluated. In this example, the test (b1) is true, so the line of code effectively becomes:

```
int x = 4;
```

Pretty simple! But this example really doesn't demonstrate the power of the conditional operator. So let's return to an earlier example and make it a little more interesting:

```
int age = 17;
String nickname = (x < 30) ? "whippersnapper" : "oldtimer";
String message = "Hello there, " + nickname + "!";
```

In this example, a relational numeric operator is used to see if the age variable is less than 30. If so, the nickname variable is set to "whippersnapper"; otherwise nickname is set to "oldtimer". In this case, the age variable is set to 17, so the conditional operator results in the nickname variable being set to "whippersnapper".

As you can probably tell, the conditional operator is somewhat of a shorthand version of the if-else branch. Consider the following if-else example code you looked at a little earlier:

```
if (isHungry)
   timeToEat = true;
else
   timeToEat = false;
```

The previous example could be shortened using the conditional operator like this:

```
timeToEat = isHungry ? true : false;
```

Actually, if you want to get down and dirty you could shorten the code to this:

```
timeToEat = isHungry;
```

When a Conditional Operator Isn't a Branch

I mentioned that the conditional operator is somewhat of a shorthand version of the if-else branch. I used the word "somewhat" because the two things aren't always equivalent. The conditional operator can only be used to conditionally execute one expression or another. The if-else branch, on the other hand, is capable of executing entire sections of code that can include multiple expressions. So, the conditional operator is only a shorthand version of the if-else branch in the most simple of examples. Beyond that, the if-else branch is capable of doing lots of things the conditional operator can't touch.

Think about it. The original example is perhaps a poor usage of the if-else branch because it could be simplified so easily, but its simplicity hopefully helps you to more easily understand how the branch works.

The switch *Branch*

Unlike the if-else branch, the switch branch is specifically designed to conditionally choose between multiple (more than two) branches of code. The syntax for the switch branch follows:

```
switch (Expression) {
   case Constant1:
      StatementList1
   case Constant2:
      StatementList2
   default:
      DefaultStatementList
}
```

As you can see, the switch branch is a little more complicated than the if-else branch. The switch branch evaluates and compares the *Expression* to all of the case constants and branches to the statement list corresponding to the matching constant. If none of the case constants match the *Expression*, the program branches to the *DefaultStatementList*, if one has been supplied. Incidentally, a statement list is simply a series of statements. Unlike the if-else branch, the switch branch doesn't require a compound statement to branch to multiple statements.

Somehow I think the previous paragraph might have lost you. Let's consider an analogy to help clear up the function of the switch branch. Imagine you're trying to drive to a friend's house based on directions given to by your friend. Now pretend you arrive at a junction where three or four roads meet. You reference your friend's directions and compare the road on which your friend said to turn with the signs in front of you. When you match a sign with the correct road name in your directions, you make a turn and are on your way. The road name in your directions is logically equivalent to the switch *Expression*, and the road signs are equivalent to the case constants. When a switch branch matches the *Expression* with a case constant, it jumps down and executes the code below the case constant.

Here's an example that will help clarify the switch branch:

```
switch (grade) {
  case 'A':
    response = "Great job!";
    break;
  case 'B':
    response = "Not bad.";
    break;
  case 'C':
    response = "I suppose average is OK.";
    break;
  case 'D':
    response = "This really isn't acceptable.";
    break;
  case 'F':
    response = "You did what?!";
    break;
  default:
    response = "The dog ate your report card?";
}
```

This example switches on a character variable and looks for a match among different character constants. In this example, the code is looking at a grade and determining the response to use based on the grade. This might serve as a good basis for a parenting Java applet! If the switch branch in the code encounters a match, it immediately starts executing the code beneath the matching case statement. It will continue executing code beneath the case statement until it reaches a break statement, at which point it jumps out of the entire switch branch. If there is not a match, program execution moves to the statement immediately following the default statement. Let's work through a hypothetical situation to see what happens.

If the grade variable is set to 'C', then the switch branch will match with the third case statement. The following line of code will then immediately be executed:

```
response = "I suppose average is OK.";
```

After executing this line of code, the program encounters a break statement and jumps out of the entire switch branch. Let's now consider what would happen if the grade variable was set to 'G'. In this case, there would be no match and the following line of code would be executed:

```
response = "The dog ate your report card?";
```

Because the default statement must appear at the bottom of the switch branch, the branch is always exited after executing any default code.

Like nested `if-else` branches, only one branch of code is executed in a `switch` branch. However, if you accidentally left out one of the `break` statements, the program would fall through and continue executing until it encountered one. The following example demonstrates:

```
switch (number) {
  case 1:
    text = "one";
  case 2:
    text = "two";
    break;
  case 3:
    text = "three";
    break;
}
```

In this example, if the `number` variable is set to 1 then you will get unexpected results. Why? Because the first `case` statement will fall through to the second `case` statement and end up setting the `text` variable to `"two"`. The missing `break` statement in the first `case` statement is the culprit. It's worth noting that there are some isolated circumstances in which you might want to purposely leave out a `break` statement to allow a `case` statement to fall through, but generally speaking it is an error.

Finding the Book's Applet and Java Application Examples on the Web

To find the applets and Java application examples provided in this book, enter the address `http://www.mcp.com/info` in the location box. Click the link called **Downloadable Code, Examples, and Info for book "Companion Sites."** In the space provided under the Book Information section, enter **0-7897-1804-9**, which is the 10-digit ISBN for this book. Click the **Search** button.

Application: ColorNames

You've covered a great deal of information in this chapter and are probably eager to see some of it pay off. Let's develop an application to put some of your newer skills to work. I thought it might be fun for the application to accept your favorite color as a command-line argument and then try to guess your name based on the color. Obviously, the accuracy of the name guessing will be a little under 100 percent, but it will still be a fun application with which to experiment.

Because you already know how to process command-line arguments in applications, let's jump straight into the code that really matters. Following is the `switch` branch that guesses a person's name based on their favorite color:

```
String color, name;
switch (args[0].charAt(0)) {
  case 'r':
    color = "red";
    name = "Fred";
```

```
      break;
    case 'g':
      color = "green";
      name = "Charlene";
      break;
    case 'b':
      color = "blue";
      name = "Lou";
      break;
    case 'y':
      color = "yellow";
      name = "Old Yeller";
      break;
    default:
      color = "a strange color";
      name = "really silly";
      break;
}
```

Because strings aren't primitive constants (they are constant objects at best), you can't use a string as the basis for a switch branch. So, I decided to just use the first character of the favorite color as the basis for the switch. The first character was plucked out of the string by calling the charAt() method on the args[0] String object. I know you haven't been formally introduced to calling methods on objects yet, but bear with me. Because there is such a thing as a constant character, the first character of args[0] is sufficient for the switch branch.

The body of the switch branch is pretty simple; each case assigns a different pair of strings to the color and name variables. Take special note of the code following the default statement; this code is executed for colors that don't match any of the case statements.

The only remaining task of the ColorNames application is to display the results. The following code accomplishes this:

```
System.out.println("You chose " + color + " so your name must be " +
name + ".");
```

Notice that the string concatenation operator (+) is used to build a sentence out of string literals and variables. The net effect is a custom sentence that relies on the color and name of the person set in the switch branch.

Following is the resulting output of the application when I entered blue as my favorite color:

```
You chose blue so your name must be Lou.
```

For more interesting results, try entering a color that isn't handled by a case state-ment. Following is the resulting output of entering a favorite color of purple:

    You chose a strange color so your name must be really silly.

Following is the complete code for the ColorNames application:

```java
import java.applet.*;
import java.awt.*;

public class ColorNames {
  public static void main(String[] args) {
    // Make sure we have the right number of args
    if (args.length != 1) {
      System.out.println("Usage: java ColorNames Color");
      System.exit(0);
    }

    // Determine the name based on the color
    String color, name;
    switch (args[0].charAt(0)) {
      case 'r':
        color = "red";
        name = "Fred";
        break;
      case 'g':
        color = "green";
        name = "Charlene";
        break;
      case 'b':
        color = "blue";
        name = "Lou";
        break;
      case 'y':
        color = "yellow";
        name = "Old Yeller";
        break;
      default:
        color = "a strange color";
        name = "really silly";
        break;
    }

    // Display the results
    System.out.println("You chose " + color + " so your name must be
    ➥" + name + ".");
  }
}
```

The Least You Need to Know

Well, it looks like you've survived another chapter detailing yet more nuts and bolts of Java. A typical Java program relies solely on expressions to perform any type of data processing or manipulation. Within an expression, operators take on the chore of performing specific functions such as adding or subtracting numbers. Beyond that, you learned that Java programs would be a lot less interesting without the benefits of branching. Let's hit the high points of what you learned in this chapter:

➤ An expression is really just a programming equation.

➤ Expressions are always evaluated from left to right, but you have to take into consideration operator precedence.

➤ The modulus operator (%) performs a division on two numbers and gives you the remainder.

➤ Concatenation is really just a fancy way of saying "stick two strings together."

➤ The conditional operator (?:) is somewhat of a shorthand version of the if-else branch.

➤ The switch branch is specifically designed to conditionally choose between multiple (more than two) branches of code.

Feeling a Little Loopy

A Loop for Every Occasion

Have you ever been talking to someone and it seems like he or she is saying the same thing over and over? I mean, you keep listening, and they keep talking, and it all sounds the same. And they talk some more and you listen some more and you wonder if it will ever end! Congratulations, you just experienced a perfect example of a verbal loop! In Java, a loop is a programming construct that enables you to repeat a section of code over and over, much like my conversation example.

Loops are very valuable in Java because they enable you to tightly control repetitive functions. Three type of loops are used in Java:

➤ for loops

➤ while loops

➤ do loops

Getting Redundant with the *for* **Loop**

Let's pretend NASA used Java applets to control the launch of the space shuttle. Any ideas on how controllers would initiate the launch sequence? With loops! Counting down from ten to one is a piece of cake with a loop. Granted, without a loop it wouldn't be too tough either, but it would require some unnecessary code. Following is code to perform the launch sequence without the use of a loop:

```
System.out.println(10);
System.out.println(9);
System.out.println(8);
System.out.println(7);
System.out.println(6);
System.out.println(5);
System.out.println(4);
System.out.println(3);
System.out.println(2);
System.out.println(1);
```

And now the loop version:

```
for (int i = 10; i > 0; i--)
   System.out.println(i);
```

See what I mean about tightening up the code? You probably wonder exactly how the loop code works. This code relies on a for loop, which is the most structured type of loop supported by Java. for loops repeat a section of code a fixed number of times. Following is the syntax for the for loop:

```
for (InitializationExpression; LoopCondition; StepExpression)
   Statement
```

The for loop repeats the *Statement* the number of times determined by the *InitializationExpression*, *LoopCondition*, and *StepExpression*:

➤ The *InitializationExpression* is used to initialize a loop control variable.

➤ The *LoopCondition* compares the loop control variable to some limit or value.

➤ The *StepExpression* specifies how the loop control variable should be modified before the next iteration of the loop.

Let's take a look at the NASA launch sequence code again to make some sense of this stuff:

```
for (int i = 10; i > 0; i--)
   System.out.println(i);
```

In this code the *InitializationExpression* is int i = 10, which is evaluated initially before the loop begins. This is the code you use to prime the loop and get it ready. The *LoopCondition* is i > 0, which is a Boolean test that is performed before each iteration of the loop. If the Boolean test result is `true`, the *Statement* is executed, which in this case prints the current value of i. After each iteration the *StepExpression* is evaluated, which is i--. This serves to decrement i after each iteration, and ultimately provides the countdown.

The loop continues to iterate and print numbers as i counts down to 0. After i reaches 0, the *LoopCondition* test fails (i > 0), so the loop bails out without printing any more numbers.

Whew, that explanation seemed a little long-winded, and that's coming from the person that wrote it! Unfortunately, it isn't always easy to verbalize the flow of program code. This is why it's easy to fall back on figures. Just ask Ross Perot, who isn't a Java programmer but who nonetheless relied on diagrams and illustrations to help us grasp his big plans for the presidency. You can feel safe and secure knowing that I'm not running for president or trying to help you visualize my answer to global trade. I just want to help you learn how loops work! To help you visualize the looping process, take a look at the following figure.

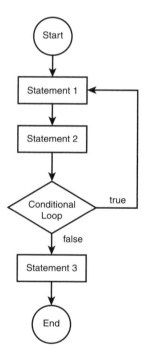

A Java program executing with a loop.

Notice in the figure that *Statement 1* and *Statement 2* will be repeatedly executed as long as the loop condition is `true`. When the loop condition goes `false`, the program falls out of the loop and executes *Statement 3*.

103

The previous figure alludes to the fact that a loop can execute multiple statements. Loops can execute as many statements as they want, provided curly braces ({}) enclose the statements. If you recall, this grouping of statements is known as a compound statement and was used in the previous chapter when dealing with if-else branches. Following is an example of a for loop with a compound statement:

```
int[] squares = new int[10];
for (int i = 1; i <= 10; i++) {
  squares[i - 1] = i * i;
  System.out.println(squares[i]);
}
```

This code calculates the squares of the numbers 1 through 10, stores them in an array, and prints each one. Notice that the loop counter (i) is used as the index (i - 1) into the squares array. This is a very popular way to handle arrays. It is necessary to subtract 1 in this case because all Java array indexes start with 0, which means they are zero based. It might be worth noting that although zero-based arrays were used in other programming languages in the 1980s and before, they have nothing to do with the 80s movie *Less Than Zero* or the 80s hit song *Saved By Zero*. Rest assured I would be the first to tell you if they did!

Looping for Just a Little While

Like the for loop, the while loop has a loop condition that controls the number of times a loop is repeated. However, the while loop has no initialization or step expression. A for loop is like one of those friends who tells you a story three or four times and then waits for a response, whereas a while loop is like one of those friends who continues to repeat himself as long as you continue to listen. They're both annoying, but in different ways. Not the loops, the people!

Following is the syntax for the while loop, which should make its usage a little more clear:

```
while (LoopCondition)
   Statement
```

If the Boolean *LoopCondition* evaluates to true, the *Statement* is executed. When the *Statement* finishes executing, the *LoopCondition* is tested again and the process repeats itself. This continues until the *LoopCondition* evaluates to false, in which case the loop immediately bails out. Because the while loop has no step expression, it is important to make sure that the *Statement* somehow impacts the *LoopCondition*. Otherwise, it is possible for the loop to repeat infinitely, which is usually a bad thing. Following is a simple example of an infinite while loop:

```
while (true)
   System.out.println("Print me infinitely!");
```

Because the loop condition in this example is permanently set to true, the loop will repeat infinitely, or at least until you manually terminate the program. Infinite loops are extremely dangerous because they can result in your computer overheating. Just kidding! Actually, infinite loops are useful in some situations; they are never truly infinite because you can typically terminate one by shutting down the application or applet containing it.

You can think of the while loop as a more general for loop. To understand what I mean by this, check out the following code:

```
int i = 10;
while (i > 0) {
  System.out.println(i);
  i--;
}
```

This is the NASA launch sequence implemented using a while loop instead of a for loop. Because while loops don't have initialization expressions, the initialization of the counter variable i had to be performed before the loop. Likewise, the step expression i-- had to be performed within the *Statement* part of the loop. Regardless of the structural differences, this while loop is functionally equivalent to the for loop you saw earlier in the chapter.

If a for loop can do everything a while loop can and in a more organized way, then why do we need while loops? Because there is a time and a place for everything, and in many situations you have no need for initialization and step expressions. A for loop is overkill in situations like this. Even more importantly, a while loop is much more readable than a for loop when you have no need for initialization and step expressions. Consider the following example:

```
boolean correct = false;
while (!correct) {
  answer = askQuestion();
  correct = isCorrect(answer);
}
```

This code demonstrates how a while loop could be used to ask a question and patiently wait for the correct answer. The loop repeats itself as long as the Boolean variable correct is false. This results in the code repeating the question as many times as necessary until the user guesses the correct answer. The details of the methods askQuestion() and isCorrect() aren't important for this example; just assume that they somehow present the user with a question, retrieve an answer, and then judge the correctness of the answer. The main concern is that the isCorrect() method returns a boolean value that indicates whether or not the answer is correct.

In this example, it is impossible to know how many times the user will miss the answer and need the question repeated. For this reason, the structured step expression of a for loop wouldn't be of much use. while loops are perfect in situations where you don't know ahead of time how many times a loop needs to be repeated.

If you aren't completely satisfied with while loops, however, there is one other option.

To Do, Or Not to Do

The while loop has a very close relative known as the do loop, or do-while loop, that is surprisingly similar to the while loop. Because you're becoming pretty loop savvy, I'll show you the syntax for the do-while loop first and see if you can figure out how it works:

```
do
   Statement
while (LoopCondition);
```

Give up? The do-while loop is basically a while loop with the *LoopCondition* moved to the end. Why is this necessary? Because there are some situations where you would like the *Statement* to execute before evaluating the *LoopCondition*, instead of afterward. This also guarantees that the *Statement* is executed at least once, regardless of the *LoopCondition*. Let's take a look at the question and answer example implemented using a do-while loop:

```
boolean correct;
do {
   answer = askQuestion();
   correct = isCorrect(answer);
}
while (!correct);
```

The code really isn't much different than before, except that you no longer need to initialize the correct variable; it is always initially set during the first pass through the loop. Although both types of loops accomplish the goal of this example, the do-while loop is a better fit because its structure more closely mimics the function of the code. What do I mean by this? Well, if you "read" the code, it is saying "ask the question and if the answer is not correct, ask it again." This makes more sense than if it read "if the answer is not correct, ask the question and then check the answer again."

Admittedly, this is a subtle difference, but a large part of successful programming is keeping things logical and straightforward. You won't always succeed because sometimes code gets complicated regardless of how you construct it, but using loops intelligently is a good start.

Applet: Countdown

Have you ever visited a Web page that directed you to another page, but informed you that if you waited a few seconds it would automatically take you there? I used to run across these pages and wonder how you could make a page wait a few seconds and then automatically navigate to a new page. After I started programming in Java,

I realized what a trivial task this is. In this section you use your knowledge of loops to build a "countdown" applet that counts down from ten to one and then navigates to a new Web page. The following figure shows the Countdown applet in action.

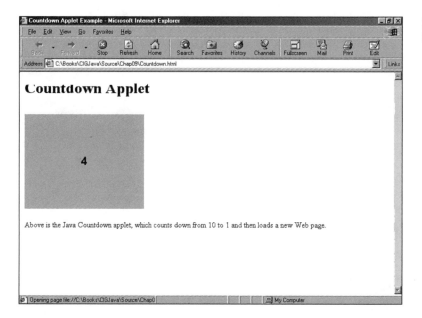

The Countdown applet in the midst of its count.

When the applet finishes counting down, it navigates to the Web page identified by the page applet parameter. As an example, what Web site could be better than NASA's to demonstrate how this applet works? Following is NASA's Web site, to which the Countdown applet will take you after it finishes its countdown.

To understand how the Countdown applet works, let's first take a look at the Countdown.html Web page that contains the embedded applet:

```
<HTML>
<HEAD>
<TITLE>Countdown Applet
➥Example</TITLE>
</HEAD>
<BODY>
<H1>Countdown Applet</H1>
<HR>
```

Finding the Countdown Applet Example on the Web

To find the Countdown applet example source code on the Web, enter the address **http://www.mcp.com/info** in the location box of your Web browser. Click the link called **Downloadable Code, Examples, and Info for book "Companion Sites."** In the space provided under the Book Information section, enter **0-7897-1804-9**, which is the 10-digit ISBN for this book. Click the **Search** button.

107

```
<APPLET CODE="Countdown.class" WIDTH=250 HEIGHT=200>
<PARAM NAME=page VALUE="http://www.nasa.gov">
</APPLET>
<P>
Above is the Java Countdown applet, which counts down from 10 to 1 and
➡then loads a new Web page.
</P>
</BODY>
</HTML>
```

NASA's Web site, to which you are automatically navigated by the Countdown applet after it counts down.

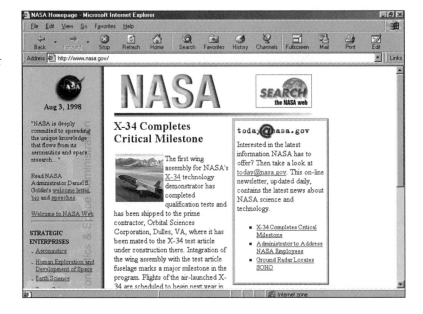

All this stuff should look pretty familiar to you by now. The main thing on which I want you to focus is the page parameter, which is defined as:

```
<PARAM NAME=page VALUE="http://www.nasa.gov">
```

Notice that the value of the page parameter is set to http://www.nasa.gov, which is the URL of NASA's Web site. Changing this value enables you to change the page that is loaded after the applet finishes counting down. This page could have easily been set as a variable within the applet code, but a recompile would be required to change the page. That is the beauty of applet parameters; they enable you to customize the function of applets without doing any real programming!

Let's move on to the actual code required of the Countdown applet. Unfortunately, the Countdown applet requires some code that is a little beyond the lesson, so I don't expect all of this applet to make sense to you. However, you can download the complete source code for the applet from the book's companion Web site, which was mentioned a little earlier in this section. Also, the core mechanics of the applet are very straightforward and should be familiar to you from your recent study of loops. Following is the run() method in the Countdown applet class, which forms the heart of the applet:

The World According to URL

URL stands for Uniform Resource Locator, which is a fancy way of saying "Web address." A URL, pronounced U-R-L, is simply the address of a Web site, such as http://www.yahoo.com or http://www.urbanlegends.com. I'll stick to using URL to refer to Web addresses because that's the way Java refers to them.

```java
public void run() {
    // Loop through the countdown
    for (count = 10; count > 0;
    ➥count--) {
      try {
        // Repaint the applet window and wait a second
        repaint();
        thread.sleep(1000);
      }
      catch (InterruptedException e) {
        System.out.println("Something interrupted the count!");
      }
    }

    // Load the Web page from the "page" applet parameter
    String newPage = getParameter("page");
    URL newPageURL = null;
    try {
      newPageURL = new URL(newPage);
    }
    catch (MalformedURLException e) {
      System.out.println("Bad URL : " + newPage);
    }
    if (newPageURL != null)
      getAppletContext().showDocument(newPageURL);
}
```

Ouch, that looks a little messy! Try not to get intimidated by any code that doesn't look familiar; just concentrate on the loop code. As you can see, the for loop counts down from 10 to 1 just like the countdown code you saw earlier in the chapter. The *Statement* part of this for loop is completely new territory, however. The call to the repaint() method is necessary to update the applet's window with the new count-down number. The call to the thread.sleep() method results in the applet waiting one second, which effectively pauses the countdown for one second between numbers.

The Need for Threads

The Countdown applet makes use of threads, which are necessary for an applet to be able to perform timing functions such as waiting or scheduling events. A major function of the Countdown applet is waiting a second between countdown numbers. This is why it requires the use of threads. You get a formal introduction to threads in Chapter 17, "Hanging by a Thread."

When the for loop finishes, the code gets the page applet parameter and proceeds to navigate to the Web page identified by it. The code required to navigate to the Web page is probably pretty strange looking to you because it has to deal with exceptions. Exceptions are errors caused by unforeseen problems such as your computer running out of memory, your modem coming unplugged, spilling coffee on your keyboard, hurling your monitor out the window, and so on. I'll explain exceptions as you encounter them throughout the book.

The complete source code for the Countdown applet follows:

```
import java.applet.*;
import java.awt.*;
import java.net.*;

public class Countdown extends Applet
➥implements Runnable {
    Thread thread;

    int    count = 10;

    public void start() {
      // Start the thread
      thread = new Thread(this);
      thread.start();
    }

    public void run() {
      // Loop through the countdown
      for (count = 10; count > 0; count--) {
        try {
          // Repaint the applet window and wait a second
          repaint();
          thread.sleep(1000);
        }
```

```
      catch (InterruptedException e) {
        System.out.println("Something interrupted the count!");
      }
    }

    // Load the Web page from the "page" applet parameter
    String newPage = getParameter("page");
    URL newPageURL = null;
    try {
      newPageURL = new URL(newPage);
    }
    catch (MalformedURLException e) {
      System.out.println("Bad URL : " + newPage);
    }
    if (newPageURL != null)
      getAppletContext().showDocument(newPageURL);
  }

  public void paint(Graphics g) {
    // Select a font and get its metrics
    g.setFont(new Font("Helvetica", Font.BOLD, 24));
    FontMetrics fm = g.getFontMetrics();

    // Prepare the display string
    String str;
    System.out.println(count);
    if (count >= 1)
      str = String.valueOf(count);
    else
      str = "Blast off!";

    // Draw the countdown number or blast off string
    g.drawString(str, (getSize().width - fm.stringWidth(str)) / 2,
      ((getSize().height - fm.getHeight()) / 2) + fm.getAscent());
  }
}
```

Although this is a longer program than you are accustomed to seeing, a lot of it should look familiar to you. For example, the paint() method code is very similar to the code used in the DateTime applet from Chapter 4, "Constructing Applets of Your Own." On the other hand, the start() method is entirely new and is related to the applet's use of threads. You don't need to understand it fully at this point.

A Vote for Practicality

The Countdown applet isn't just a cute example for you to study. It's actually a very useful applet that you can start using immediately on your own Web development projects. By altering the page applet parameter, you can direct the applet to any Web page after the countdown finishes. You can also change the duration of the countdown by altering the initial value of the count variable. Just a thought to help you start applying what you've learned in a practical manner!

Breaking Away

If you recall from the previous chapter, each case section of a switch branch ends with a break statement. Following is an example to recap:

```
switch (grade) {
  case 'A':
    response = "Great job!";
    break;
  case 'B':
    response = "Not bad.";
    break;
  case 'C':
    response = "I suppose average is OK.";
    break;
default:
    response = "The dog ate your report
    ➥card?";
}
```

The purpose of the break statement in this example is to bail out of the switch branch so that no other code is executed. The break statement serves a similar purpose in loops; it breaks out of a loop regardless of the loop condition. Following is an example of circumventing an infinite loop with a break statement:

```
int i = 0;
while (true) {
  System.out.println("Print me infinitely!");
  if (++i > 99)
    break;
}
```

Without the assistance of the break statement, this while loop would continue forever thanks to the permanent true loop condition. The break statement sidesteps this problem by breaking out of the loop after one hundred iterations (0–99). Of course, it is rare that you would purposely create an infinite loop and then use a break statement to bail out of it. However, the break statement can be very useful in some tricky loops when you need to exit at an otherwise inconvenient time.

A close relative of the break statement is the continue statement, which is used to skip to the next iteration of a loop. The following example shows how a continue statement can be used to print only the even numbers between 1 and 100:

```
for (int i = 1; i <= 100; i++) {
  if ((i % 2) != 0)
    continue;
  System.out.println(i);
}
```

Having trouble seeing how this one works? Think back to the modulus operator (%), which returns the remainder of a division. Now consider what the remainder of a division by 2 yields for even and odd numbers. Aha! Even numbers divided by 2 always yield a remainder of 0, and odd numbers always leave a remainder of 1! The example code exploits this characteristic of even and odd numbers to skip to the next iteration of the loop when it encounters an odd number. Skipping to the next iteration bypasses the println() call, which prevents odd numbers from being printed. Pretty tricky!

The Least You Need to Know

Computers are often called upon to perform tasks we humans find to be utterly redundant. As dull as some humans can be, I guarantee you computers are much duller when it comes to repeating the same thing over and over. Java enables you to build programs that repeat themselves through the use of loops. The different types of loops basically perform the same function; they repeat a section of code over and over. Let's go over the main points you learned about loops in this chapter:

➤ Loops can execute as many statements as you want them to, provided the statements are grouped together as a single compound statement enclosed by curly braces ({}).

➤ A for loop is used to repeat a section of code a given number of iterations.

➤ A while loop is a more general for loop.

➤ A do-while loop is a while loop with the loop condition moved to the end.

➤ The break statement is used to break out of a loop regardless of the loop condition.

➤ The continue statement is used to skip to the next iteration of a loop.

Chapter 10

Why Classes Appeal to the Architect in All of Us

In This Chapter

➤ Classes as Object Blueprints

➤ Creating Objects

➤ Packaging Objects

➤ Controlling Access

➤ Interfacing Objects

How to Be the Frank Lloyd Wright of Programming

I used to live in Scottsdale, Arizona, and one day while living there I ventured on my bicycle to Taliesan West, the original western home of famed architect Frank Lloyd Wright. Frank Lloyd Wright is probably known best for his cantilevered architectural designs that blended incredibly well with their natural surroundings. As natural and awe inspiring as Mr. Wright's finished products might appear after completion, they all originated as detailed technical specifications and intricate blueprints.

In spite of the obvious differences between the architectural and software development trades, Java classes aren't really that different from blueprints for physical structures. Physical blueprints consist of lines and measurements, and Java classes consist of Java code. This Java code is used as the basis for creating a Java object, just as a blueprint is used as the basis for constructing a house or museum. Perhaps the biggest difference between the two is that with Java you are typically both the architect and the builder.

If you want to become a productive Java programmer, you must become proficient at designing and developing useful, efficient Java classes. I can't make any promises about you becoming the Frank Lloyd Wright of Java programming, but I can assure you that becoming proficient at class design and development will help you immensely in building useful Java applets and applications.

Classes Are Just Object Blueprints

Okay, so I've pounded it into your head that a class is just a blueprint for an object, but how does that translate into code? Let's take a look at a simple class definition:

```
class Alien {
  Color color;
  int   energy;
  int   aggression;
}
```

This class is named `Alien` and might be suited for a space game applet. As the code demonstrates, the keyword `class` precedes the class name in the class definition; this is how all Java classes are defined. The state of the `Alien` class is defined by three data members, which represent the color, energy, and aggression of the alien. The fact that these variables appear within the curly braces ({}) indicates that they are member variables of the `Alien` class.

A Class or an Object?

The concept of a class named `Object` might seem a little strange at first. As you learn a little later in the chapter, an object is just an instance of a class. The `Object` class is a very special class, however, because it serves as the base class for all Java classes. If you were to make a Java family tree, the `Object` class would be at the top as the great-great-great-grandparent of all classes.

Now that you've seen a specific class definition, let's take a look at the general syntax used to define all classes:

```
class ClassName {
  ClassBody
}
```

The `ClassName` is an identifier that specifies the name of the class. The `ClassBody` is the code that actually defines the functionality of the class and includes member variables and methods for the class.

Inheritance

By looking at the code for the `Alien` example class, you wouldn't think that it has any relationship to any other classes. However, all classes in Java derive either directly or indirectly from the `Object` class. The `Object` class forms the root of the Java class hierarchy, which means that it serves as the basis for all

Java classes, including the classes in the Java API. When I say that a class is derived from another class, I mean that it inherits properties and methods from the class. The following figure illustrates the relationship between the Object class and other Java classes.

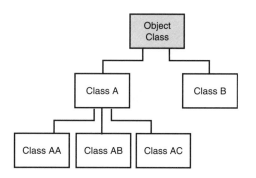

The relationship between the Object class and other Java classes.

The preceding figure shows how inheritance is used in Java to form a hierarchy of classes. As you can see in the figure, the Object class serves as the root parent class for all Java classes. That sounds fine, but how does that apply to the Alien example class? Simple: When a class doesn't explicitly declare its parent class, it is implicitly derived from Object. This means that the Alien class definition could have also been written like this:

```
class Alien extends Object {
   Color color;
   int   energy;
   int   aggression;
}
```

I mentioned a little earlier that the Alien class implicitly derives from the Object class because it doesn't explicitly extend any other class. What does this really mean? Well, when a class derives from another class, it inherits the member variables and methods of that parent class. In other words, you add everything in the parent class to the child class. Of course, the child class also adds its own member variables and methods to the mix.

A class is identified as the child of a parent class by using the extends keyword. The following code shows how the Alien class might explicitly derive from a class other than the Object class:

```
class Alien extends Enemy {
   Color color;
   int   energy;
   int   aggression;
}
```

117

The Parents and Children in an OOP Family

Incidentally, the parent/child OOP metaphor is not just something invented to make things sound cute. Class inheritance actually works quite similarly to biological inheritance.

When two people have a child, the child inherits many of the physical and personality traits of the two parents. However, the child also develops its own unique traits that are present along with the inherited traits. This mixture of inherited traits and new traits is what makes us all so unique.

Although Java classes aren't quite as unique as people, they do benefit from a similar form of inheritance. I suppose in this sense Java is an asexual programming language, however, because only one class can be the parent of a child class.

As you can see, the Enemy class is identified as the parent of the Alien class, which means that the Alien class inherits all of the member variables and methods defined in the Enemy class. Of course, at some point the Object class still appears as a parent of the Alien class because all classes ultimately derive from Object. In this case it's possible that the Enemy class derives directly from Object.

Adding Class Behavior with Methods

If you recall from Chapter 5, "Let's Try and Be Objective," a method is an isolated section of code that can be called to perform a specific function. Speaking of methods, let's examine the syntax used to define methods:

```
ReturnType MethodName(Parameters) {
   MethodBody
}
```

Methods are capable of returning data. For example, a method that performs a calculation would probably return the result of the calculation as a number. The *ReturnType* specifies the data type that a method returns. The *MethodName* is the name of the method. Methods are also capable of receiving parameters that are somehow used by the method. Method parameters are identified in the *Parameters* of the method definition. Finally, the *MethodBody* is the actual code for the method.

Geez, I'm starting to feel like we're lost in a computer science textbook! I apologize, but sometimes there just isn't a good way to liven up a dry topic. However, an example is often sufficient to break the tension:

```
void morph(int aggression) {
   if (aggression < 10) {
     // morph into a small size
   }
   else if (aggression < 20) {
     // morph into a medium size
   }
   else {
```

```
    // morph into a huge size (yikes!)
  }
}
```

This method makes a good addition to the Alien class. Let's analyze its vitals! The name of the method is morph(), and it returns data of type void.

The morph() method accepts one parameter, aggression, which is of type int. The code in the morph() method uses this parameter as a basis for determining how the alien should be morphed. Incidentally, just in case you are science fiction impaired, morphing is when a creature transforms itself into another shape or size. It's actually pretty common among aliens.

Do you see anything wrong with the morph() method? I don't really expect you to, but there is a subtle problem that has to do with the fact that the method is a part of the Alien class. Allow me to explain. Because aggression is a member variable of the Alien class, it isn't necessary to provide it as a parameter to the

Type void?

Hold it right there! I distinctly remember *not* covering any such data type back in Chapter 7, "Jumping into Java," when we talked about numbers, strings, and characters. That's because void doesn't actually represent any data. Sure, void is a valid data type, but it represents the absence of data. In other words, a return type of void indicates that the morph() method doesn't return any data.

morph() method. Instead, the morph() method can directly access the aggression member variable to determine how to morph the alien. The following code shows the Alien class with the newly modified morph() method:

```
class Alien extends Enemy {
  Color color;
  int   energy;
  int   aggression;

  void morph() {
    if (aggression < 10) {
      // morph into a small size
    }
    else if (aggression < 20) {
      // morph into a medium size
    }
    else {
      // morph into a huge size (yikes!)
    }
  }
}
```

Method Trickery

You can do some pretty neat things with methods. One interesting OOP feature is the ability to override methods, which is when you supersede an inherited method with a newer version. As an example, if the Enemy class defined a move() method, you might want the movement to vary based on the type of enemy. To allow the Alien class to manage its own movement, you would override the move() method in the Alien class. So, the Enemy class might look something like this:

```
class Enemy {
...
  void move() {
    // move the enemy
  }
}
```

The Alien class with an overridden move() method would look like this:

```
class Alien extends Enemy {
  Color color;
  int    energy;
  int    aggression;

  void move() {
    // move the alien
  }

  void morph() {
    if (aggression < 10) {
      // morph into a small size
    }
    else if (aggression < 20) {
      // morph into a medium size
    }
    else {
      // morph into a huge size (yikes!)
    }
  }
}
```

When you create an alien based on the Alien class, you are free to call the move() method to make the alien move. But which move() method is called, the one in the Enemy class or the one in the Alien class? Overridden methods are always given precedence within the context of the class in which they are defined. So, the move() method in the Alien class would be called when you are dealing with an Alien object. If this wasn't the case, inheritance wouldn't be of much use!

Method Overloading

Another interesting thing associated with methods is method overloading, which involves the use of multiple methods with the same name. How can that happen? Aren't all methods supposed to be unique? Yes, but how do you define unique? If you're talking about uniqueness and Java methods, you must factor in not only the name of a method, but also its parameter list. To understand what I'm talking about, let's again consider the move() method in the Alien class.

It is possible to provide two different versions of the move() method: one for general movement and one for moving to a specific location. The general version is the one you've already defined; it moves the alien based on its current state. This method definition follows:

```
void move() {
  // move the alien
}
```

The move() method for moving the alien to a specific location requires two parameters, the new x and y positions of the alien:

```
void move(int x, int y) {
  // move the alien to position x, y
}
```

The only identifiable difference between the two methods is the parameter list for each. The Java compiler keeps up with both the name and parameter list of a method when it comes to identifying the method. The appropriate method is executed based on the type and number of parameters provided in a call to the method. For example, the following code calls the generic move() method:

```
myAlien.move();
```

Likewise, the following code calls the other move() method:

```
myAlien.move(4, 11);
```

From Blueprint to Concrete

The bulk of the work in developing any Java program is creating all of the classes required to make it work. However, classes by themselves don't accomplish much because they act only as object blueprints. It's when you create an object from a class that things really get interesting. An object created from a class is known as an *instance* of the class. The process of creating an object instance is known as *instantiating* an object.

The creation of an object begins with the object's constructors. A *constructor* is a special method that is called when an object is first created. Constructors are a good place to perform any initialization required to get an object up and running properly. Constructors are easy to spot in code because they are named the same as the class to which they belong. The following code shows the Alien class, complete with two constructors:

```
class Alien extends Enemy {
  Color color;
  int    energy;
  int    aggression;

  public Alien() {
    Alien(Color.green, 100, 15);
  }

  public Alien(Color c, int e, int a) {
    color = c;
    energy = e;
    aggression = a;
  }

  void move() {
    // move the alien
  }

  void morph() {
    if (aggression < 10) {
      // morph into a small size
    }
    else if (aggression < 20) {
      // morph into a medium size
    }
    else {
      // morph into a huge size (yikes!)
    }
  }
}
```

This code makes use of method overloading to provide two different Alien constructors. This is a nice class feature because it gives you more flexibility in creating objects from the class. The first constructor is considered the default constructor for the Alien class because it takes no parameters. The second constructor is more detailed in that it accepts parameters for setting each of the three alien properties. Notice that the default constructor actually calls the detailed constructor and passes along default values for the alien properties. This is a common approach used to implement default constructors in Java classes.

There are some situations where you might want a class's constructor to call the constructor of its parent class. Java supports a special method named super() that represents a parent class's constructor. As an example, the default Alien constructor could call the default Enemy constructor like this:

```
public Alien() {
  super();
  Alien(Color.green, 100, 15);
}
```

The constructors for the Alien class come into play when you start creating Alien objects. The following code creates a few different Alien objects:

```
Alien myAlien = new Alien();
Alien yourAlien = new Alien(Color.blue, 50, 500);
Alien otherAlien;
```

The first alien created, myAlien, uses the default constructor to create an alien with default property settings. The second alien, yourAlien, uses the detailed constructor so that it can provide specific property values for the alien's various attributes. The last alien hasn't actually been created yet; the otherAlien variable acts as a placeholder awaiting an Alien object to be created via the new operator. You could also assign an Alien object to the otherAlien variable like this:

```
otherAlien = yourAlien;
```

Speaking of the new operator, it is the primary means by which you create objects from classes. The new operator allocates memory for an object's member variables, and then makes sure to call the object's appropriate constructor to properly initialize everything.

The Importance of this

There are some situations where it is necessary for a class to reference itself. For example, you might call a method within a class that requires an instance of the class as a parameter. Java provides a keyword called this that is used to reference an object within itself.

You can think of the this keyword as being logically equivalent to the word "I" in the English language; we use the word "I" to refer to ourselves. In the short novel *Anthem*, by Ayn Rand, the word "I" is never used because the characters have no concept of individuality. Without the this keyword, Java classes would suffer from the same problem.

Preventing Memory Loss

People new to Java programming are often puzzled by the fact that memory management is handled automatically by Java. Other programming languages such as C and C++ push the responsibility of memory management onto programmers. Although this ultimately gives you more flexibility, it comes at a huge cost: memory leaks! No, I'm not referring to silicon oozing out of your computer case. Instead, I'm talking about memory that is allocated and then forgotten; this memory is effectively lost to the system.

Java avoids the whole issue of memory leaks by taking charge of memory management. When you create an object from a class using the new operator, Java automatically allocates memory for the object and keeps track of it. Later when you are finished with the object, Java will free the memory up automatically. Java periodically looks for objects that are no longer being used so that it can free the memory associated with them. This process is known as garbage collection. And you thought computers were clean!

Organizing Your Blueprints

My dad is an architect, so I grew up amid piles of drawings and sketches. One thing I've always marveled at is my dad's ability to know where certain drawings are located when he doesn't seem to store them according to any organizational plan. A box full of blueprints in a closet doesn't really qualify as an organizational scheme. Classes, which are Java's equivalent of blueprints, benefit from a more structured approach to organization than my dad's closet scheme.

In Java, packages are used to group related classes. Packages are useful in providing more structure to Java classes. The Java API itself is implemented as a group of packages. You can organize your own classes into packages to help your own internal organization or possibly to make them commercially available to others. The Alien and Enemy classes are good examples of classes that would go well together in a package.

You identify the package for a class at the beginning of the source code file for the class. The package syntax follows:

```
package PackageName;
```

The *PackageName* is an identifier that specifies the name of the package. Following is an example of a package declaration:

```
package spacewar;
```

This package declaration would need to be placed at the top of both the Alien and Enemy class source code files for the classes to be included in the package.

To use the classes stored in a package, you must import the classes individually or the package as a whole using the import keyword. You've already been importing entire packages in the sample applets throughout the book thus far. Remember the following lines of code?

```
import java.applet.*;
import java.awt.*;
```

These two lines indicate that all of the classes in the `java.applet` and `java.awt` packages are to be imported into the applet. If you needed only a specific class in a package, you could just import the class by itself, like this:

```
import java.applet.Applet;
```

This can get tedious, however, if you're using lots of different classes, so it's often more convenient to use a wildcard (*) and import all of the classes in a given package.

Class Access

An important topic relevant to the discussion of classes and packages is access. Access refers to the ability of different parts of a Java program to view and manipulate other parts. For example, what determines if an object can access member variables within another object? There are actually very strict rules governing access and which areas different parts of a program can access. These rules revolve around access modifiers.

Access modifiers define varying levels of access between class members and other classes. Access modifiers are declared immediately before the type of a member variable, the return type of a method, or the definition of a class. There are four different access modifiers in Java: `default`, `public`, `protected`, and `private`.

The `default` access modifier applies to classes, variables, and methods that don't explicitly indicate any particular access characteristics. The `default` access modifier indicates that only classes in the same package can have access to each other's member variables and methods.

The Complete Idiot's Guide to Package Naming

Although you are free to name packages just about anything you want, there is an established scheme for coming up with unique package names. This scheme involves using your domain name as part of the package name, followed by any other series of names that describes the set of classes you are packaging. As an example, my Web site is located at `http://www.thetribe.com`, which means that my domain name is `thetribe.com`.

If I had some custom security classes I wanted to package, I might name the package `com.thetribe.security`. If I had different sub-packages for different levels of security, I might have two packages: `com.thetribe.security.tight` and `com.thetribe.security.loose`. Placing my classes in these packages guarantees uniqueness because the domain name `thetribe.com` is not used by anyone else.

The public access modifier indicates that classes, member variables, and methods are completely accessible. For a class, this means that it is recognized by all other objects, regardless of their package affiliation. For a member variable or method, it means that all other objects are capable of directly accessing the public member variable or calling the public method.

The protected access modifier indicates that member variables and methods are only accessible to child classes (subclasses) and classes in the same package as the class. This means that no other class can access a protected member variable or method unless it is a child of the given class or it is in the same package as the class.

Finally, the private access modifier provides the most restriction of them all. private member variables and methods are only accessible within the class they are defined. No other class has access to private member variables and methods, not even child classes.

Don't worry if access modifiers don't make total sense to you just yet. You'll revisit them a few times throughout the rest of the book in contexts that will help make their usage more clear. I mainly wanted to cover them here so that you would at least have some familiarity with how they relate to classes and packages.

Interfacing to Other Architectural Masterpieces

The last topic you're going to tackle in this chapter is interfaces, which play an important role in Java's support for OOP. An interface is like a class that has been stripped of the majority of its code. If a class is a blueprint, then an interface is a rough sketch. Interfaces are used to define general class characteristics that are shared among multiple classes. As an example, interfaces declare method names and parameter lists, but they don't ever include actual method code.

How could interfaces possibly be useful? Interfaces are important because they enable you to define the general design for a class without worrying about the implementation details. This seemingly small abstraction can make a huge difference in managing large programming projects. If you begin with a set of well-designed interfaces, the classes often just fall into place.

Because an interface isn't a full-blown class, you don't extend them like you would a class. Instead, you "implement" them using the implements keyword, like this:

```
public class Countdown extends Applet implements Runnable {
  ...
}
```

This is actual code from the Countdown applet you developed in the previous chapter. Although you didn't know it at the time, the Countdown applet implements an interface named Runnable. This interface defines the methods required to make threads function. More specifically, the Runnable interface defines a single method, run(). All a class must do to implement the Runnable interface is provide a run() method. That's exactly what the Countdown applet did!

You declare an interface much like a class declaration, except there is much less code. Following is the syntax for declaring interfaces:

```
interface InterfaceName {
   InterfaceBody
}
```

The *InterfaceName* is an identifier that specifies the name of the interface. The *InterfaceBody* is the code that actually declares the member variables and methods in the interface. Following is an example of how the Enemy class might be implemented as an interface:

```
interface Enemy {
   void move();
   void move(int x, int y);
}
```

Notice that the methods listed in the Enemy class are purely method declarations; there is no place for adding code to the methods. The Alien class already contains move() methods that match those in the Enemy interface, so the only real change for the Alien class comes in the initial class definition:

```
class Alien implements Enemy {
   ...
}
```

You'll encounter more interfaces throughout the rest of the book, in which case I'll clarify exactly which methods must be implemented to fulfill the implementation requirements of each interface.

The Least You Need to Know

Although you immersed yourself in object-oriented programming theory back in Chapter 5, you didn't look into any of the practical implications of how classes and objects work. You now know that classes serve as blueprints for objects; and, fortunately, they are pretty straightforward to design and develop. Objects, on the other hand, are just instances of classes created in memory. With these facts in mind, let's go over what you learned in this chapter:

➤ The Object class serves as the root parent class for all Java classes.

➤ The void data type represents the absence of data.

➤ When a class derives from another class, it inherits the member variables and methods of that parent class.

➤ An inherited method is overridden when you supersede it with a newer version.

➤ A constructor is a special method named after an object that is called when the object is created.

➤ There are four different access modifiers in Java: `default`, `public`, `protected`, and `private`.

➤ If a class is a blueprint, then an interface is a rough sketch; interfaces define general class characteristics that are shared among multiple classes.

Part 3
The Beauty of Java

If beauty is in the eye of the beholder, then I'll let you judge for yourself whether Java is a beauty or a beast. Actually, you are ready to learn about graphics and how to put them to work in Java. Java has several neat graphics features that you are sure to find useful as you build your own Java applets. If you aren't an aspiring artist, it's not a problem, because graphical user interfaces in Java practically design themselves. Ready to learn how?

Java as an Artist's Canvas

It All Starts with the AWT

This chapter marks your first official foray into Java graphics, which is one of the most rewarding areas of Java programming because you get to visualize the fruits of your labors. Because Java applets are graphical in nature, you can't get too far without relying on Java's graphics capabilities in one way or another. Java's support for graphics starts with the AWT, which stands for Abstract Windowing Toolkit. The Java AWT is a vast set of classes and interfaces devoted to building graphics into Java applets and applications.

All of the graphics within a Java applet or application are drawn with respect to a window, hence the name Abstract *Windowing* Toolkit. The AWT not only supports simple graphics operations such as drawing lines and text, but it also provides a framework for building graphical user interfaces. For example, the AWT includes a Button class for creating push buttons. You'll explore different parts of the AWT throughout the remainder of the book, as they become needed. You'll quickly learn that the AWT plays a vital role in just about every Java applet you build.

The Java Graphics Coordinate System

When you draw a picture on a piece of paper, you make some assumptions about the orientation of the paper and the manner in which it is being viewed. Additionally, if you wanted to center the picture, you might measure in from the edges of the paper to determine the paper's center, and then draw from there. When you make considerations such as these, you are effectively utilizing your own primitive graphics coordinate system.

Graphical computing systems also rely on graphics coordinate systems, and Java is no exception. Coordinate systems typically specify the axes (x and y) and directions of increasing value for each of the axes. It is also important for a coordinate system to indicate the location of the origin, which is the reference point (0, 0). Coordinate values increase and decrease from this point along the coordinate axes. Has all this mathematical talk confused you yet? I hope not, but just in case it has, check out the following figure.

The traditional mathematical coordinate system.

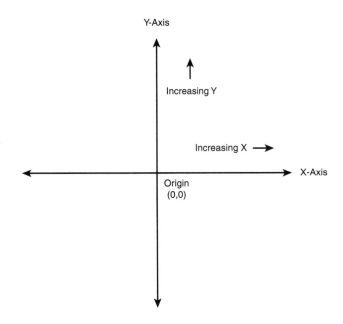

Notice in the above figure that there are x- and y-axes that increase in value from the origin to the right and from the origin up. Coordinate values to the left of the origin or below the origin have negative values. The Java graphics coordinate system is shown in the following figure.

132

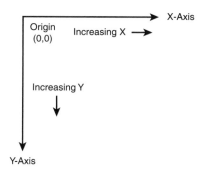

The Java graphics coordinate system.

As the figure shows, the Java graphics coordinate system doesn't support negative coordinate values. Its x-axis increases to the right, and its y-axis increases down. When you map this coordinate system to an applet or application window, the origin ends up being located in the upper left corner of the window. This means that all Java graphics coordinates are specified relative to the upper left corner of a window.

Understanding Color

You can't get very far in discussing graphics without taking a moment to explore color and how it affects graphics in Java. To fully understand the role color plays in Java graphics, you have to take a step back and examine color in computer systems in general. The main function of color in a computer system is to accurately reflect the physical nature of color within the confines of a graphical system.

What do I mean by "the physical nature of color"? Well, think back to your formative years and you might recall a wonderful invention called Play-Doh. Anyone who has experienced the thrill of Play-Doh can tell you that colors react in different ways when different colors are combined. I can still remember the elegantly simple instructions on the box: "Yellow plus blue makes green." Much like Play-Doh, a computer system must be able to mix colors with accurate, predictable results.

Monitoring Colors

Your color monitor provides a very useful insight into how computer systems handle color. A color monitor has three electron guns: red, green, and blue. The output from these three guns converges on each pixel of the screen to produce a color. The color itself is determined by the intensity of each of the guns. Going back to the Play-Doh analogy, the intensity of each electron gun is a lot like the amount of Play-Doh you use of a given color. As a matter of fact, you could simulate your monitor with Play-Doh by combining different amounts of the colors red, green, and blue. The following figure illustrates how electron guns combine colors in a monitor.

133

Electron guns are used to combine colors in a color computer monitor.

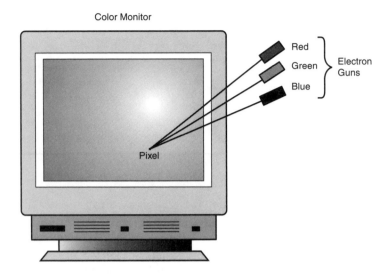

Color in Java

The software color system used by Java is very similar to the hardware color system used by color monitors; unique colors are formed by combining varying intensities of the colors red, green, and blue. Java programs use numeric color intensities to determine the mix of a color; these intensities tell the monitor how hard to fire each electron gun. Combinations of the numeric intensities of the primary colors red, green, and blue therefore represent Java colors. This color system is known as RGB (Red Green Blue) and is standard across most graphical computer systems.

Each component (red, green, and blue) of a Java color is represented by a number in the range 0–255. The table below shows the numeric values for the color components of some basic colors. If you pay attention to the primary colors red, green, and blue, you'll see that they consist solely of one color component at the maximum value of 255.

Play-Doh Break!

The biggest difference between Play-Doh and your monitor is that when you mix a bunch of different Play-Doh colors together, it somehow always ends up being a strange brown color. When you mix a bunch of colors on a monitor, you get white. Take a break and experiment with some Play-Doh to learn more about color; you probably never knew it could be so educational!

RGB Color Component Values and `Color` Class Constants for Some Basic Colors

Color	Red	Green	Blue
Red	255	0	0
Green	0	255	0
Blue	0	0	255
Black	0	0	0
White	255	255	255
Light Gray	192	192	192
Dark Gray	128	128	128
Yellow	255	255	0
Purple	255	0	255

Colors are represented in Java programs by the `Color` class. The `Color` class packages the three components of an RGB color and provides methods for extracting and manipulating the components individually. You typically use the `Color` class to identify colors when you are using one of Java's many graphics functions. For example, you might want to draw your name in red, in which case you would create a `Color` object that represented the color red. Following is an example of creating a red `Color` object:

```
Color c = new Color(255, 0, 0);
```

As a little bonus, the `Color` class defines constant `Color` objects that represent some of the more commonly used colors. Following is a list of these constants:

➤ `Color.black`

➤ `Color.blue`

➤ `Color.cyan`

➤ `Color.darkGray`

➤ `Color.gray`

➤ `Color.green`

➤ `Color.lightGray`

More than One Way to Look at Colors

Although RGB is the most popular computer color system in use, there are others. One other popular color system is HSB, which stands for Hue Saturation Brightness. Another color system that sees a great deal of use in print-related computer systems is CMYK, which stands for the colors Cyan, Magenta, Yellow, and Black. The HSB color system is directly supported by Java; CMYK currently is not.

➤ Color.magenta

➤ Color.orange

➤ Color.pink

➤ Color.red

➤ Color.white

➤ Color.yellow

You can use any of these constants in lieu of creating your own `Color` objects:

```
Color c = Color.red;
```

Applet: Colorize

To visualize how RGB color values result in physical colors, let's create an applet that fills its background with a solid color. Since it wouldn't be any fun to have to recompile the applet each time you want to change the color, you can make the RGB color components applet parameters. This allows you to set the applet's background color in the HTML code for the page containing the applet.

Finding the Colorize Applet Example on the Web

To find the Colorize applet example source code on the Web, enter the address
http://www.mcp.com/info in the location box of your Web browser. Click the link called
Downloadable Code, Examples, and Info for book "Companion Sites." In the space provided under the Book Information section, enter **0-7897-1804-9**, which is the 10-digit ISBN for this book. Click the **Search** button.

Enough talk, let's take a look at the Colorize applet. The first step in creating the applet is to define the member variables that hold the RGB color components:

```
private int red = 0,
            green = 0,
            blue = 0;
```

Notice that the color components are stored as integers. Integers are sufficient because each color component is in the range 0–255. Let's move on to the `init()` method, which is where all the action takes place:

```
public void init() {
    // Get the red color parameter
    String s = getParameter("red");
    if (null != s)
      red = Integer.parseInt(s);

    // Get the green color parameter
    s = getParameter("green");
    if (null != s)
      green = Integer.parseInt(s);

    // Get the blue color parameter
    s = getParameter("blue");
```

```
      if (null != s)
        blue = Integer.parseInt(s);

      // Set the background color
      setBackground(new Color(red, green, blue));
  }
```

The `init()` method is responsible for two jobs: retrieving the color parameters and setting the applet's background color. The `init()` method grabs the color parameters by calling `getParameter()`. The only hitch here is that `getParameter()` deals solely in strings, which means you have to convert the string parameters to numbers before they can be used. This is easily accomplished with a call to `Integer.parseInt()`, which extracts integers from strings.

With the color parameters in place, you're ready to set the background color. This is accomplished with a single line of code, thanks to the `setBackground()` method. A `Color` object is created based on the color parameters and then passed into `setBackground()` as the background color.

Because the Colorize applet uses parameters, it's worth taking a look at the HTML code that displays it:

```
<APPLET CODE="Colorize.class" WIDTH=200 HEIGHT=200>
<PARAM NAME=red VALUE="255">
<PARAM NAME=green VALUE="128">
<PARAM NAME=blue VALUE="255">
</APPLET>
```

Notice that each color component is set using a <PARAM> tag. In this case, the RGB values result in purple. The following figure shows the Colorize applet. You'll have to use your imagination a little and pretend that the gray color you are seeing in the figure below is actually a vibrant purple practically jumping off the page!

The Colorize applet.

137

The Colorize applet is great for experimenting with different colors. For example, try changing the color parameters to the following:

```
<PARAM NAME=red VALUE="255">
<PARAM NAME=green VALUE="128">
<PARAM NAME=blue VALUE="64">
```

This results in an orange background. Another interesting thing you can try is eliminating the color parameters altogether. Because the color member variables are initialized to zero in the `Applet` class, the resulting color is black if you don't supply any parameters.

Digging into the Graphics Class

Although the Java AWT encompasses a large number of classes, the `Graphics` class can be used to perform a great many graphics functions. The `Graphics` class is located in the `java.awt` package. The `Graphics` class represents a graphics context—an abstract representation of a graphical drawing surface. You can think of a graphics context as being roughly equivalent to a piece of paper.

Who's the Painter?

A `Graphics` object is passed into an applet's `paint()` method for the applet to use for drawing operations. That's easy to understand, but when should you call the `paint()` method, and how do you pass along the `Graphics` object? This question brings up an interesting point regarding the `paint()` method—you are never responsible for calling it! Java automatically calls the `paint()` method for an applet when it detects that the applet needs to be repainted. Java also takes care of supplying the `Graphics` object to the `paint()` method, so you never have to worry about from where it came.

Graphics contexts are necessary in Java because drawing can take place on a variety of different "surfaces" such as monitors, printers, and even memory. The `Graphics` class provides you with a generic graphics context to which you perform all graphics functions.

How does the `Graphics` class come into play in a practical setting? I'm glad I asked! A `Graphics` object is passed into an applet's `paint()` method, which is where an applet typically does all of its drawing. Following is the code for an empty `paint()` method, which shows the `Graphics` object being passed in as a parameter:

```
public void paint(Graphics g) {
}
```

Graphics contexts have a few different attributes that are useful when performing drawing operations. Following are three of the more commonly used attributes in the `Graphics` class:

➤ Color

➤ Background color

➤ Font

The Color attribute determines the color used in graphics operations such as drawing lines and filling rectangles. You can get and set the color attribute of a Graphics object using the getColor() and setColor() methods. Not surprisingly, the background color attribute determines the background color of the graphics surface. You get and set it using the getBackgroundColor() and setBackgroundColor() methods. Finally, the Font attribute determines the font used to draw text onto the graphics surface. You get and set this attribute using the getFont() and setFont() methods.

Let me cover one last thing about the Graphics object before you start putting it to work. Although I've been alluding to graphics ultimately being drawn to an applet window, a graphics context is really tied to a component. A component is a generic graphical window that forms the basis for all other graphical elements in the Java AWT. All graphical Java components are modeled at the highest level by the Component class, which is defined in the java.awt package. Thinking of graphics in terms of the Component class instead of an applet window helps illuminate the fact that any object derived from Component can be used for drawing. An applet window is just a specific type of component.

Getting Primitive with Graphics

Although Java is a modern programming language, its graphics operations are actually quite primitive. I'm referring to graphics primitives, which consist of lines, rectangles, squares, ovals, circles, polygons, and arcs. Although these graphics primitives are admittedly pretty simple, you can create impressive graphics by using them together.

The methods required to draw graphics primitives are included in the Graphics class. Let's explore some of the more commonly used graphics primitives!

Lines

Unlike drawing a freehand line on paper, it is really easy to draw a straight line in Java. The drawLine() method enables you to draw lines and is defined as follows:

```
public void drawLine(int x1, int y1, int x2, int y2)
```

The first two parameters, x1 and y1, specify the starting point for the line, and the second two parameters, x2 and y2, specify the ending point. Following is an example of drawing a diagonal line using the drawLine() method:

```
public void paint(Graphics g) {
  g.drawLine(0, 0, 100, 100);
}
```

Rectangles

A rectangle is defined by its upper left coordinate along with a width and height. The drawRect() method is used to draw rectangles:

```
public void drawRect(int x, int y, int width, int height)
```

The first two parameters, x and y, specify the upper left corner of the rectangle. The width and height parameters specify the width and height of the rectangle. No surprises there! Following is an example of drawing a rectangle using the drawRect() method:

```
public void paint(Graphics g) {
    g.drawRect(5, 20, 55, 80);
}
```

More Fun with Rectangles

The drawRect() method draws the outline of a rectangle using the Color attribute of the Graphics object; black is the default. You can also draw filled rectangles using the fillRect() method, which takes the same parameters as drawRect(). The fillRect() method simply draws a filled rectangle using the Color attribute of the Graphics object. If that's not enough, you can also clear a rectangle using the clearRect() method. The clearRect() method draws a rectangle filled with the background color of the Graphics object.

You can also draw squares using the drawRect() method; just enter the same value for the width and height.

Ovals

Ovals are rounded shapes that include both circles and ellipses. Think of an oval as a rectangle with extremely rounded corners. This idea forms the basis for how an oval is drawn; you specify a bounding rectangle for an oval to draw it. The drawOval() method is used to draw ovals:

```
public void drawOval(int x, int y, int
➥width, int height)
```

The first two parameters, x and y, specify the upper left corner of the oval's bounding rectangle. The width and height parameters specify the width and height of the bounding rectangle. Following is an example of drawing an oval using the drawOval() method:

```
public void paint(Graphics g) {
    g.drawOval(30, 25, 45, 20);
}
```

Just as passing the same values for the width and height in the drawRect() method results in a square, the same technique can be used with drawOval() to produce a circle. This makes sense because a circle's radius determines both its width and its height—these two values are the same!

Other Primitives

The Graphics class also supports a few other graphics primitives that you aren't likely to use as often as the previously covered ones. I'm referring to polygons, arcs, and rounded rectangles. A polygon is a closed shape made of lines with an unlimited number of sides. An arc is a partial oval, meaning that it doesn't form a closed shape. Finally, a rounded rectangle is a rectangle with rounded corners. You can control how rounded the corners are when you draw a rounded rectangle. Keep in mind that a rectangle with corners that are very rounded starts to look a lot like an oval.

Filling Ovals

Similar to the fillRect() method, there is also a fillOval() method that is used to draw filled ovals. The fillOval() method takes the same parameters as drawOval() and simply draws a filled oval using the Color attribute of the Graphics object.

The mechanics of the methods used to draw polygons, arcs, and rounded rectangles are similar to those for the graphics primitives about which you've already learned. So, I'll let you explore them on your own if you're just dying to see how they work.

Applet: Minnesota

Let's take a moment to create an applet that uses some of your newly found graphics knowledge. Minnesota is known as the land of a thousand lakes, which makes it an ideal basis for an example applet. How is this so? Well, lakes often have a rounded shape, which makes it possible to draw a rough equivalent in Java using ovals. The Minnesota applet draws a bunch of randomly shaped "lakes" in random positions. The following figure shows what the Minnesota applet looks like.

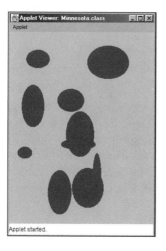

The Minnesota applet and its many "lakes."

Finding the Minnesota Applet Example on the Web

To find the Minnesota applet example source code on the Web, enter the address **http://www.mcp.com/info** in the location box of your Web browser. Click the link called **Downloadable Code, Examples, and Info for book "Companion Sites."** In the space provided under the Book Information section, enter **0-7897-1804-9**, which is the 10-digit ISBN for this book. Click the **Search** button.

Admittedly, this applet isn't quite as accurate as a map of Minnesota, but you get the general idea. The complete source code for the Minnesota applet follows:

```java
import java.applet.*;
import java.awt.*;
import java.util.*;

public class Minnesota extends Applet {
  Random rand = new
  ➥Random(System.currentTimeMillis());

  public void init() {
    // Set the background color to green
    setBackground(Color.green);
  }

  public void paint(Graphics g) {
    // Set the color of the lakes to blue
    g.setColor(Color.blue);

    // Draw the lakes
    for (int i = 0; i < 10; i++) {
      int x = getRandomNum(200),
          y = getRandomNum(300),
          width = getRandomNum(100),
          height = getRandomNum(100);
      g.fillOval(x, y, width, height);
    }
  }

  private int getRandomNum(int range) {
    return Math.abs(rand.nextInt() % range);
  }
}
```

The Minnesota applet makes use of random numbers, which are generated by the Random class, located in the java.util package. An instance of the Random class is created as a member variable of the Minnesota applet class. It is necessary to create the Random object with a seed, which is a number used to get the random number generator started; in this case the seed is the current system time. The seed for the Random object is necessary to help make sure that it randomly generates numbers.

The background color (green) of the Minnesota applet window is set by calling the setBackground() method in the init() method. The lakes are then drawn in the paint() method. The current drawing color is first set to blue with a call to setColor(). A for loop is then used to draw 10 different lakes via the fillOval() method. Increasing the for loop counter will result in more lakes being drawn.

The Minnesota applet also includes a private method, getRandomNum(), that is used to help obtain random numbers. The paint() method calls the getRandomNum() method in order to get the random position and size of each lake. The getRandomNum() method takes a parameter that determines the range of the random number it returns. For example, if you pass in 50, getRandomNum() will return a number between 0 and 49. This magic is made possible thanks to the modulus operator (%).

I encourage you to experiment with the for loop counter and the random number ranges to get different results. This is a good applet with which to tinker because the results are entirely graphical.

Graphically Speaking with Text

The downside to applets being so graphical is that you can't just draw text using the simple println() method you used earlier in command-line applications. No, even text must be drawn using a special method in the Graphics class. The upside to drawing text as graphics, however, is that you can use different fonts, sizes, and styles. This is something that is not possible in non-graphical applications. Did you ever use a word processor prior to graphical operating systems? I did, and I'm here to tell you that it was no fun. So, please appreciate the fact that text in a graphical environment is so rich and can be viewed in such a variety of ways.

The font attribute of a graphics context is the primary factor in determining the appearance of text. The Font class models a font and includes members that represent the name, size, and style of a font. There are three different font styles supported by the Font class: BOLD, ITALIC, and PLAIN.

Member Constants

A member constant is a data member of a class that has a fixed value; it can never change. The font styles in the Font class are good examples of member constants. Member constants are declared using the final keyword and must be initialized upon declaration. Member constants are often referenced outside of the class where they are defined, in which case you must provide the full class name. For example, in a program you must reference the font styles as Font.BOLD, Font.ITALIC, and Font.PLAIN. Member constants are also usually declared as static, which means that there is only one copy of the members to be shared by all instances of the class.

The constructor for the Font class follows:

```
public Font(String name, int style, int size)
```

The name parameter is the string name of the font, style is one or more of the style constants added together, and size is an integer font size. Although there might be a wide variety of fonts available on a given system, it is generally safer to stick with one of the following font names: Times Roman, Courier, or Helvetica. Following is an example of creating a Font object:

```
Font f = new Font("Helvetica", Font.BOLD + Font.ITALIC, 24);
```

This code creates a bold, italic, 24-point Helvetica font. Before actually using this font, you might want to learn details about its size and how big text drawn in it will be. The size attributes of a font are known as font metrics and are retrieved using the FontMetrics class. You get the font metrics for a font by creating a FontMetrics object, like this:

```
FontMetrics fm = new FontMetrics(f);
```

The FontMetrics class provides methods such as getHeight() and getStringWidth(), which can be used to get the height of text or the width of a specific string drawn in a particular font. This is often useful when you need to center a string within a certain space.

Getting back to the Font object created a little earlier, to select the font into a graphics context, you must call the setFont() method on a Graphics object, like this:

```
g.setFont(f);
```

After calling this method, any text drawn using the Graphics object will be drawn using the new font. Drawing text is as simple as calling the drawString() method:

```
drawString("Honey, I'm home!", 5, 15);
```

The last two parameters to the drawString() method are the x and y positions of the string. The x position of a string of text is the left edge of the text, and the y position is the baseline of the text. The baseline of the text is the bottom of the text, not including the descent required for letters such as y and g. The following figure shows the relationship between the height, baseline, ascent, and descent of text, which are all considered font metrics.

The relationship between different font metrics.

Applet: Ransom

I would never encourage criminal activity, but let's just suppose you had the need for an applet that displayed a ransom note. Traditionally, at least in the movies, ransom notes are created using words cut from different sources to disguise a kidnapper's handwriting. You can accomplish the same look by using different fonts in a Java applet. For the record, there are much smarter ways than a Java applet to issue a ransom request. But, of course, I'm not at liberty to elaborate.

The Ransom applet, shown in the following figure, displays a sentence of text using various fonts.

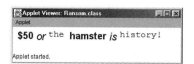

The Ransom applet and its many fonts.

Following is the complete source code for the Ransom applet.

```
import java.applet.*;
import java.awt.*;

public class Ransom extends Applet {
  public void paint(Graphics g) {
    // Create the fonts and font
    ➥metrics
    Font f1 = new Font("Helvetica",
    ➥Font.BOLD, 20),
        f2 = new Font("Times Roman",
        ➥Font.ITALIC, 22),
        f3 = new Font("Courier",
        ➥Font.PLAIN, 18);
    FontMetrics fm1 =
    ➥g.getFontMetrics(f1),
            fm2 =
            ➥g.getFontMetrics(f2),
            fm3 =
            ➥g.getFontMetrics(f3);
    int xPos = 10;
```

Finding the Ransom Applet Example on the Web

To find the Ransom applet example source code on the Web, enter the address
http://www.mcp.com/info in the location box of your Web browser. Click the link called
Downloadable Code, Examples, and Info for book "Companion Sites." In the space provided under the Book Information section, enter **0-7897-1804-9**, which is the 10-digit ISBN for this book. Click the **Search** button.

145

```
        // Draw the ransom note
        g.setFont(f1);
        g.drawString("$50 ", xPos, fm1.getHeight());
        xPos += fm1.stringWidth("$50 ");
        g.setFont(f2);
        g.drawString("or ", xPos, fm2.getHeight());
        xPos += fm2.stringWidth("or ");
        g.setFont(f3);
        g.drawString("the ", xPos, fm3.getHeight());
        xPos += fm3.stringWidth("the ");
        g.setFont(f1);
        g.drawString("hamster ", xPos, fm1.getHeight());
        xPos += fm1.stringWidth("hamster ");
        g.setFont(f2);
        g.drawString("is ", xPos, fm2.getHeight());
        xPos += fm2.stringWidth("is ");
        g.setFont(f3);
        g.drawString("history! ", xPos, fm3.getHeight());
    }
}
```

The paint() method is the only method defined in the Ransom applet class. The paint() method starts off by creating three different Font objects and their associated FontMetrics objects. It also declares an x position member variable, xPos, which is used to keep track of the word position when drawing the individual words of the ransom note. The rest of the paint() method is devoted to setting each font, drawing a word, and updating the word position. This process repeats until the entire sentence is drawn.

Just as an added precaution, let me reiterate that kidnapping is against the law and I don't encourage it as a profession. In fact, I doubt you could make much money kidnapping hamsters, as the Ransom applet suggests.

The Least You Need to Know

You were probably anxious to reach this chapter because graphics play a very important role in the vast majority of Java applets. Graphics also tends to be one of the more rewarding areas of Java programming, at least for me, simply because you get to immediately view the results of your hard work. This chapter laid the groundwork for you to start using Java graphics in your own applets. Let's recap what you learned in this chapter:

➤ The Java AWT (Abstract Windowing Toolkit) is a vast set of classes and interfaces devoted to building graphics into Java applets and applications.

➤ Specific colors in Java are formed by combining varying intensities of the colors red, green, and blue.

➤ The Graphics class represents a graphics context, which is a graphical drawing surface roughly equivalent to a piece of paper.

➤ Java automatically calls the paint() method for an applet when it detects that the applet needs to be repainted.

➤ Java graphics primitives include lines, rectangles, squares, ovals, circles, polygons, and arcs.

➤ The Font class models a font and includes members that represent the name, size, and style of a font.

➤ The size attributes of a font are known as font metrics and are retrieved using the FontMetrics class.

Your Next Work of Art

Understanding Images

It has been said that a picture is worth a thousand words. If that were true, I might have considered giving you half a picture of the Java logo and saved you the time in reading this book. Even if you can't make a reliable picture-to-word comparison, there is no doubting the power of imagery in stirring human emotions and conveying ideas. Consequently, images have become standard fare in modern computer software. The inherently graphical nature of the Web has made digital images commonplace. So, what does all this have to do with Java?

Although Web pages provide a great framework for displaying graphical images, there are certainly situations in which you might want to view and manipulate images interactively. Java fully supports images and enables you to draw and manipulate images at will. In fact, there is an `Image` class in the `java.awt` package that models a digital image. But I'm getting a little bit ahead of myself. Let's take a moment to clarify exactly what I'm referring to when I talk about images.

You learned in the previous chapter that the primary colors red, green, and blue converge inside your monitor to produce different colored pixels on the screen. An image is just a rectangular grouping of pixels. To better understand this, consider the image in the following figure.

A rectangular image.

At this size it's hard to visualize the fact that an image is just a grouping of pixels. But when you zoom in, things take on a whole new perspective. The following figure shows a magnified portion of the same image.

As you can see, an image is just a bunch of different colored pixels arranged in a rectangular shape. Why does this matter? Well, by understanding the composition of an image, you have a better idea of the way in which images can be used in applets.

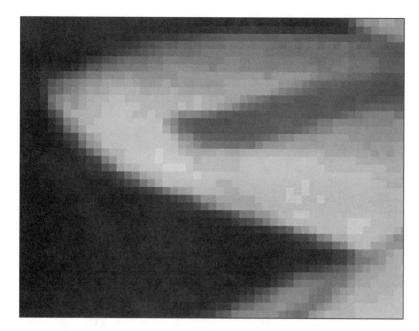

Zooming in on an image reveals that it is just a rectangular grouping of pixels.

Types of Images

Although images are just rectangular groupings of pixels, all images aren't created equal. There are many different image formats used to specify the structures of images. These formats arose out of the need to share images across different computers and also to help reduce image file size. I don't want to get into the gory details of the different image formats available, but I would like to point out the two major image formats supported by Java:

➤ **GIF—Graphics Interchange Format** The internal structure of GIF images makes them useful for storing images other than photographs. For example, illustrations and diagrams are great for the GIF image format because it is very effective at reducing the file size for these types of images.

➤ **JPEG—Joint Photographic Experts Group** As the acronym suggests, the JPEG format was created for the sole purpose of providing a highly efficient means of storing photographic images. If you are using scanned photographic images, make sure to store them in the JPEG image format.

There are plenty of graphics utilities available that support both of these image types. You can use such a utility to scan or draw images and save them in the GIF or JPEG format.

Displaying Your Masterpiece with Java

Now that you have an idea of what images are and how they are stored, let's focus on how to load and display them. Before you can display an image, you must first load it into the computer's memory. If you don't see the significance of loading an image before displaying it, imagine trying to view a slideshow without loading slides into the slide projector. You would see a splendid display of nothing, and the slide show would quickly erode into a room full of people making animal shapes with their hands. And we know how annoying that can be!

So you get the idea that loading images is necessary. The Applet class provides a couple of methods you can use to load images from a file:

```
public Image getImage(URL url)
```

or

```
public Image getImage(URL url, String name)
```

These two methods are actually overloaded versions of the same method, getImage(). The first version expects an image filename to be packaged into a full URL. The second version enables you to specify the base URL for the image file separately from the filename. I find the second version more useful because the Applet class has a method you can use to determine in which URL the applet is stored. Let me demonstrate with an example:

```
Image img = getImage(getCodeBase(), "Skate.gif");
```

Invisible Images

Although images are inherently rectangular in nature, it is possible to simulate an irregularly shaped image by making use of transparency. Transparency involves specifying a given color as transparent, which means that the background behind an image will show through this color. Any part of an image with the transparent color will appear transparent when the image is drawn.

This line of code loads the image named Skate.gif from the directory in which the applet class file is stored. The getCodeBase() method returns the URL specifying the applet's directory. Now that the image is loaded, you're ready to draw it from within the paint() method.

The Graphics class provides a few different overloaded methods named drawImage() that you can use to draw images. They all function similarly in that they draw an image at a specified position. The difference between them is how they size the image, how they interpret transparent parts of the image, and whether they support clipping or flipping the image. After you learn how to use the most basic of the drawImage() methods, you'll be able to use the others without much trouble.

The most basic `drawImage()` method follows:

```
public boolean drawImage(Image img, int x, int y, ImageObserver
observer)
```

This method accepts an `Image` object and an x,y position as its first three parameters. This x,y position specifies the location of the upper left corner of the image. The last parameter is an `ImageObserver` object, which is a special object used to help keep track of images as they are loading. Because the `Applet` class implements the `ImageObserver` interface, it can serve as the image observer for loading images. Passing `this` as the last parameter to `drawImage()` is sufficient for passing the `Applet` object.

Following is an example of drawing an image using the `drawImage()` method:

```
public void paint(Graphics g) {
   drawImage(img, 0, 0, this);
}
```

Incorporating this code with the earlier image-loading code enables you to build a simple image-drawing applet. The complete source code for the DrawImage applet follows:

```
import java.applet.*;
import java.awt.*;

public class DrawImage extends Applet {
  public void paint(Graphics g) {
    // Load the image
    Image img = getImage(getCodeBase(), "Skate.jpg");

    // Draw the image
    g.drawImage(img, 0, 0, this);
  }
}
```

The following figure shows the DrawImage applet in action.

On the Outside Looking In

Keep in mind that applets are loaded over the Web, along with any images they display. Because even the smallest of images still takes up a reasonable amount of space, you can't expect images to load immediately when you run an applet. Consequently, Java relies on the notion of image observers to help make this a smooth process. Image observers are responsible for determining how an image is displayed when it is only partially loaded. The `Applet` class implements the `ImageObserver` interface, so you can use it as the image observer for loading images.

The DrawImage applet.

A Nerd Daredevil

Just in case you're curious, that's me in the skateboarding image displayed in the DrawImage applet. I thought it might be fun to share with you one of my other passions outside of my nerdly interests in Java!

Applet: SlideShow

Although the DrawImage applet certainly succeeds in displaying an image using Java, it isn't all that big of a breakthrough. If all you need to do is simply display an image, why not just use HTML and stick an image right on the Web page? As much as I like Java, I could never endorse using it when there is a simpler way to accomplish a task.

Having said that, let's now focus on a task that isn't really possible in HTML: a slide show. Before I go any further, let me address what you're already thinking. Yes, it is possible to construct a slideshow in HTML, but it involves navigating through multiple Web pages to view the next images, which is a pain. A Java slideshow applet could provide forward and backward buttons that enable you to gingerly move through a slideshow and stay on a single Web page. Or you could simplify things by just allowing the user to click the mouse button to move through the slides. This latter approach is the one you use to build the SlideShow applet in a moment.

Incidentally, I got the idea for a slideshow applet because I recently built a koi pond and I thought it would be neat to document the construction of the pond with a slideshow. So, I took a series of pictures, scanned them, and saved them in the JPEG image format. The following figure shows the SlideShow applet with one of the pond slides being displayed. You could easily substitute your own images to create a slideshow for a vacation or some other pictorial adventure. Just let your creativity lead you!

Now that you've seen the SlideShow applet, let's think about the specifics of how it might work. This hypothetical design approach makes it much easier to follow the actual code for the applet. First, the applet could store the individual slide images in an array, which makes it easier to change the number of slides in the slideshow. You would have to first load the images into the array, possibly using a `for` loop to simplify the process. You would then need to draw the current slide image in the `paint()` method by indexing into the array of images.

Curious About Koi

I've made mention of my koi pond a couple of times throughout the book thus far. In case you aren't familiar with koi or koi ponds, allow me to fill you in. A koi is an ornamental Japanese carp (fish) that can have very unusual color patterns and grow to nearly three feet in length. Koi can live 60 years or more and can also be quite expensive because they are valued as collector's items in Japan and to a lesser extent in the U.S. A koi pond is a pond specially designed as a home for koi and is usually constructed at least three feet in depth.

Navigating through the images would somehow involve detecting when the user clicked the mouse button and then incrementing the image array index. Got all that?

The SlideShow applet.

Finding the SlideShow Applet Example on the Web

To find the SlideShow applet example source code on the Web, enter the address
http://www.mcp.com/info in the location box of your Web browser. Click the link called
Downloadable Code, Examples, and Info for book "Companion Sites." In the space provided under the Book Information section, enter **0-7897-1804-9**, which is the 10-digit ISBN for this book. Click the **Search** button.

Instead of delving into any more design specifics, let's go ahead and peek at the source code for the SlideShow applet:

```java
import java.applet.*;
import java.awt.*;
import java.awt.event.*;

public class SlideShow extends Applet {
    final int SLIDETOTAL = 5;
    Image[]   slides = new Image[SLIDETOTAL];
    int       slideNum = 0;

    public void init() {
        // Register the mouse event handler
        addMouseListener(new MouseHandler());

        // Load the slide images
        for (int i = 1; i <= SLIDETOTAL; i++)
            slides[i - 1] = getImage(getCodeBase(),
            ➥"Pond" + i + ".jpg");
    }

    public void paint(Graphics g) {
        // Draw the current slide image
        if (slides[slideNum] != null)
            g.drawImage(slides[slideNum], 0, 0, this);
    }

    class MouseHandler extends MouseAdapter {
        public void mouseClicked(MouseEvent e) {
            // Move to the next slide
            if (++slideNum == SLIDETOTAL)
                slideNum = 0;

            // Draw the next slide
            repaint();
        }
    }
}
```

The SlideShow applet class declares three data members:

➤ **SLIDETOTAL** This member is actually a constant that stores the total number of slides in the slideshow. The final modifier is used to indicate that SLIDETOTAL is constant. To change the number of slides in the slideshow, you would simply modify the SLIDETOTAL member.

➤ **slides** This member variable is an array of Image objects that contains the individual slide images.

➤ **slideNum** This member variable keeps track of the current slide being viewed.

The init() method takes on the chore of loading all the slide images. A for loop iterates through the slides array and loads each image one at a time. The image files are named Pond1.jpg, Pond2.jpg, and so on, which is why the for loop is able to build the filename for each image. Also notice at the beginning of the init() method that there is a call to the addMouseListener() method. This method call is necessary to process mouse clicks; don't worry about this method right now because the next chapter explains all about it.

The paint() method is pretty simple—it draws the current slide image from the slide array. Notice that the paint() method first checks to make sure that the image is not equal to null. This touches on a subtle but important issue relating to the paint() method and the loading of the images. Because this is an applet and the images are likely to be loaded over an Internet connection, it is possible for the paint() method to get called before the images have finished loading. This means that the slides array will contain null values for its images, resulting in a big problem if you try to draw one of them. So, it is necessary to check and make sure an image isn't null before drawing it. After the images are loaded this isn't a problem, but checking for null makes things safer when the applet starts.

The last section of code in the SlideShow applet class handles mouse clicks, which is necessary to move to the next slide in the slideshow. The code essentially responds to a mouse click event, which is sent to the applet whenever the mouse button is clicked. Because you don't learn about events until the next chapter, it isn't important that you follow this code exactly. What is important, however, is the small section of code that moves the slideshow to the next slide:

```
if (++slideNum == SLIDETOTAL)
   slideNum = 0;
```

This code simply increments the slideNum variable and makes sure it isn't equal to SLIDETOTAL. If slideNum equals SLIDETOTAL, it means you've moved past the last slide, in which case the slideshow rolls back to the first slide. That way you can loop through the slideshow just like you were controlling a real slide projector. See, modeling the real world in a Java applet isn't all that difficult!

The Least You Need to Know

To me, images are the most compelling graphics to use in Java applets because they can convey such a sense of realism. Although graphics primitives such as lines and circles certainly have their place, images reign supreme in most applets. And I'm not just talking about photographic images, but also artistically rendered images such as clip art. I could go on and on, but I think you get the idea that I think images are a good thing. This chapter covered the basics of images and how they are used in Java. More specifically, you learned that:

➤ An image is a rectangular grouping of pixels.

➤ GIF and JPEG are the two types of images directly supported by Java.

➤ The JPEG image format is more useful for storing photographic images, and the GIF format is useful for storing other types of non-photographic images.

➤ The `getImage()` method is used to load images from disk.

➤ The `drawImage()` method is used to draw images to a graphics context.

Interacting with the User

Meeting the Demands of the User

I was fortunate enough a few years ago to see my favorite comedian, George Carlin, live in Las Vegas. George is fond of picking apart euphemisms and misuses of the English language. In his act he talked about how the word "event" is used to try to dramatize everyday occurrences. For example, on local news you commonly hear a thunderstorm referred to as a "weather event." Similarly, some department stores talk about their huge weekend "sales event." George pondered the question of where one would buy tickets to attend a weather event.

Although I agree completely with George's commentary on the misuse of the word "event," I can't say that he would be too pleased with Java in this regard. You see, events are a major part of Java. An event is defined in Java as something that occurs in a program that you might want to know about and respond to. Even though attending a mouse click or key press event might not sound like much excitement, they are nonetheless important within the realm of Java programming. Let's take a step back and get a grasp on exactly what Java events are.

Interacting with the user via a Java program involves knowing when the user has done something meaningful, such as moving the mouse or pressing a key on the keyboard. Granted, it's entirely possible to move the mouse around and bang on the keyboard without it being meaningful, but for the purposes of this discussion let's assume all user input is worth knowing about. When the user does something like moving the mouse or pressing a key, it is considered an event. It's not quite on the same scale as a tornado ripping down your street (a weather event), but an event all the same. Writing Java code to handle events is known as event-driven programming.

Say It with an Event

In the event-driven world of Java, the flow of a program often follows events that occur externally. In other words, the user can do something that generates an event and effectively interrupts the linear flow of your program. This might sound like a problem, but it's actually the way event-driven programs are designed to function. An event-driven Java program is really in a constant state of responding to events. The most visible events are things such as mouse clicks and key presses, which are known as input events. You respond to these events by writing special methods known as event handlers.

Events and Components

All events in Java are processed through the AWT, which means that they are tightly linked with graphical components. Although you aren't formally introduced to components until the next chapter, you might as well go ahead and start getting accustomed to them. Graphical user interface elements such as buttons and scrollbars are referred to as components. Components form the basis for the entire Java AWT. In fact, the Applet class is itself a type of component.

Because of the inherently graphical nature of Java applets, it will eventually become obvious to you why event-driven programming is not only convenient, but also downright vital to the function of applets. When you consider all the types of things that can take place within an applet (such as button presses, scroll bar movement, mouse clicks, and key presses to name a few), it only makes sense that events are used to coordinate it all.

Java supports two different types of events:

➤ Low-level events—Events fired in response to a low-level input or visual user interface interaction such as a mouse drag, mouse button click, or a key press.

➤ Semantic events—Events fired when an action occurs that is based on the semantics of a particular component. An example of a semantic event is an item selection event, which is related to the specific function (semantics) of a component that manages a list of items, such as a list box.

Semantic events only make sense within the context of a specific component, whereas low-level events are all-purpose events understood by all.

There are classes defined in the Java AWT that represent each type of low-level and semantic event. You learn about some of these classes a little later in the chapter when you find out how to handle events in Java code. For now, let's move on to learning about event sources and listeners.

Listening for Events

Have you ever seen a movie in which an undercover stakeout takes place? Usually it involves some undercover cops in a van listening to a tapped phone line and watching their targets with binoculars. The cops are armed and ready for the criminal targets to make a move, in which case they respond by attempting an arrest. As strange as it might sound, this popular movie scenario is not very far off from the way event handling works in Java. A Java program sits around waiting for something to happen; when it happens, the program jumps into action and somehow responds.

A program or object that receives and responds to events is referred to as an event listener. Event listeners are required to implement interfaces that formally define how events are received and processed. Huh? Read on, it will get clearer, I promise! An event listener interface has an individual method for each event type it is capable of catching and responding to. Related events are usually grouped together in a single event listener interface. Following are a few of the more commonly used event listener interfaces:

➤ `KeyListener`

➤ `MouseListener`

➤ `MouseMotionListener`

➤ `WindowListener`

➤ `ActionListener`

➤ `ItemListener`

You learn how to use a few of these event listener interfaces a little later in the chapter. For now, let's take a look at another major issue related to event delivery: event sources.

Where Do Events Come From?

Event listeners provide half of the event delivery equation; event sources provide the other. Put simply, an event source is an object (component) capable of generating events. Event sources must provide a means of registering listeners, which is how the sources know where to send event notifications. When an event occurs within an event source, the source is responsible for examining the registered listeners and sending event notifications appropriately. Similar to event listeners, event sources can be distinguished by whether they generate low-level or semantic events.

Now that you understand the specific relationships between events, event sources, and event listeners, let's take a moment to ponder the big picture of event delivery. The event delivery process can be broken down into three basic steps:

1. An event listener registers itself with an event source as wanting to receive event notifications.

2. An event occurs within an event source.

3. The event source notifies the event listener of the event by calling an event response method and passing information about the event.

Handling Mouse Input

For an applet to handle events, it must register itself as an event listener by calling an event listener registration method. Additionally, event-handling applets must implement an event listener interface, which involves implementing the event response methods defined in the interface. As an example, the following code shows how an applet registers itself by calling an event listener registration method:

```
addMouseListener(this);
```

This code, which would appear in the applet's `init()` method, registers the applet as a mouse event listener. Any mouse events that occur in the applet window are sent to the `Applet` object for handling.

After registering an application as an event listener, you must implement the appropriate event listener interface. The `addMouseListener()` method requires that the object passed in implement the `MouseListener` interface. This is accomplished in the applet class definition like this:

```
class MyApplet extends Applet implements MouseListener {
    ...
}
```

The applet then must implement all of the event response methods defined in the `MouseListener` interface. These methods follow:

➤ mouseClicked()

➤ mousePressed()

➤ mouseReleased()

➤ mouseEntered()

➤ mouseExited()

The `mouseClicked()` method is called whenever the user clicks a mouse button. In some situations it might be useful to break a mouse click down into a button press and button release. The `mousePressed()` and `mouseReleased()` methods are called in each of these situations. Finally, the `mouseEntered()` and `mouseExited()` methods are called whenever the mouse pointer enters and exits the applet's window, respectively.

Following is an example of how the applet would implement one of these methods:

```
public void mouseClicked(MouseEvent e) {
  System.out.println("Mouse clicked!");
}
```

This method prints a message to standard output any time the user clicks the mouse button while the mouse is over the applet. Unfortunately, because interfaces must be fully implemented in order for a class to be instantiable, the applet must implement all of the event response methods in the `MouseListener` interface even if it does not need them all. This is a problem that can be easily solved with event adapters, which are covered in the next section.

You might be curious about the `MouseEvent` object that is passed into the mouse event handler methods. This object contains information about the mouse event that occurred. For example, the `MouseEvent` class provides two methods, `getX()` and `getY()`, for determining the x and y positions of the mouse pointer when the mouse event occurs.

So far I've only discussed the `MouseListener` interface. Although this interface is certainly used a great deal to handle mouse events, there is also a `MouseMotionListener` interface that is used to deal with events related to the mouse moving. Following are the event handler methods defined in the `MouseMotionListener` interface:

➤ `mouseMoved()`

➤ `mouseDragged()`

The `mouseMoved()` method is called whenever the mouse is moved across the applet window. The `mouseDragged()` method is similar to `mouseMoved()`, but it is only called if the mouse is being moved while a mouse button is held down.

Let's take a moment to try out a simple example applet that demonstrates how to handle mouse events. Following is the source code for the Mousy applet:

```
import java.applet.*;
import java.awt.event.*;

public class Mousy extends Applet implements MouseListener,
➡MouseMotionListener {
  public void init() {
    // Register the mouse event handlers
    addMouseListener(this);
```

163

```
      addMouseMotionListener(this);
   }

   public void mouseClicked(MouseEvent e) {
      System.out.println("The mouse button was clicked at: " +
         e.getX() + ", " + e.getY());
   }

   public void mousePressed(MouseEvent e) {
      System.out.println("The mouse button was pressed at: " +
         e.getX() + ", " + e.getY());
   }

   public void mouseReleased(MouseEvent e) {
      System.out.println("The mouse button was released at: " +
         e.getX() + ", " + e.getY());
   }

   public void mouseEntered(MouseEvent e) {
      System.out.println("The mouse entered the applet window.");
   }

   public void mouseExited(MouseEvent e) {
      System.out.println("The mouse exited the applet window.");
   }

   public void mouseDragged(MouseEvent e) {
      System.out.println("The mouse was dragged to: " +
         e.getX() + ", " + e.getY());
   }

   public void mouseMoved(MouseEvent e) {
      System.out.println("The mouse was moved to: " +
         e.getX() + ", " + e.getY());
   }
}
```

This code begins by defining the Mousy applet class as implementing the
MouseListener and MouseMotionListener interfaces. The init() method then takes
on the task of registering the applet as an event listener for both types of events.
Please take note that the event registration in the init() method must be performed.
Without it, the applet will never receive mouse events.

Beyond the init() method, every other method in the Mousy applet is an event handler. Each method simply outputs a string indicating the event that took place. Notice that some of the methods use the MouseEvent object to determine the position of the mouse pointer within the applet window. When you run the Mousy applet, it's interesting to move and click the mouse over the applet window and watch the events in the command-line window as they are generated.

Efficiency Events

The primary reason for having to register event listeners is to improve the efficiency of event delivery. If an applet doesn't need to receive certain kinds of events, it would be very wasteful to send the events anyway. So, you must always register an applet so that it can receive the type of event in which you are interested. This clarifies exactly which events you are handling, and it helps Java run more efficiently.

Adapting to Events

Implementing event listener interfaces to handle events is often annoying because it requires that you implement all of the event response methods in an interface, regardless of which ones you need. To alleviate this problem, Java supplies event adapters, which are helper classes that make the handling of events much cleaner. Event adapters enable you to implement only the event response methods you need, freeing you from the hassle of writing empty methods you do not need just to conform to an interface.

Event adapters are classes, not interfaces. This is what enables you to override only the methods you need in them. There is a unique event adapter class for each low-level event listener interface. There are no event adapter classes for semantic event listener interfaces because the interfaces define only one method each.

Because event adapters are classes and not interfaces, they are a little tricky to use; you cannot just implement them in an applet class. To use an adapter class, you can create an inner class within the application class that derives from the adapter class. You then implement only the event response methods you need in the inner class. Following is an example of such an inner class called MouseHandler:

```
class MyApplet extends Applet {
  ...
  class MouseHandler extends MouseAdapter {
    public void mouseClicked(MouseEvent e) {
      System.out.println("Mouse clicked!");
    }
  }
  ...
}
```

Inner Classes

Although it might seem like a weird prospect, it is possible in Java to define a class within a class. A class defined within another class is known as an inner class and can actually be quite useful in some situations. One of these situations is event handling, where inner classes give you the freedom of responding to a single event without having to fully implement an event listener interface.

The MouseHandler inner class, which is located within the applet class definition, extends the MouseAdapter class and implements only one method, mouseClicked(). With this approach you still have to register an event listener, but this time the listener is specified as an instance of the adapter-derived inner class instead of the applet object itself:

```
addMouseListener(new MouseHandler());
```

Incidentally, this code is still located in the init() method for the applet, which is usually the most convenient place to register event listeners.

The following code is a modified version of the Mousy applet, named Mousy2, that relies on event adapters to handle events:

```
import java.applet.*;
import java.awt.event.*;

public class Mousy2 extends Applet {
  public void init() {
    // Register the mouse event handlers
    addMouseListener(new MouseHandler());
    addMouseMotionListener(new MouseMotionHandler());
  }

  class MouseHandler extends MouseAdapter {
    public void mouseClicked(MouseEvent e) {
      System.out.println("The mouse button was clicked at: " +
        e.getX() + ", " + e.getY());
    }


  }

  class MouseMotionHandler extends MouseMotionAdapter {
    public void mouseMoved(MouseEvent e) {
      System.out.println("The mouse was moved to: " +
        e.getX() + ", " + e.getY());
    }
  }
}
```

The Mousy2 applet functions much the same as Mousy, except for the fact that it uses event adapters to handle the mouse events. However, because Mousy2 uses event adapters, it is free to use only the event handler methods it needs. In this case it overrides the mouseClicked() and mouseMoved() methods from the adapter class.

Getting back to the Mousy2 applet class, notice that the class doesn't implement the mouse event listener interfaces. Additionally, the init() method registers event listeners by creating event handler objects and passing them into the event registration methods.

The event handler objects are the real workers in this program. The event handler classes, MouseHandler and MouseMotionHandler, derive from event adapter classes and override the same methods defined in the respective event listener interfaces. The difference in this case is that you are free to override only the methods you need. This isn't possible when dealing with interfaces because you always have to fully implement an interface in order to create a class that can be instantiated.

So that you can see the real benefit of event adapters, you'll return to them a little later in the chapter when you build the Scribbler applet.

Handling Keyboard Input

Keyboard input is handled much like mouse input, except that there is a different event listener interface devoted to keyboard events. This interface is named KeyListener and defines the following event handler methods:

➤ keyTyped()

➤ keyPressed()

➤ keyReleased()

The keyTyped() method is called whenever a key is typed on the keyboard. A typed key can be broken down into a key press and a key release. The keyPressed() and keyReleased() methods are called in response to each of these events.

In all three of the key event handler methods, a KeyEvent object is passed along containing information about the key event. The main piece of information contained in this object is the identity of the key that was typed, pressed, or released. Either of the two methods in the KeyEvent class can be used to determine the key identity: getKeyChar() and getKeyCode(). The getKeyChar() method returns the key identity as a character, and the getKeyCode() method returns an integer code representing the key. Because it is possible for a Java applet to run in environments that support different languages with different character sets, it isn't very reliable to use the getKeyChar() method. For this reason you should try to stick with the getKeyCode() method to check for the identity of a key.

The following table lists some examples of key codes associated with the getKeyCode() method:

Key Codes Associated with the `getKeyCode()` Method

Key Code	Key
VK_INSERT	Insert
VK_DELETE	Delete
VK_HOME	Home
VK_END	End
VK_PAGE_UP	Page Up
VK_PAGE_DOWN	Page Down
VK_ENTER	Enter
VK_ESCAPE	Escape
VK_UP	Up Arrow
VK_DOWN	Down Arrow
VK_LEFT	Left Arrow
VK_RIGHT	Right Arrow
VK_A	A
VK_B	B
VK_C	C
VK_1	1
VK_2	2
VK_3	3
VK_F1	F1
VK_F2	F2
VK_F3	F3

Checking to see if a certain key or group of keys has been pressed is a very straightforward process. The following code demonstrates:

```
public void keyPressed(KeyEvent e) {
  // Handle the arrow keys
  switch (e.getKeyCode()) {
    case VK_UP:
      System.out.println("The Up Arrow key was pressed.");
      break;
    case VK_DOWN:
      System.out.println("The Down Arrow key was pressed.");
      break;
    case VK_LEFT:
      System.out.println("The Left Arrow key was pressed.");
      break;
```

```
        case VK_RIGHT:
          System.out.println("The Right Arrow key was pressed.");
          break;
      }
    }
```

Of course, this code requires that you first register the applet by calling `addKeyListener()`. Additionally, the applet would need to implement the `KeyListener` interface. Of course, you could also use the `KeyAdapter` event adapter class to make things a little cleaner.

Applet: Scribbler

Now that you feel pretty comfortable with handling events and dealing with user input, let's tackle an applet that does some interesting things with user input. The Scribbler applet accepts mouse input and uses it as the basis for allowing the user to draw pictures. By holding the mouse button down and dragging the mouse, you can draw lines. Letting go of the mouse button stops the drawing. You can think of the mouse button as working a lot like the nozzle on a can of spray paint; if you hold down the nozzle, paint comes out. It's pretty simple, really.

The following figure shows an artistic piece I worked on for a few hours using the Scribbler applet. I think you'll agree I have some artistic talent just waiting to burst out.

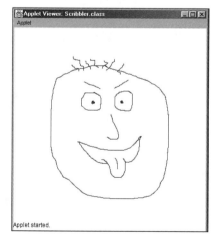

A stunning work of art created in the Scribbler applet.

Finding the Scribbler Applet Example on the Web

To find the Scribbler applet example source code on the Web, enter the address `http://www.mcp.com/info` in the location box of your Web browser. Click the link called **Downloadable Code, Examples, and Info for book "Companion Sites."** In the space provided under the Book Information section, enter **0-7897-1804-9**, which is the 10-digit ISBN for this book. Click the **Search** button.

As you'll soon learn, the code behind the Scribbler applet is almost as masterful as the art that can be created with it. Seriously, parts of the code look a little complicated, but I want to focus primarily on the event handling aspects of it. Before I jump into the code, however, I want to explain the theory behind how the Scribbler applet actually stores drawings.

When you press the mouse button and hold it down, Scribbler draws a continuous line until you let go of the button. You can think of this continuous line as a stroke, kind of like a stroke of a paintbrush. Because it is possible to track the movement of the mouse with events, you can model a stroke as a series of connected points. So, as the user drags the mouse, the Scribbler applet stores every point the mouse traverses. The applet then connects lines between this list of points to create a graphical stroke. The following figure illustrates this concept.

The figure shows the word "Hi" written in freehand. Notice how straight line segments of the drawing are connected by points. Realistically, enough mouse motion events would be generated during the drawing process to generate more points, but this figure helps illustrate the general idea.

A stroke in the Scribbler applet is just a series of points connected by lines.

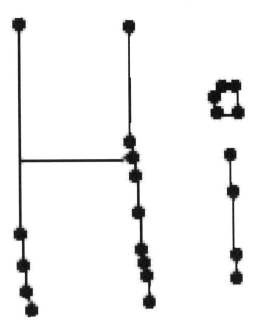

The only hitch with this approach to representing a stroke with a list of points is that there is no way to know how many points a stroke consists of. Quicker mouse movements will generate more mouse move events, and therefore more points. Also, the longer you hold the button down, the more points you accumulate. Because Java arrays are fixed in length, you really need a better way to store the list of strokes. I'll show you how to get around this problem a little later when you dig into the code for the applet.

The other thing to keep in mind about the applet is that there can be multiple strokes. So, not only do you need to store a series of points in a given stroke, but you also need to store all of the strokes in some kind of list. Fortunately, Java provides a way to conveniently solve these problems, as you shall soon see.

Following is the complete source code for the Scribbler applet:

```java
import java.applet.*;
import java.awt.*;
import java.awt.event.*;
import java.util.*;

public class Scribbler extends Applet {
  Vector strokes = new Vector();
  Vector curStroke;

  public void init() {
    // Register the mouse event handlers
    addMouseListener(new MouseHandler());
    addMouseMotionListener(new MouseMotionHandler());
  }

  public void paint(Graphics g) {
    // Draw the list of strokes
    for (int i = 0; i < strokes.size(); i++)
      for (int j = 1; j < ((Vector)strokes.elementAt(i)).size(); j++)
        g.drawLine(
          ((Point)((Vector)strokes.elementAt(i)).elementAt(j - 1)).x,
          ((Point)((Vector)strokes.elementAt(i)).elementAt(j - 1)).y,
          ((Point)((Vector)strokes.elementAt(i)).elementAt(j)).x,
          ((Point)((Vector)strokes.elementAt(i)).elementAt(j)).y);
  }

  class MouseHandler extends MouseAdapter {
    public void mousePressed(MouseEvent e) {
      // Create a new stroke
      curStroke = new Vector();

      // Add the current stroke to the list of strokes
      strokes.addElement(curStroke);
```

```
        }
    }

    class MouseMotionHandler extends MouseMotionAdapter {
        public void mouseDragged(MouseEvent e) {
            // Add the mouse position to the current stroke
            curStroke.addElement(new Point(e.getX(), e.getY()));

            // Update the drawing
            repaint();
        }
    }
}
```

Can I Get the Vector Victor?

The movie *Airplane!* has a classic scene where the pilot is trying to get the position vector for the plane from a copilot, whose name is Victor. The words "Victor" and "Vector" repeatedly interchanged made for pretty funny dialogue. The vector they were referring to in the movie is used in engineering and aeronautics to represent an XY quantity such as speed or position. In Java, however, a vector represents a list of items. You can think of a vector as a more powerful array, because it ultimately performs the same function as an array. However, vectors have the important ability to dynamically grow in size.

The `Scribbler` applet class contains two member variables, `strokes` and `curStroke`. The `strokes` member is a `Vector` object used to store the list of strokes that make up a Scribbler drawing. The `Vector` class is provided in the `java.util` package, and serves as a container for holding a list of items. Unlike arrays, vectors can grow in size to accommodate as many items as you need. This makes it ideal as a container to hold the list of strokes.

The `curStroke` member is also a `Vector` object, but it is used to hold a list of points. As the mouse is dragged, its position is added to the `curStroke` vector as a point. The `Point` class, which is provided in the `java.awt` package, is used to represent an x,y point.

The applet's `init()` method is used to register event adapters for mouse and mouse motion events. As you learned earlier in the chapter, this is necessary for mouse events to be sent to the applet.

The `paint()` method is admittedly the most complex method in the Scribbler applet because it has to do some interesting things with the `strokes` vector. Although the code looks tricky, the function of the method is actually quite simple. The first `for` loop iterates through the strokes stored in the `strokes` vector. This stroke is used as the basis for the second `for` loop, which iterates through the points stored in the stroke. Inside the second `for` loop, a line is drawn between each successive point in the `strokes` vector. If you take some time to study the code, this will make more sense. Or you could just take my word for it and move on to the event handling code, which is primarily what I'm interested in showing you.

The MouseHandler class is an inner class that serves as an event adapter for dealing with mouse events. Within it, the mousePressed() method creates a new stroke and adds it to the vector of strokes. This method is called when you first press the mouse button to draw a new stroke.

The MouseMotionHandler class is an inner class that serves as an event adapter for dealing with mouse motion events. Within it, the mouseDragged() method retrieves the current mouse position and adds it to the current stroke. The repaint() method is then called to update the drawing with the new point. The mouseDragged() method is called when you drag the mouse around within the applet window.

That's really all there is to the Scribbler applet. I know the code probably looks a little intimidating, but you have to consider the fact that it is doing some interesting things. I encourage you to take some time and study the code a little more to try and get comfortable with how the applet works. Also try out the applet and observe how it functions. You might think of a few enhancements!

The Least You Need to Know

As much fun as it might be to create applets that do nothing more than display cute graphics, the vast majority of applets require some degree of user interaction. All user interaction in Java is detected and responded to via events. This includes user input associated with the mouse, the keyboard, and any other input device dreamed up in the future. This chapter explored Java events and how applets can respond to them in interesting ways. To recap, you learned that:

➤ An event is something that occurs in a Java program that you might want to know about and respond to.

➤ Writing Java code to handle events is known as event-driven programming.

➤ A program or object that receives and responds to events is referred to as an event listener.

➤ An event source is an object capable of generating events.

➤ For an applet to handle events, it must register itself as an event listener by calling an event listener registration method.

➤ Event adapters are helper classes that make the handling of events much cleaner.

➤ Java uses integer key codes to identify keys on the keyboard in a language-independent manner.

Making a Great First Impression

The Importance of User Interfaces

This chapter explores user interfaces and the role they play in Java applets. To be able to create effective user interfaces, you must fully understand their significance in Java programming. One interesting way to approach this topic is to consider the ideal user interface. Putting aside all technical limitations, what is the ideal manner in which humans could communicate with computers?

To me, the ideal user interface would be one that interpreted your brain waves and was able to understand your thoughts. I imagine that a computer that understood your thoughts would be pretty intuitive and simple to use. For example, can you picture yourself working away on a computer with no keyboard or mouse? Your sole interface with the computer in this hypothetical scenario is your thought process.

Unfortunately, this ideal user interface is still on the level of science fiction. However, it does provide some insight into how a user interface should work. More specifically, user interfaces should be oriented more toward people, not computers, and should be very intuitive and easy to use.

Studying User Interfaces

If you're concerned about learning how to design effective user interfaces, let me assure you that you don't have to look far for inspiration. Because major software publishers spend lots of money researching user interface design, their software tends to have very effective user interfaces. So, spend some time running a few commercial applications and studying the user interfaces. What do you like and dislike about each of them?

There is no right or wrong user interface; user interface design is an art form that is dictated by aesthetics just as much as practical function.

Until my brain wave user interface becomes technologically feasible, we are left to make the most of graphical user interfaces that are manipulated with the mouse and keyboard. Fortunately, Java comes standard with a rich set of graphical user interface classes that you can use to build effective user interfaces.

Components Are at the Heart of It All

User interfaces in Java begin and end with components, which are Java objects that represent graphical user interface elements such as buttons, menus, and scrolling lists. The Java API provides a large set of components in the java.awt package that are used to build user interfaces. The AWT (Abstract Windowing Toolkit) is actually a set of nested components that represent practically every visible user interface element used in Java, along with some other elements that aren't readily visible.

AWT components are structured in a nested hierarchy that begins with the Component class. The Component class defines general properties required of all components such as width, height, background color, and so on. The component hierarchy not only defines the relationship between component classes, but also the way components are arranged on the screen and the order in which they are painted.

Basically all windows you see in a Java applet are components of some sort. There is a special type of component called a container that is used to hold other components and containers. The main window in an applet is a good example of a container because it contains all of the components that make up the user interface for the applet. Another type of component is a canvas, which is a basic drawing surface on which you can perform drawing operations. The AWT provides the classes Container and Canvas to represent container and canvas components, respectively.

Digging into User Interface Components

One good thing about Java components is that they are all handled in a very consistent manner; after you learn how to create and add a component to an applet, you can figure out how to work with other components without much trouble. To see what I mean by this, check out the following code:

```
public void init() {
   Button button = new Button("Click me");
   add(button);
}
```

This code demonstrates how to create and add a button to an applet's user interface. A Button object is created by providing the label for the button in the Button constructor. Adding the button to the applet is as simple as calling the add() method and passing in the Button object. The add() method, which is defined in the Container class, is used to add components to a container. Because applets themselves are containers, you can call the add() method anywhere from within an applet. It usually makes sense to construct the user interface for an applet in the init() method.

The previous piece of code is a very good example of how you add components to an applet to construct a user interface. Just to make sure you understand what is taking place, let me clarify that adding a component to an applet is a two-step process:

1. Create a component object.
2. Call the add() method on the applet and pass in the component object.

When you add a component to an applet using this approach, the component is automatically sized and positioned. Components appear in an applet's user interface in the same order that they were added. The applet's layout manager controls the specific positioning of components, which is an inherited container property that describes the way components are positioned relative to each other. For example, there is a grid layout manager that arranges components in a grid pattern from left to right and top to bottom. You learn more about layout managers later in the chapter.

As I mentioned earlier, the AWT is vast and contains lots of different components. For this reason, I won't try to exhaustively cover every AWT component. Rather, I want to focus on the ones you are most likely to use. Following is a list of the more commonly used AWT user interface components:

➤ Labels
➤ Buttons
➤ Checkboxes and Radio Buttons
➤ Choices
➤ Lists
➤ Text Fields and Text Areas

The next few sections explore these different components and show you how to create and use them.

Labels

Label components are used to display text. Labels come in handy when you want to provide text that describes another user interface component, such as a text entry field. The following figure shows what a label component looks like.

A label component.

You create a Label object by providing a string label to its constructor, like this:

```
Label label = new Label("This is my label.");
```

The text appearing in a label is left justified by default. You can create a label with other justification by using a different constructor and passing one of the constants Label.LEFT, Label.CENTER, or Label.RIGHT. Following is an example of how to create a label with its text centered:

```
Label label = new Label("This is another label.", Label.CENTER);
```

Of course, you are also free to create labels that initially have no text associated with them:

```
Label label = new Label();
```

You can use the getText() and setText() methods to get and set the text in a label. You can also use the getAlignment() and setAlignment() methods to get and set the alignment of a label after it has been created. Keep in mind that adding a label to an applet is a two-step process: create the Label object and then add it to the applet. Following is an example of doing this:

```
public void init() {
  Label label = new Label("I'm a label!");
  add(label);
}
```

If you don't need to keep the reference to the Label object around, you can create and add the label to the applet in one line of code, like this:

```
add(new Label("I'm a label!"));
```

The problem with this approach is that you can't manipulate the label because you aren't keeping a reference to it in a variable. This is often okay because many labels are created and forgotten.

Buttons

Button components are very useful in enabling the user to invoke a process. Like labels, button components contain a text label that is displayed on the surface of the button. The following figure shows what a button component looks like.

A button component.

You create a `Button` object by providing a string label to its constructor, like this:

```
Button button = new Button("Start");
```

You can also create buttons that initially have no text associated with them, in which case they appear as empty buttons:

```
Button button = new Button();
```

This might be useful in situations where you don't know the button name when you first create the button. The `Button` class provides `getText()` and `setText()` methods that you can use to get and set the text in a button. Like labels and all other components, adding a button to an applet involves creating the `Button` object and then adding it to the applet. You saw an example of this earlier in the chapter when I explained the `add()` method.

Checkboxes and Radio Buttons

Checkboxes are components used to represent two-state properties such as on/off, true/false, hot/cold, and so on. A checkbox consists of a text label and a small box that is either checked or unchecked. The following figure shows what a checkbox component looks like.

You create a `Checkbox` object by providing a string label to its constructor, like this:

```
Checkbox check = new Checkbox("Automatically save");
```

A checkbox component.

Checkboxes default to being unchecked when you create them. You can initially set their state by using a different constructor, like this:

```
Checkbox check = new Checkbox("Automatically save", true);
```

The Checkbox class provides a setState() method that you can use to set the state of the checkbox to checked (true) or unchecked (false). You can also get the state of a checkbox using the getState() method. Adding a checkbox to an applet is as easy as creating a Checkbox object and adding it to the applet, like this:

```
add(check);
```

The Checkbox class can also be used to create radio buttons, which are small two-state buttons organized in a group. The significance of radio buttons is that only one of the buttons can be set at a time. This relationship is known as mutual exclusion, which means that it only makes sense for one of the buttons to be active (set) at a time.

To better understand this, consider an applet that converts measurements. It might make sense to support different units such as inches, feet, meters, and so on. Because it only makes sense to have one unit of measurement active at a time, this is a good situation in which to use a group of radio buttons. The following figure shows what a group of radio buttons looks like.

A group of checkbox components used as radio buttons.

You create a group of radio buttons by first creating a CheckboxGroup object, like this:

```
CheckboxGroup group = new CheckboxGroup();
```

The CheckboxGroup class is used as a container for grouping radio buttons. Radio buttons are actually implemented through the Checkbox class, which provides a special constructor for creating radio buttons. Following is an example of creating radio buttons and adding them to a checkbox group:

```
add(new Checkbox("Inches", true, group));
add(new Checkbox("Feet", false, group));
add(new Checkbox("Yards", false, group));
add(new Checkbox("Miles", false, group));
add(new Checkbox("Centimeters", false, group));
add(new Checkbox("Meters", false, group));
add(new Checkbox("Kilometers", false, group));
```

As you can see, the checkboxes are actually added to the applet like normal, except that the checkbox group is specified as the last parameter to the constructor. This is important because the checkbox group manages the mutual exclusion of the radio buttons. The second parameter to the Checkbox constructor is the initial value of the radio button. Keep in mind that it doesn't make sense to specify more than one of the radio buttons as initially set to true.

Choices

Choices are components used to represent a pop-up menu containing a list of selectable items. A choice consists of a menu title that displays the currently selected item. When you click on that item, the choice menu opens to reveal a list of items from which you select one. The following figure shows what a choice component looks like.

A choice component.

You create a Choice object by simply calling its default constructor, like this:

```
Choice choice = new Choice();
```

Choices default to being empty when you create them, which means that they don't initially contain any items to select. You add items by calling the add() method and identifying each item as a string:

```
choice.add("Larry");
choice.add("Curly");
choice.add("Moe");
```

The add() method results in items being added to the end of the choice menu. You can also insert an item at a specific location in the menu by using the insert() method. The getItemCount() method returns the number of items in a choice menu. To determine which item is currently selected, you call the getSelectedItem() method, like this:

```
String selItem = choice.getSelectedItem();
```

You can also select an item by calling the select() method and providing the name of the item, like this:

```
choice.select("Curly");
```

Adding a choice to an applet is as easy as creating a Choice object and adding it to the applet, like this:

```
add(choice);
```

Lists

Lists are components used to represent a scrolling list of selectable items. Unlike choices, lists always display a list of items. Additionally, lists can be created to support the selection of either one item or multiple items. The following figure shows what a list component looks like.

A list component.

The easiest way to create a List object is to call its default constructor, like this:

```
List list = new List();
```

By default, lists are created empty and with no visible rows of items. As you add items, the list will grow in size to accommodate the items. However, at some point the applet's layout manager will constrain the list, at which point scroll bars will appear to enable you to view more items. You can initially specify how many rows of items a list is to show by using a different constructor, like this:

```
List list = new List(8);
```

This constructor creates a list with the specified number of rows visible at creation. Adding items to the list won't affect the size of the list. This constructor and the default constructor both create lists that only support the selection of one item at a time.

You can create a multiple selection list by using yet another constructor:

```
List list = new List(8, true);
```

This constructor allows you to specify the number of visible rows along with whether the list supports multiple selection (`true`) or not (`false`). Because a multiple selection list is toggled, you click an item in the list to select it and click it again to deselect it.

You add items to a list by calling the `add()` method and identifying each item as a string:

```
list.add("John Galt");
list.add("Dagney Taggart");
list.add("Hank Rearden");
list.add("Francisco d'Anconia");
list.add("Midas Mulligan");
```

When a List Isn't a List

As of Java 2, the `List` graphical user interface class in the Java AWT isn't the only thing in the Java API named `List`. There is also a `List` interface in the `java.util` package that defines a data structure for organizing objects into an ordered list. The `java.awt` `List` class and the `java.util` `List` interface perform very different functions, so it's unlikely that you'll mistake one for the other in the context of a Java program. However, I wanted to let you know about them both to help avoid any future confusion.

The `add()` method results in items being added to the end of the list. You can also insert an item at a specific location in the list by using the `add()` method and providing the integer index as the second parameter. The `getItemCount()` method returns the number of items in a list. To determine which item is currently selected, you call the `getSelectedItem()` method, like this:

```
String selItem = list.getSelectedItem();
```

If the list is a multiple selection list, you can determine which items are selected using the `getSelectedItems()` method, like this:

```
String[] selItems = list.getSelectedItems();
```

This method returns an array of strings, which makes sense because a multiple selection list is designed to support the selection of multiple items at once. You can select items by calling the `select()` method and providing the integer index of the item, like this:

```
choice.select(0);
```

This code selects the first item in the list. If you want to clear out a list so that you can refill it, you can remove all of the items by calling the `removeAll()` method. This is also a `remove()` method that enables you to remove individual items.

Adding a list to an applet simply involves creating a `List` object and adding it to the applet, like this:

```
add(list);
```

Text Fields and Text Areas

The last user interface components you need to learn about are text fields and text areas. Both of these components are used as a means of enabling the user to input text. Let's first take a look at text fields because they are a little simpler than text areas. Text fields present a text entry field that enables the user to enter a single line of text. The following figure shows what a text field component looks like.

A text field component.

You can create an empty `TextField` object by using its default constructor, like this:

```
TextField text = new TextField();
```

If you want to provide default text in the text field, then you can use a different constructor that accepts a string as its only parameter:

```
TextField text = new TextField("Your Name Here");
```

By default, the size of a text field is determined by the applet's layout manager. However, you can set a specific size for a text field by using a different constructor. The following code shows how to create a text field that is 20 characters wide:

```
TextField text = new TextField(20);
```

You can also set a text field width and provide a default string by using yet another constructor, like this:

```
TextField text = new TextField(20, "Your Name");
```

To get or set the text in a text field, you can use the `getText()` and `setText()` methods. There is also another neat feature of text fields that enables you to hide the characters that are being entered. This is useful if you are using a text field to enable someone to enter a password. By calling the `setEchoChar()` method, you can make it so that the text entered appears as asterisks (*), for example, when typed. Following is an example of how this is accomplished:

```
text.setEchoChar('*');
```

Like all of the other components you've seen, adding a text field to an applet involves creating the `TextField` object and then adding it to the applet, like this:

```
add(TextField);
```

Although text fields are very useful for enabling users to enter single lines of text, there are times when you'd like to provide the user with a means of entering multiple lines of text. This is where text areas come in handy. For example, a chat applet might use a text area to provide a user interface for entering chat messages. The following figure shows what a text area component looks like.

A text area component.

You can create an empty `TextArea` object by using its default constructor, like this:

```
TextArea text = new TextArea();
```

If you want to provide default text in the text area, then you can use a different constructor that accepts a string as its only parameter:

```
TextArea text = new TextArea("Enter your message here.");
```

Similar to text fields, the default behavior for text areas is for their size to be determined by an applet's layout manager. It is often useful to provide a specific size for a text area. You do this by providing the number of rows and columns for the text area to a different `TextArea` constructor, like this:

```
TextArea text = new TextArea(10, 40);
```

This code creates a text area with 10 rows and 40 columns. You can also use a similar constructor to provide default text along with the number of rows and columns:

```
TextArea text = new TextArea("Enter your message here.", 10, 40);
```

Measuring Text Areas

The number of rows and columns in a text area determines the number of characters that can be displayed in the text area. More specifically, the number of rows equals the number of lines of text that can be displayed, and the number of columns equals the number of characters that can be displayed on each line. So, the text area in the previous example that had 10 rows and 40 columns could display 10 lines of text with 40 characters on each line.

Similar to text fields, you can get or set the text in a text area using the getText() and setText() methods. Also similar to text fields, you add a text area to an applet by creating the TextArea object and then adding it to the applet, like this:

```
add(TextArea);
```

Understanding Panels

Now that you have an idea of the basic types of user interface components supported by Java, let's take a closer look at how they fit together within an applet. When describing the components throughout the chapter thus far, I've talked about adding components to an applet's window. What I didn't talk about is how an applet window enables you to add components to it. The Applet class derives from the Panel class, which is a container class used to manage user interface components.

One interesting way to think of a panel is as a refrigerator door. Sound crazy? Well read on! Just like the magnets you stick to a refrigerator door, components are similarly added to panels. Refrigerator magnets aren't capable of doing much without a metallic surface on which to stick. The same is true of Java components; they aren't of much use without a panel to hold them. So, when you add a component to an applet window you are really adding them to a panel. Why is this important? Because panels determine the layout of components.

A panel always has a layout manager associated with it that determines how components are arranged. You can create panels within panels to facilitate a more elaborate organization of components. Admittedly, the concepts of layout managers and panels are a little abstract, so you really need to see them in action to understand how they work. The next section addresses this by examining layout managers.

Taking Advantage of Layouts

You just learned that layout managers are used to physically arrange the user interface components that are contained within a panel. Layout managers serve an important role in designing the user interface for an applet because they greatly simplify the organization of user interfaces. The basic layout managers supported by Java follow:

➤ Flow

➤ Grid

➤ Border

➤ Card

➤ Grid Bag

The next few sections explore these layout managers. A little later in the chapter you put one of them to use in a user interface for an investment calculator applet.

Flow Layouts

The FlowLayout class supports the simplest of layout managers. In a flow layout, components are arranged from left to right in rows as they are added to a panel. When a component doesn't fit along the right side of a panel, it is wrapped around and appears on the next row. You can arrange the rows in a flow layout to be aligned left, right, or centered.

Relative Positioning

The primary reason Java relies on panels and layout managers to position user interface components is because it doesn't directly support absolute positioning. Did you happen to notice in the earlier discussion of components that none of them allow you to specify an absolute x and y position? In Java, components are positioned relative to each other and are rarely given absolute positions within a panel.

The primary reason for Java's avoidance of absolute positioning is because it is more predictable to automatically position components using a layout manager. This alleviates the problems associated with trying to support absolute positioning on different computing platforms, because the display characteristics of different platforms can vary widely.

To set the layout of an applet to a flow layout, you call the setLayout() method, like this:

```
setLayout(new FlowLayout());
```

Although this code works perfectly well, it isn't necessary because the flow layout manager is the default layout manager for all panels. In other words, if you don't specify a layout manager for an applet, it will automatically use the flow layout manager. Following is an example of an applet's init() method that arranges a few buttons using a flow layout:

```
public void init() {
  setLayout(new FlowLayout());
  add(new Button("green"));
  add(new Button("eggs"));
  add(new Button("and"));
  add(new Button("ham"));
}
```

The following figure shows the results of this example code.

Some buttons arranged using a flow layout manager.

Grid Layouts

The GridLayout class supports a layout manager that arranges components in a grid of rows and columns. Similar to the flow layout manager, components are arranged from left to right in a grid layout, but they conform to the fixed cell arrangement of the grid. This means that components in a grid layout are always lined up according to the arrangement of the cells in the grid. Similar to setting the flow layout manager, you set an applet to a grid layout by calling the setLayout() method, like this:

```
setLayout(new GridLayout(2, 2));
```

The GridLayout constructor takes two parameters, which are the number of rows and columns in the grid. So, in this case the grid layout forms a 2×2 grid. Following is an example of an applet's init() method that arranges some buttons using a grid layout:

```
public void init() {
  setLayout(new GridLayout(2, 2));
  add(new Button("green"));
  add(new Button("eggs"));
  add(new Button("and"));
  add(new Button("ham"));
}
```

The following figure shows the results of this example code.

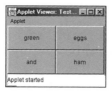

Some buttons arranged using a grid layout manager.

Border Layouts

The Border class supports a layout manager that is totally different from the layout managers you've seen so far. The border layout manager arranges components in the geographic directions north, south, east, and west, along with another component in the center. You set an applet to a border layout by calling the setLayout() method, like this:

```
setLayout(new BorderLayout());
```

You specify the direction location of a component when you add it to a panel. For example, to place a component in the north position of a border layout, you call a different version of the add() method and pass the string "North" as the first parameter, like this:

```
add("North", new Button("Look up here."));
```

Following is an example of an applet's init() method that arranges some buttons using a border layout:

```
public void init() {
  setLayout(new BorderLayout());
  add("North", new Button("green"));
  add("West", new Button("eggs"));
  add("South", new Button("and"));
  add("East", new Button("ham"));
  add("Center", new Button("sam I am"));
}
```

Notice that the last button in the example uses the string "Center" to specify that the button is to be positioned in the center position of the border layout. The following figure shows the results of this example code.

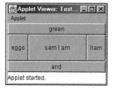

Some buttons arranged using a border layout manager.

189

Card Layouts

The CardLayout class is used to arrange multiple panels so that they act much like a stack of cards. If you've ever seen a tabbed dialog box in an application, then you're familiar with how this works. Basically a group of panels is added to a card layout, but only one at a time is visible. You can maneuver through the cards as if you're viewing a slideshow. Each panel card can use its own layout manager to arrange the components it contains.

Because card layouts are more complicated to use than the flow, grid, and border layouts, I won't go into any more detail. You might want to look into them after you've gained some experience with building user interfaces and working with the other layout managers.

Grid Bag Layouts

The GridBagLayout class provides the most powerful means of laying out components in an applet, but not without a price. Grid bag layouts take a significant amount of effort to put together, so I don't want to jump into how they work and overburden you with complex example code. I do want you to understand the general idea behind grid bag layouts, however, just in case you should need them somewhere down the road.

A grid bag layout is similar to a grid layout, except that you have a lot more control over the size and position of the cells in the grid bag layout than you do in a grid layout. For example, in a grid bag layout you can specify that some cells span multiple columns. You can also control the arrangement of components within specific cells in the grid.

Applet: InvestmentCalc

Your head is no doubt spinning from all the AWT components I've thrown at you in this chapter thus far. The good news is that all AWT components are used in much the same way. I thought it might be a good idea to work through an example applet to help put AWT components into perspective. Unlike most of the applets you've developed throughout the book to this point, This example applet has a user interface that requires components. I thought an investment calculator applet might be a good idea.

The investment calculator applet calculates the return on an investment based on a periodic investment over a period of time. You can alter the investment amount, investment frequency, investment return, and duration of investment. The following shows the investment calculator applet busy at work making money.

As you can see in the figure, the InvestmentCalc applet makes use of a variety of different AWT components to present its user interface. More specifically, it uses label components for identifying the different parts of the user interface. The applet also uses text fields and choice menus to enable the user to enter the different investment parameters. Finally, a button component is used to calculate the total investment. The total investment itself is displayed using a label component.

Following is the source code for the InvestmentCalc applet:

Finding the InvestmentCalc Applet Example on the Web

To find the InvestmentCalc applet example source code on the Web, enter the address `http://www.mcp.com/info` in the location box of your Web browser. Click the link called **Downloadable Code, Examples, and Info for book "Companion Sites."** In the space provided under the Book Information section, enter **0-7897-1804-9**, which is the 10-digit ISBN for this book. Click the **Search** button.

```java
import java.applet.*;
import java.awt.*;
import java.awt.event.*;

public class InvestmentCalc extends
➥Applet implements ActionListener {
  TextField amountField, returnField,
  ➥durationField;
  Choice    amountPeriod,
  ➥durationPeriod;
  Button    calcButton;
  Label     totalInvestment;

  public void init() {
    // Create the user interface
    setLayout(new GridLayout(4, 4));
    add(new Label("Invest $", Label.CENTER));
    amountField = new TextField("100");
    add(amountField);
    add(new Label("Per", Label.CENTER));
    amountPeriod = new Choice();
```

```
        amountPeriod.add("Month");
        amountPeriod.add("Year");
        add(amountPeriod);

        add(new Label("At An", Label.CENTER));
        returnField = new TextField("8");
        add(returnField);
        add(new Label("% Return", Label.CENTER));
        add(new Label());

        add(new Label("For", Label.CENTER));
        durationField = new TextField("12");
        add(durationField);
        durationPeriod = new Choice();
        durationPeriod.add("Months");
        durationPeriod.add("Years");
        add(durationPeriod);
        add(new Label());

        add(new Label("Yields", Label.CENTER));
        totalInvestment = new Label();
        add(totalInvestment);
        add(new Label());
        calcButton = new Button("Calculate");
        add(calcButton);

        amountField.requestFocus();

        // Register the button event handler
        calcButton.addActionListener(this);
    }

    public void actionPerformed(ActionEvent evt) {
        Button source = (Button)evt.getSource();
        if (source.getLabel().equals("Calculate")) {
            // Calculate the total investment
            totalInvestment.setText("$" + String.valueOf(calcInvestment()));
        }
    }

    private int calcInvestment() {
        float amount, invReturn, total = 0.0f;
        int   duration;

        // Get the values required for the calculation
        amount = (Float.valueOf(amountField.getText())).floatValue();
```

```
invReturn = (Float.valueOf(returnField.getText())).floatValue()
➥/ 100;
duration = (Integer.valueOf(durationField.getText())).intValue();

// Prepare to perform the calculation in terms of months
if (durationPeriod.getSelectedItem().equals("Years"))
  duration *= 12;
invReturn /= 12;

// Calculate the total investment
for (int i = 0; i < duration; i++) {
  if (amountPeriod.getSelectedItem().equals("Year")) {
    // Amount is invested yearly
    if (i % 12 == 0)
      total += (total * invReturn) + amount;
    else
      total += total * invReturn;
  }
  else
    // Amount is invested monthly
    total += (total * invReturn) + amount;
}

// Return the result as an integer
return (int)Math.rint(total);
  }
}
```

The bulk of the user interface code in the InvestmentCalc applet takes place in the init() method, which is responsible for setting up the user interface. The applet uses a grid layout manager to arrange the components in a 4×4 grid. The different components are then added to the grid in order from left to right. You might notice that there are a few empty label components thrown in to correctly space the different parts of the user interface.

The actionPerformed() method is an event handler method that responds to the **Calculate** button being pressed. It calls the calcInvestment() method and displays the result using the totalInvestment label component.

The calcInvestment() method is where the actual investment calculation is performed. Because text fields are used to store text, not numbers, it is necessary to perform a few conversions to extract numeric values out of the text fields. After that is accomplished, the calcInvestment() method goes about calculating the total investment with a for loop that iterates through the total number of investment months. The end result is rounded off to an integer and returned from the method.

Swing and the AWT

As of Java 2, Java's support for graphical user interfaces has undergone a major enhancement. An entirely new suite of graphical user interface components has been added to Java as part of the Swing library. Swing consists of a new set of components that can take on the look and feel of the native platform on which it is running. For example, a Java applet running on a Macintosh will look noticeably different than the same applet running on a Windows PC. This is because each platform has different ways of presenting elements of its graphical user interfaces.

Swing also dramatically increases the choices you have in terms of components. Swing includes new versions of the standard AWT components you learned about in this chapter, along with brand new components such as borders, icons, progress bars, tables, trees, and HTML viewers. Swing is a little beyond the scope of this book, but I wanted to mention it so that you would know what it was. Fortunately, when the time comes for you to explore Swing, you'll have the basic AWT skills required to understand how to use its components.

The Least You Need to Know

Graphical user interfaces are the heart and soul of modern software applications. Because Java is a modern programming language, it only makes sense that it would have a rich suite of components for building applets with advanced graphical user interfaces. You learned in this chapter about some of the more basic components provided with the standard Java AWT. With this knowledge you should be ready to build some pretty nifty user interfaces of your own, as well as explore more advanced GUI programming areas such as Swing. Let's recap what you learned in this chapter:

➤ AWT components are structured in a nested hierarchy that begins with the Component class.

➤ The add() method, which is defined in the Container class, is used to add components to a container such as an applet.

➤ The Applet class derives from the Panel class, which is a container class used to manage user interface components.

➤ A panel always has a layout manager associated with it that determines how components are arranged.

➤ The flow layout manager is the default layout manager for all panels.

➤ Swing consists of a new set of components that can take on the look and feel of the native platform on which it is running.

Part 4

Is Java More than a Pretty Face?

Although Java certainly has a penchant for pretty graphics, that's not all it has to offer. Java's communication facilities are quite impressive, including built-in support for networking. Other features—such as streams and threads—add to Java's utility arsenal and offer opportunities for building interesting applets.

Speaking of interesting, how much fun would Java be without multimedia? Although Java is in the midst of getting a multimedia overhaul, you can do lots of cool things with it right now, including animation and digitizing files. Brace yourself, because you're about to learn how to really have fun with Java!

Reading, Writing, and Java?

I/O Basics

As you learned in Chapter 13, "Interacting with the User," input and output (I/O) are significant concerns for just about all Java programs. However, I/O isn't confined to user input devices such as the keyboard and mouse. Every hardware device connected to your computer can be considered an I/O device of some sort. Following is a list of devices, along with an indication of whether they are used for input, output, or both:

➤ Monitor—output

➤ Printer—output

➤ Scanner—input

➤ Speakers—output

➤ Hard disk—input/output

➤ Floppy disk—input/output

➤ CD-ROM—input

➤ Joystick—input

In addition to these tangible devices, there are also other logical devices with which you can interact from a Java program. For example, it is possible to treat memory as an I/O device, or a specific string in memory. The concept of logical devices might sound confusing right now, but it will make sense later in the chapter. For now, let's move on to the key issue at the heart of Java I/O: streams.

Jumping into Streams Without Getting Wet

Although devices play an important role in I/O, they don't directly come into play at the programming level. How could this be? Well, the same way you don't deal directly with the monitor to draw graphics in Java, you also don't deal directly with I/O devices to input or output data. Java provides an intermediary that insulates you from dealing directly with I/O hardware. The reason for this is because it alleviates the hassles of having to factor in the nuances of different types of hardware devices.

The intermediary to which I'm referring is the stream, which is an abstraction of a medium through which data is transferred. I know that's a high brow explanation, so let's consider an analogy to simplify the function of streams. Pretend that you're living in the lost city of Atlantis, which just so happens to be located on the bottom of the ocean. Ignoring the challenges of learning how to breathe underwater, let's focus on using a computer designed for underwater use. More specifically, imagine a computer that uses water instead of electricity to transfer information.

Water Isn't Just for Drinking

If the aquatic computer analogy has gotten you excited about interesting uses of water, you might want to watch the movie *The Abyss*. In the movie an underwater alien life form is able to control water and make it do all kinds of neat things. The movie was written and directed by James Cameron, of *Titanic* fame.

Instead of wires, your aquatic computer would consist of an intricate set of pipes connecting devices to each other. To transfer information to or from a device, data would be pumped through a pipe and flow to or from the device. And what flows through the pipe to carry the data? Of course, a stream of water. Aha, the analogy is starting to make sense! The stream of water that shuttles data around in your hypothetical aquatic computer acts very much like the software streams used to move data around in a Java program.

Continuing with the stream analogy, data moving through a Java stream can be directed in many different ways. Also, data in a Java stream is transferred one byte (8 bits) at a time, which is like the drops of water moving through a pipe containing water. Okay, I think I've sufficiently worn out the water/stream analogy, so let's move on to the specific types of streams used in Java.

Not surprisingly, Java streams are divided into input streams and output streams. There is a variety of different types of streams, but it isn't imperative that you understand them all at this point. In fact, most Java streams are derived from two fundamental stream classes, InputStream and OutputStream. These two classes, along with all of Java's I/O support classes, are located in the java.io package. Java also supports two other I/O classes, Reader and Writer, that perform a function very similar to InputStream and OutputStream.

Input Streams and Readers

The InputStream class is an abstract class that defines the basic functionality of an input stream. Because the InputStream is abstract, you can't actually create instances (objects) of it. Even so, the InputStream class is extremely important because it defines the general interface used to input data from all of Java's input streams. Following are some of the more important methods defined in the InputStream class:

➤ **read()** This method reads a byte or series of bytes of data from an input stream.

➤ **skip()** This method skips over bytes of data in an input stream.

➤ **mark()** This method marks the current point in the input stream and is sort of like placing a bookmark in the stream.

➤ **reset()** This method resets the stream to the "bookmark" point previously set by a call to mark().

Although input streams are very useful in retrieving data from a device, they are sometimes limiting in that they deal solely in bytes of data. It is often more useful to input data in a given data format, such as an integer or a string. Fortunately, Java provides an interface to make just this sort of thing possible. This interface is called DataInput and is useful for reading data from an input stream into a specific data type. Because DataInput is an interface, you can't actually create instances of it. However, there are other standard classes that implement DataInput.

The importance of the DataInput interface is that it defines the manner in which data is retrieved from an input stream into a standard

Abstract Classes

An abstract class is a class that contains unimplemented methods, which means you must derive from the class and implement the methods in order to create an instance of the class. Abstract classes are similar to interfaces, but they can contain member variables and implemented methods in addition to the unimplemented methods. Interfaces consist solely of unimplemented methods.

199

Java data format. Following are some of the more important methods defined in the `DataInput` interface:

➤ `readBoolean()`

➤ `readShort()`

➤ `readByte()`

➤ `readInt()`

➤ `readLong()`

➤ `readFloat()`

➤ `readDouble()`

➤ `readChar()`

These methods are pretty self explanatory; they each read data from an input stream into a standard Java data format.

In addition to the input classes that are based on `InputStream`, Java also provides a suite of reader classes that are based on the `Reader` class. The `Reader` class was added in Java 1.1 as an alternative to using input streams. Technically speaking, the `Reader` class functions very much like an input stream, but it doesn't derive from `InputStream`. The `Reader` class was added to Java primarily to help support internationalization, which involves developing programs that can have different character sets based on different languages. For the most part, the methods in the `Reader` and `InputStream` classes function in the same manner.

Output Streams and Writers

Output streams are the logical counterpart to input streams. Consequently, the Java classes and interfaces used to support output streams mirror those used for inputting data from streams. The `OutputStream` class forms the basis for outputting data to Java streams. Like its counterpart, the `InputStream` class, the `OutputStream` class is abstract. Following are some of the more important methods defined in the `OutputStream` class:

➤ **write()** This method writes a byte or series of bytes of data to an output stream.

➤ **flush()** This method forces data to be written to an output stream if it hasn't been already.

The purpose of the `flush()` method might not be clear to you because the `write()` method is supposed to have already written data to an output stream. The `flush()` method is necessary because it is possible for data to be buffered, which means that it isn't actually written to an output stream immediately after you call the `write()` method. Instead, buffered data is first output to a memory buffer where it accumulates until the buffer fills up, the output stream is closed, or you call the `flush()` method.

The `OutputStream` class suffers from the same limitation as the `InputStream` class in that it only deals with data in byte form. I mentioned earlier in the chapter that it is often more useful to input data in a given data format, such as an integer or a string. The `DataOutput` interface makes this possible by performing the output equivalent of the `DataInput` interface you learned about a little earlier.

The `DataOutput` interface defines the manner in which data is written to an output stream from a standard Java data format. Following are some of the more important methods defined in the `DataOutput` interface:

➤ `writeBoolean()`

➤ `writeShort()`

➤ `writeByte()`

➤ `writeInt()`

➤ `writeLong()`

➤ `writeFloat()`

➤ `writeDouble()`

➤ `writeChar()`

➤ `writeChars()`

The Reason for Buffered I/O

Buffered I/O involves the use of a memory buffer to serve as a middleman for data that is being input or output. The primary reason for using buffered I/O is performance.

Allow me to explain by using buffered output as an example. Let's pretend you have a Java application that for some reason needs to write out a bunch of data to a hard disk in single bytes. If the application is writing tons of data, it puts a big strain on the hard disk because the drive has to perform thousands of individual write operations. A much more efficient approach is to collect the data in a memory buffer and then write out larger chunks to the hard disk, resulting in fewer overall write operations. That's where buffered output comes into play!

Like their `DataInput` counterparts, these methods are fairly self explanatory; they each write data to an output stream from a standard Java data format. The last method, `readChars()`, is a little different in that it writes a string of text from a `String` object to the output stream.

Like the `Reader` class that provides an alternative to `InputStream`, Java also provides a `Writer` class. The `Writer` class was added in Java 1.1 as an alternative to using output streams that supports internationalization. The `Writer` class functions very much like an output stream, but it doesn't derive from `OutputStream`. You can use most of the methods in the `Writer` and `OutputStream` classes in the same manner.

Reading and Writing Files

Okay, I've given you the goods on input and output streams, along with the Java classes that make them tick. But I still haven't shown you how to do anything practical with streams. Not wanting to run the risk of you thinking I'm an impractical guy, please allow me to shift the discussion toward a common usage of streams.

Not surprisingly, one of the most common uses of streams is reading and writing files. Although there are security issues associated with applets reading and writing files, file I/O is nevertheless something you are likely to need at some point in your Java endeavors. So, I want to give you the ground rules necessary to perform basic I/O with files.

The first two classes associated with file I/O are `FileInputStream` and `FileOutputStream`, which are streams that use files as the basis for reading and writing data. These classes derive from `InputStream` and `OutputStream`, respectively, and therefore support the same functions defined in each. The reader equivalents of `FileInputStream` and `FileOutputStream` are `FileReader` and `FileWriter`, which are based on the `InputStreamReader` and `OutputStreamWriter` classes. The `FileReader` and `FileWriter` classes support similar methods as the `FileInputStream` and `FileOutputStream` classes.

While we're on the subject of files, it's worth pointing out that Java applets are subjected to very stringent security limitations that don't allow them to write to files under normal circumstances. For example, if you try to create a `FileWriter` object in an applet, you are likely to trigger an exception. Your options are to either forget about writing to files or digitally sign the applet so that it can legally pass through Java security.

Getting Down to Business with Files

A little later in the chapter you create an applet that reads lines of text from a file. The applet relies on the `FileReader` class to pull this off. Let's take a look at how a `FileReader` object is created. There are two main constructors used to create `FileReader` objects:

```
public FileReader(File file)
```

and

```
public FileReader(String name)
```

The second version is a little easier to use, so I'll focus on it. The `name` parameter to the constructor is simply the name of the file from which you want to read or to which you want to write.

Following is an example of creating a `FileReader` object that can be used to read from the file named `People.txt`:

```
FileReader file = new FileReader("People.txt");
```

Let's pretend the file `People.txt` contains a list of names of people with each name on a single line by itself. Any guess as to how you might read the names from the list? Well, the `FileReader` class doesn't provide a really clean way of making this happen because it requires you to read a file one character at a time. However, Java provides a class named `BufferedReader` that supports reading lines of text from a file. You create a `BufferedReader` object by passing in a `Reader` object such as a file reader, like this:

```
BufferedReader in = new BufferedReader(new FileReader("People.txt"));
```

Now that you have your hands on a buffered reader, you can simply call the `readLine()` method to read lines of text. Following is some code that reads each name from the `People.txt` file and prints them to standard output:

```
String s;
while ((s = in.readLine()) != null)
  System.out.println(s);
```

Are you surprised by the simplicity of this code? To be honest, I am too. Allow me to explain just in case the simplicity of the code is creating a mental stumbling block. The `while` loop conditional checks to see if the end of the file has been reached, as indicated by the `readLine()` method returning `null`. This results in the loop not bailing out until the end of the file has been reached. The `readLine()` method returns each line of text as a `String` object, which is perfect for outputting via `println()`. There's nothing to this file stuff!

Applet: Fortune

Now that you have some understanding of how files are manipulated, let's take a look at a practical example. One of the first programs I ever wrote was a Fortune program, which displays a random quote, or fortune. The name of the program originally comes from Chinese fortune cookies because they often contain insightful quotes. Besides, "Fortune" sounds a lot more exciting than "Quote." Anyway, the following figure shows the contemporary version of my Fortune program, which now appears as a Java applet.

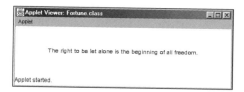

The Fortune applet.

Finding the Fortune Applet Example on the Web

To find the Fortune applet example source code on the Web, enter the address **http://www.mcp.com/info** in the location box of your Web browser. Click the link called **Downloadable Code, Examples, and Info for book "Companion Sites."** In the space provided under the Book Information section, enter **0-7897-1804-9**, which is the 10-digit ISBN for this book. Click the **Search** button.

The Fortune applet displays a random fortune each time you run it. You can view a new fortune by clicking the mouse button on the applet. I know, the Fortune applet isn't all that flashy, but it's a great way to champion your political views by passing them off as fortunes. Seriously, the importance of the Fortune applet is that it reads the fortunes from a text file named Fortunes.txt. This is far better than hard-coding the fortunes into the program because you can add, remove, or modify the fortunes simply by editing the Fortunes.txt file. Incidentally, the Fortunes.txt file should be placed in the same directory on a Web server as the Fortune applet class file.

The fortunes are listed in the Fortunes.txt text file as individual lines of text. Following are the contents of the Fortune.txt file:

```
We learn from history that we do not learn
from history.
Few men have virtue to withstand the highest
bidder.
Petty laws breed great crimes.
The right to be let alone is the beginning of all freedom.
America's one of the finest countries anyone ever stole.
What's the Constitution between friends?
The highest result of education is tolerance.
Tyranny is always better organized than freedom.
```

Notice that there is nothing special about the formatting of the fortunes except that they appear on separate lines. The Fortune applet is smart enough to count how many fortunes there are and then retrieve them appropriately. Speaking of how smart the applet is, let's go ahead and dig into the code that makes it tick:

```java
import java.applet.*;
import java.util.*;
import java.awt.*;
import java.awt.event.*;
import java.io.*;

public class Fortune extends Applet {
    int     curFortune = 0;
    Vector fortunes = new Vector();
    Random rand = new Random(System.currentTimeMillis());

    public void init() {
```

```
        // Register the mouse event handler
        addMouseListener(new MouseHandler());

        // Initialize the fortunes
        try {
          // Determine the number of fortunes
          BufferedReader in = new BufferedReader(new
          ➡FileReader("Fortunes.txt"));
          String        s;
          while ((s = in.readLine()) != null)
            fortunes.add(s);

          // Pick the first fortune
          curFortune = Math.abs(rand.nextInt() % fortunes.size());
        }
        catch (IOException e) {
          fortunes.clear();
          fortunes.add("Error loading fortunes.");
        }
      }

      public void paint(Graphics g) {
        // Draw the current fortune
        if (fortunes.size() > 0) {
          FontMetrics fm = g.getFontMetrics();
          g.drawString((String)fortunes.get(curFortune),
          ➡(getSize().width -
            fm.stringWidth((String)fortunes.get(curFortune))) / 2,
            ➡((getSize().height -
            fm.getHeight()) / 2) + fm.getAscent());
        }
      }

      class MouseHandler extends MouseAdapter {
        public void mouseClicked(MouseEvent e) {
          // Pick another fortune
          curFortune = Math.abs(rand.nextInt() % fortunes.size());
          repaint();
        }
      }
    }
```

The first thing to notice about the code is the fortunes member variable, which is a
Vector object used to contain strings. This member variable is used to store the fortunes as a list of strings. The curFortune member keeps track of the fortune currently
being displayed and is really just an index into the fortunes array. Finally, the rand
member you are already familiar with from earlier examples in the book is used to
generate random numbers.

205

As in all applets, everything begins with the init() method. The init() method first registers the mouse event handler so that the applet can respond to mouse clicks. Then comes the important part, reading the fortunes from the Fortunes.txt file. You might notice that the fortunes aren't stored in an array. Because it is difficult to determine how many fortunes there are before you've finished reading them, it is much simpler to use a data structure that can grow in size. I chose the Vector class to hold the fortunes because it is basically an array that can grow in size. You were introduced to the Vector class while building the Scribbler applet in Chapter 13.

Not surprisingly, a BufferedReader object is used to read from the file. A while loop moves through the file a line at a time, adding each line of text to the fortunes vector. The resulting size of the fortunes vector indicates the number of fortunes. After the fortunes are read into the fortunes vector, the current fortune is randomly selected using the rand member variable.

One thing worth pointing out about the code that reads in the fortunes is that it is capable of throwing exceptions if the Fortunes.txt file doesn't exist or if there is some other problem reading from the file. So, it is necessary to place the code within a try clause and also to provide a catch clause to handle any exceptions. If there is a problem reading the fortunes, the catch clause sets an error message as the only fortune so that the applet plainly displays the problem.

The only other methods in the Fortune applet are paint() and mouseClicked(), which are very similar to versions you've seen in other applets, so I won't spend any time boring you with explanations of these.

The Least You Need to Know

Although user interaction via the keyboard and mouse is probably the most obvious form of input you associate with Java programs, they only scratch the surface in terms of what you can do with input and output in Java. As you learned in this chapter, Java provides a rich set of classes and interfaces in the java.io package that enables you to perform I/O in a variety of different ways. Let's go over the main points of what you learned:

➤ A stream is an abstraction of a medium through which data is transferred; more simply put, data flows through a Java stream much like water flows through a stream in nature.

➤ Java streams are divided into input streams and output streams.

➤ The InputStream and OutputStream classes define the basic functionality of input and output streams.

➤ Readers and writers function much like input and output streams, but they also support internationalization.

➤ Java applets are subjected to very stringent security limitations that don't allow them to write to files under normal circumstances.

Java and the Global Village

The World at Your Fingertips

Believe it or not, there was a time when the vast majority of computers operated in complete isolation, unaware of the existence of other computers. Because computers aren't exactly the most social of animals, they never really knew what they were missing. People, on the other hand, started realizing that an interconnected world of computers had a lot to offer. Now that we've had some time to absorb the full impact of global computing (thanks to the Internet), it's hard to imagine why anyone would ever want to use a computer in isolation.

Few people can resist the allure of the Internet after they've had a taste; the sheer quantity and variety of information is just too compelling. Add to that the ability to interact with other people and share information, and there is just no arguing the importance of networking to the present and future of computing. This chapter explores the role of networking in Java and includes examples of some things you can do in Java to manipulate Web sites.

Before we get into Java networking, however, let's take a moment to get up to speed on networking in general. More specifically, let's analyze the mother of all networks, the Internet. As you are no doubt already aware, the Internet is a global network of many different types of computers connected in various ways. Because it is no trivial task to get a bunch of different computers to communicate with each other, the pioneers of the Internet decided to establish some ground rules, called standards.

Addressing the Internet

Because every computer on the Internet must be uniquely distinguishable, one of the first areas of standardization involved IP addresses. IP addresses are numbers used to uniquely identify computers connected to the Internet. The easiest way to understand IP addresses is to compare them to the physical mailing address of your house or apartment. If you think about it, physical mailing addresses work in very much the same way as IP addresses—they uniquely identify the place where you live. A mailing address is guaranteed to only identify one physical location. Likewise, an IP address uniquely identifies one computer on the Internet. By the way, the "IP" in IP address stands for Internet Protocol.

IP addresses are actually 32-bit numbers that look like this: 243.37.126.82. You're probably more familiar with the symbolic form of IP addresses, which looks like this: sincity.com. Keep in mind that without IP addresses there would be no way to distinguish between different computers on the Internet.

Locating Resources with URLs

If IP addresses uniquely identify computers on the Internet, then URLs identify resources on those computers. More specifically, URLs (uniform resource locators) serve as pointers to Web pages, binary files, and other information objects on the Web. When you manually enter the name of a Web site such as http://www.mind-spring.com/index.html, you are really just providing the URL for the site's home page.

In case you didn't notice, IP addresses play an important role in URLs. Because a Web page ultimately resides on a computer connected to the Internet, it is necessary to identify the computer when referencing the page. Therefore, a URL inherently includes the IP address of the computer containing a given resource. Incidentally, the computer that contains a resource is known as the resource's host. Let's analyze the earlier URL, http://www.mindspring.com/index.html, to see exactly what information it contains:

➤ **http** the protocol used by the resource (HTTP).

➤ **mindspring.com** the IP address of the computer on which the resource is stored.

➤ **index.html** the resource, in this case a Web page.

Rules to Surf By

The concept of communicating among different computers on the Internet might not sound like such a big deal now that you understand how IP addresses work. However, computers can communicate with each other in a variety of different ways. Each type of communication between computers on the Internet requires a network protocol, which is a set of rules and standards that governs how the communication works. For example, a protocol specifies the format of data sent over the Internet, along with how and when the data is sent. On the other end of the communication, the protocol also defines how the data is received and interpreted.

You might have heard that the Internet is really just a bunch of bits flying back and forth through cyberspace. That's a very realistic statement; and without protocols, those bits wouldn't mean a thing.

For the record, protocols aren't groundbreaking or even new to computers. We use protocols all the time in everyday situations; we just don't call them protocols. Consider the following dialogue:

"Hi, may I take your order?"

"Yes, I'd like the poached ostrich and a soda."

"Thank you, I'll put your order in and bring you your drink."

"Thanks, I can't wait to taste that ostrich!"

Although this conversation might not look like anything special (other than the poached ostrich!), it follows a very definite social protocol used to place orders for food at a restaurant. Social protocols are important because they give us familiarity and confidence in knowing what to do in certain situations. Have you ever been nervous when entering a new social situation where you didn't quite know how to act? A lack of familiarity with the proper protocol is typically the source of the anxiety in situations like that. For networked computers, "protocol anxiety" reveals itself in the form of errors and data transfer failures.

Of all the protocols in use on the Internet, the one getting the most attention these days is HTTP, which stands for Hypertext Transfer Protocol. HTTP is the protocol used to transfer HTML documents across the Web. Another important protocol is FTP, which stands for File Transfer Protocol. FTP is used to transfer binary files over the Internet. These two protocols have their own unique sets of rules and standards defining how information is transferred.

Of Clients and Servers

There is one more important networking topic to cover before you learn how Java fits into everything. I'm referring to the client/server architecture that lies at the very heart of the Web. You've no doubt heard of clients and servers before, but you might not fully understand their importance in regard to the Web. The client/server architecture of the Web involves thinking of computing in terms of a client, who is essentially in need of some type of information, and a server that has information to offer the client. A client typically connects to a server and asks for a certain piece of information. The server sends the information to the client and everyone lives happily ever after.

I know you're probably thinking that I'm oversimplifying things here, but I'm really not; client/server computing is as simple as a client asking for information and a server returning it. In the context of the Web, client computers use Web browsers to get information from servers, which are usually large computers with lots of disk space on which Web sites are stored. The following figure graphically shows the relationship between Web clients and servers.

A Web server connected to multiple clients.

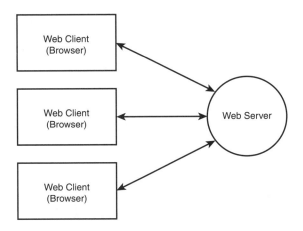

Client/Server Everywhere

Although I've described clients and servers in the context of the Web, they are actually used heavily in all kinds of software systems. The majority of database applications developed these days are entirely client/server. Additionally, Internet services such as FTP are based on a client/server architecture.

You might wonder why I've bothered explaining the Web's client/server architecture, because you aren't planning to develop your own Web browser. Although you might not directly need to rely on your newfound client/server knowledge at this very moment, it subtly plays into Java network programming at almost every level. Don't forget that a Java applet is technically a part of a Web page that was transferred from a Web server to a client Web browser. This fact affects the manner in which you perform network operations from within a Java applet.

Java Networking Basics

Now that you've made it through all the conceptual network stuff, you're probably itching to find out about networking and Java. As always, I'm eager to oblige! You'll be pleased to know that Java's support for networking follows very closely with the concepts you just learned. Following are some of the basic network classes provided by the Java network API, which is contained in the `java.net` package:

➤ **InetAddress** represents an IP address and contains methods for viewing either the numeric (raw) or symbolic representation of an address.

➤ **URL** represents a URL and includes methods for breaking up a URL into its different parts. You can also use the URL class to open a connection to a URL.

➤ **URLConnection** represents a URL connection through which a resource can be accessed.

Perhaps more interesting than being able to connect to a URL is the ability to open a URL as a stream from which you can read data. You use this capability of the URL class a little later in the chapter. This capability isn't very useful, however, until you've successfully created a URL. Let's examine how that's done.

The URL class provides a number of constructors that you can use to create a URL. The simplest constructor to use requires that you provide a string representation of the URL resource:

```
public URL(String spec)
```

Following is an example of creating a URL object using this constructor:

```
URL url = null;
try {
  url = new URL("http://www.learn2.com");
}
catch (MalformedURLException e) {
  System.out.println("Bad URL: " + url);
}
```

Because the URL constructor is capable of throwing an exception if it runs into trouble, you must construct URL objects within a `try-catch` construct. Fortunately, as the example code shows, this isn't too terribly difficult.

After you've successfully created a URL object, you're ready to move on to more interesting Java networking endeavors. For example, you can redirect a Web browser to another Web page from within an applet. Following is code to do exactly this:

```
getAppletContext().showDocument(url);
```

Of course, this code must be placed within a method in a class derived from `Applet`, because the `getAppletContext()` method is defined in the `Applet` class. The showDocument() is actually doing the work of navigating to another Web page. You simply pass a URL and everything else is automatic!

A more interesting usage of a URL is reading data from a resource on the Web. This is accomplished by connecting an input stream to a URL that is then used to read data from the resource pointed to by the URL. You learn how to do this a little later in the chapter.

Applet: Searcher

You're probably starting to see a teaching pattern forming in this book—theory is always followed up by application. It turns out that this is a great way to learn Java programming, because concepts often don't make sense until you see them in the context of a working example. Continuing on with this teaching approach, let's take a look at a Java applet that uses URLs to navigate to different Web sites based on user interaction.

The following figure shows the Searcher applet, which presents a list of search engine Web sites from which the user can select. After selecting a search engine, the user presses the **Go Search!** button to send the Web browser to that Web site.

The Searcher applet.

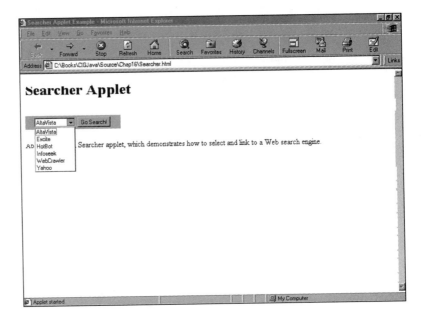

Finding the Searcher Applet Example on the Web

To find the Searcher applet example source code on the Web, enter the address **http://www.mcp.com/info** in the location box of your Web browser. Click the link called **Downloadable Code, Examples, and Info for book "Companion Sites."** In the space provided under the Book Information section, enter **0-7897-1804-9**, which is the 10-digit ISBN for this book. Click the **Search** button.

The source code for the Searcher applet uses the URL class to navigate to different Web pages. Following is the complete source code for the applet:

```java
import java.applet.*;
import java.awt.*;
import java.awt.event.*;
import java.net.*;

public class Searcher extends Applet implements ActionListener {
  static String[] siteNames = { "AltaVista",
                                "Excite",
                                "HotBot",
                                "Infoseek",
                                "WebCrawler",
                                "Yahoo" };
  static String[] siteURLs = { "http://www.altavista.com",
                               "http://www.excite.com",
                               "http://www.hotbot.com",
                               "http://www.infoseek.com",
                               "http://www.webcrawler.com",
                               "http://www.yahoo.com" };
  Choice   searchChooser;
  Button   searchButton;

  public void init() {
    // Create the user interface
    searchChooser = new Choice();
    for (int i = 0; i < siteNames.length; i++)
      searchChooser.add(siteNames[i]);
    add(searchChooser);
    searchButton = new Button("Go Search!");
```

```
      add(searchButton);
      searchChooser.requestFocus();

      // Register the button event handler
      searchButton.addActionListener(this);
   }

   public void actionPerformed(ActionEvent evt) {
      Button source = (Button)evt.getSource();
      if (source.getLabel().equals("Go Search!")) {
         // Obtain a URL for the selected site
         URL url = null;
         try {
          System.out.println(siteURLs[searchChooser.getSelectedIndex()]);
           url = new URL(siteURLs[searchChooser.getSelectedIndex()]);
         }
         catch (MalformedURLException e) {
           System.out.println("Bad URL: " + url);
         }

         // Jump to the search site
         getAppletContext().showDocument(url);
      }
   }
}
```

The Searcher applet class first defines two string array member variables, siteNames and siteURLs, which are used to store the names and URLs for the search engine Web sites. You can easily add new sites to the applet by adding strings to both of these arrays. The applet class also defines two user interface member variables, searchChooser and searchButton, which are used to store the list of search engine choices and the buttons used to navigate to them, respectively.

The init() method is used to initialize the user interface for the applet by creating a Choice object and a Button object. Notice that the Web site names are added to the Choice object by iterating through the siteNames string array. The last step in the init() method is to register the applet class as an action listener for the button. This is necessary so that the applet receives an event notification when the button is pressed.

Speaking of event notifications, the button's action event is handled by the actionPerformed() method. After checking to make sure the correct button was pressed, the actionPerformed() method creates a URL object by indexing into the siteURLs string array. This index is determined by getting the index of the currently selected Web site name in the Choice control.

After successfully creating a URL object, the actionPerformed() method calls the showDocument() method to direct the Web browser to the search engine Web page. Navigating the Web with Java is not difficult at all!

Scanning the Web

Admittedly, the Searcher applet is pretty simple in terms of demonstrating what can be accomplished with Java's networking facilities. Let's consider an example that does a little more. The PageScan application scans a Web page and counts the number of other pages referenced by the page. You could use the PageScan application as the basis for a Web crawler application that follows linked pages looking for information. Following is an example of running the PageScan application from a command line:

```
java PageScan http://www.usatoday.com
```

The results of this scan follow:

```
Working...
Pages referenced: 117
```

In this example, the PageScan application is reporting that the *USA Today* home page contains 117 references to other pages. What does this really mean? Well, in HTML terms it means that the Web page contains 117 HREF tags, which are used to link to other pages. The HREF tag is in fact how the PageScan application looks for page references when analyzing a Web page.

Why an Application?

You might wonder why PageScan is implemented as a Java application instead of a Java applet. The primary reason is because Java's default security limitations don't allow an applet to read data from a computer other than the server computer from which the applet came. Also, the PageScan application functions better as a command-line utility and really wouldn't make sense running within a Web browser.

I mentioned earlier in the chapter that you could read data from a Web page by connecting an input stream to a URL object. This is precisely the technique used by the PageScan application. Let's examine the source code for the application to see how this is possible:

```java
import java.net.*;
import java.io.*;

class PageScan {
  public static void main (String args[]) {
    // Let the user know we're working
    System.out.println("Working...");

    // Make sure we have the right number of args
    if (args.length != 1) {
      System.out.println("Usage: java PageScan URL");
      System.exit(0);
    }

    // Obtain the URL
    URL url = null;
    try {
      url = new URL(args[0]);
    }
    catch (MalformedURLException e) {
      System.out.println("Bad URL: " + url);
    }

    // Open the URL and read its contents into a string
    StringBuffer page = new StringBuffer();
    try {
      InputStream in = url.openStream();
      BufferedReader reader = new BufferedReader(new
        InputStreamReader(in));
      int data;
      while ((data = in.read()) != -1)
        page.append((char)data);
    }
    catch (IOException e) {
      System.out.println("I/O Error: " + e.getMessage());
    }

    // Count the number of document references in the page
    int refCount = 0;
    for (int i = 4; i < page.length(); i++)
      if (page.substring(i - 4, i).equalsIgnoreCase("HREF"))
        refCount++;
    System.out.println("Pages referenced: " + refCount);
  }
}
```

The first thing the application does is print a message informing the user that the application is busily working away. Next the application looks for the single command-line argument containing the URL for the page to be scanned. If the user has provided the wrong number of arguments, PageScan prints a help message and exits.

You must first create a URL object before you can read data from a URL. This URL creation code is very similar to the code you saw in the Searcher applet earlier in the chapter. Now comes the good stuff!

The approach taken by the PageScan application is to read an entire Web page into a string and then search the string for occurrences of the HREF tag. The string is first created as a StringBuffer object. Unlike String objects, StringBuffer objects can easily be appended to and grow in size. An input stream is first attached to the URL object with a call to the openStream() method. Because buffered I/O is more efficient, a BufferedReader object is created to actually read the data from the URL. The read() method is called within a while loop to read the Web page one character at a time. Each character is appended to the string buffer, which eventually contains the complete contents of the Web page.

After the Web page is read into a string buffer, it determines the number of page references by counting the number of occurrences of the tag HREF. The substring() method is used to move through the string buffer, analyzing four-character strings at a time and comparing them to the word HREF. The page reference count is incremented each time an HREF tag is encountered.

A Really Fancy Electrical Socket

You've learned a lot about Java networking in this chapter, but I've deliberately avoided a very large topic, sockets. Java performs all of its low-level network communication using sockets. A socket is a software abstraction for a medium of network communication. Because that definition is a little stuffy, let's relate sockets to something you already understand.

If you recall from the previous chapter, streams are used as the medium through which data is sent. Knowing that, you can think of a socket as the fitting that connects a stream of network data to a Java program. Or, to return to the water analogy, sockets are the glue and fittings that connect a pipe between its source and destination.

Java supports different types of sockets. In fact, not all sockets are associated with streams. Although I'd love to show you a complete socket example requiring four pages of Java code, I'll spare you. In all fairness, sockets are a little beyond the scope of this book, but I didn't want to let you escape this chapter without at least learning what they are.

The Least You Need to Know

Because of its inherent association with the Internet, Java includes lots of features for communicating information between computers on a network. Unfortunately, network programming can get hairy, even in Java, simply due to the complexities associated with networks. For this reason, I tried to make the examples in this chapter as interesting as possible, without letting you get in over your head. Let's recap what you learned:

➤ IP addresses are numbers used to uniquely identify computers connected to the Internet.

➤ URLs serve as pointers to Web pages, binary files, and other information objects on the Web.

➤ A network protocol is a set of rules and standards that governs how network communication works.

➤ HTTP is the network protocol used to transfer HTML documents across the Web.

➤ FTP is the network protocol used to transfer binary files over the Internet.

➤ Java's default security limitations don't allow an applet to read data from a computer other than the server computer from which the applet came.

➤ A socket acts as the fitting that connects a stream of network data to a Java program.

Hanging by a Thread

A Tale of Two Threads

In the movie *Multiplicity*, the character played by Michael Keaton was overwhelmed with family and career commitments, and ultimately didn't have enough time in the day to accomplish everything he needed to. His solution was to create clones of himself who could fill in for him and take care of many of his commitments. The theory was that with the clones taking care of a lot of his day-to-day hassles, he would have more time to do the things more important to him. Of course, trying to manage a group of human clones is bound to get troublesome, as the movie demonstrates.

Although this movie reference might seem a little out of place, it happens to demonstrate the significance of Java multithreading. Multithreading is a feature of Java that enables a program to perform multiple tasks at once. A multithreaded Java program creates worker threads that take care of tasks on their own while the main program gets down to serious business. In this way, Java threads function much like the human clones in the movie except that they aren't necessarily alike. The real key to multi-threading is that threads execute concurrently, meaning that you can have multiple threads running at the same time. The human clone analogy applies to this aspect of multithreading as well, because the clones perform tasks independently of each other.

Now that I've met my movie analogy quota for this chapter, let's look a little deeper into multithreading. Multithreading is closely related to multitasking, of which you have probably at least heard. All modern operating systems are multitasking, which means that they can run multiple applications at once. As an example, I regularly run Microsoft Word, Microsoft Outlook, Windows Explorer, and of course CD Player at the same time in Windows 98. It is the multithreading support built into Windows that enables me to run these applications together.

Multithreading revolves around the concept of a thread, which is a single sequence of code executing within a program. Every Java program follows a path of code execution; threads make it possible to have multiple paths of execution. As an example, you might have an applet that performs a complex mathematical calculation that takes a while to finish. You could create a thread to perform the calculation in the background, thereby freeing up the applet to do other things until the calculation finishes. The thread would work on the calculation at the same time that the main applet code is being executed.

Are Threads Really That Important?

Although the complex calculation example certainly reveals the benefits of multi-threading, you might be wondering just how useful threads really are. I have to admit I once asked the same question. It wasn't until I saw other applications of threads that I fully realized their significance. I think another example might help clarify this point.

If you recall, you developed an applet called Countdown back in Chapter 9, "Feeling a Little Loopy," that performed a countdown similar to the kind used in space shuttle launches. You might remember that I briefly mentioned the fact that the Countdown applet is multithreaded. I didn't make a big deal about it because you hadn't learned about threads at that point. Do you have any idea why it was necessary to make that applet multithreaded? It's all in the timing! The golden rule of comedy also applies to threads. Threads serve as a great way to set up timers in applets so that you can wait for a few seconds or perform things at regular intervals. The Countdown applet used a thread to wait for one second before counting down a number. You use a thread in the next chapter to control the timing of animations.

Although multithreading is an important feature of Java, it isn't useful in all situations. In fact, there are many Java programs that are better off not being multi-threaded because multithreading code can add complexity and overhead that isn't always warranted. To determine if a program would benefit from being multi-threaded, assess it based on the following questions:

➤ Does the program perform lengthy calculations or processes?

➤ Is the user ever left waiting for a command or operation to finish?

➤ Are there program tasks that need to be taking place in the background?

➤ Is there a high-speed program task that needs to maximize processor resources?

If the answer is "yes" to any of these questions, your program is probably a good candidate for multithreading. A multithreaded program performing a lengthy calculation might display a meter bar as the calculation is carried out. A multithreaded game might use a thread to control the timing of frames of animation, as you do in the next chapter. A virus detection program might use multiple threads to patrol the system for invalid memory and file writes.

Some other programs don't necessarily benefit from multithreading. For example, the added complexity and overhead of multithreading support might not be worth the tradeoff in a program performing a moderate operation of a few seconds. In this case, it might make sense to carry out the operation without using a thread because it isn't likely the user could perform any other useful actions in the program anyway. Likewise, a visual meter would appear and disappear so rapidly that it could possibly confuse the user.

All Java Programs Are Multithreaded

In this chapter I refer to a multithreaded Java program as a program that includes special code to create and manage threads. Although this statement is accurate, it is potentially misleading because technically, all Java programs are multithreaded due to the architecture of the Java runtime system. However, for our purposes you can think of a multithreaded Java program as one that makes use of more than one thread

There are no hard and fast rules regarding the types of programs that benefit from being made multithreaded. Experience is the only true guide to determining when to leverage the use of multithreading support in a Java program. The good news is that you will gain much more insight into how and when to use threads as you learn more about building multithreaded programs.

The Darker Side of Multithreading

In an ideal world, threads would have good manners and always allow each other to finish a given task before interrupting. Unfortunately, this isn't an ideal world and threads aren't necessarily this well mannered. Consider a situation in which two threads share a common piece of data. If one thread is in the midst of updating the data, it is entirely possible for the other thread to interrupt and access the data. Unpredictable behavior can result from this type of situation, which is not a good thing.

Aside from being the name of a popular album by The Police, *synchronicity* (or *synchronization* in this case) refers to the structuring of threads so that they never interrupt each other at inopportune times. There are different ways to synchronize threads, and some of them can get pretty complicated. One approach is to declare a section of code or a method as being synchronized, which means that it cannot be interrupted; the code in a synchronized method is guaranteed to fully execute before another thread has an opportunity to interrupt.

Synchronization solutions are powerful, but this power comes at the expense of complexity. For this reason, you won't get into the details of thread synchronization in this book. Fortunately, it isn't an area of Java programming you are likely to encounter until you start developing heavily multithreaded programs.

Creating and Using Threads

For all the power they provide, threads are surprisingly easy to create and use in Java. The Java API provides a Thread class in the default java.lang package that is used to represent threads. The Thread class provides lots of methods for finding out information about a thread, such as whether it is running or not. Although the Thread class is certainly important to multithreaded Java programming, it only tells half of the story. The other half of the multithreaded story is in the Runnable interface, which the Thread class implements.

You'll be glad to know that the Runnable interface is extremely simple. In fact, it only defines one method, run(). Every thread must implement the Runnable interface, which means it must provide a run() method. The run() method is where you place code that is to be executed in a thread. For example, to perform a lengthy calculation in a thread, you place the calculation code in the run() method of your Thread class. This brings us to the topic you've probably been waiting for—how to create threads.

Java provides two different approaches to thread creation:

1. Derive a class from Thread.
2. Implement the Runnable interface in a class.

The next couple of sections demonstrate how to create threads using each of these approaches.

Deriving from the Thread *Class*

Deriving from the Thread class is as simple as defining a class that extends the Thread class and also overriding the run() method. The actual code for the thread should be placed in the run() method. Following is a skeletal example of a thread class that is derived from Thread:

```
class Calculation extends Thread {
   public Calculation() {
      // Initialization calculation parameters
```

```
    }

    public void run() {
      // Perform the calculation
    }
  }
```

The key to this code is the run() method, which in a real thread class would contain the threaded code to execute. The Calculation thread class looks simple enough, but how hard is it to actually create an instance of it and get the thread running? The following code shows how easy it is to get a Calculation thread up and running:

```
Thread calc = new Calculation();
calc.start();
```

As the code demonstrates, all you have to do to get a thread running is create a thread object and call its start() method. The start() method, which is defined in the Thread class, performs all of the necessary overhead required to start the thread. The threaded run() method is automatically called as a result of calling the start() method to start a thread.

Although deriving from the Thread class is a perfectly suitable way to create threads, it isn't always an option. Consider the situation where your thread class is already derived from some other class. Because Java doesn't allow multiple inheritance, you simply don't have the option of deriving the class from Thread. The solution is to implement the Runnable interface in the class. This is the approach you must take when an applet class contains a thread.

Your Threads Are Not Alone

In addition to any threads that you create, the Java runtime system has some threads of its own that it uses to perform chores in the background. One of these threads listens for events from the keyboard and mouse and is ultimately responsible for your applets successfully receiving keyboard and mouse events. There is also a garbage collection thread that throws away objects that are no longer being used and are just taking up space in memory.

Don't Stop That Thread!

Prior to Java 2, the Thread class supported a stop() method that could be used to stop a thread dead in its tracks. After some debate, the architects at Sun decided that the stop() method was inherently unsafe. You can still pause a thread using the sleep() method, which you learn about a little later in this chapter, but you aren't supposed to use the stop() method.

Implementing the Runnable Interface

Warning: if you like complicated solutions to simple problems, then this section is probably not for you.

The Runnable interface provides such an easy way to create threads that you might start taking threads for granted. I suppose that's the risk we'll have to take!

Not surprisingly, to create a thread via the Runnable interface, you must implement the Runnable interface in a class. However, this can be any class, even an applet class. In fact, applet classes are commonly used to implement the Runnable interface so that the code for the thread is kept close to the applet code. If you recall from my earlier mention of the Runnable interface, it only requires you to implement one method, run(). Rather than blabber on about the Runnable interface, let's go ahead and look at some skeletal applet code that creates a thread using it:

```java
public class MyApplet extends Applet implements Runnable {
  Thread thread;

  public void start() {
    if (thread == null) {
      thread = new Thread(this);
      thread.start();
    }
  }

  public void run() {
    // Do anything you like!
  }
}
```

There you go, an applet just waiting for some threaded code to execute. I purposely kept the applet code skeletal so that you could see the minimum code required to create a thread using the Runnable interface. Beyond implementing the run() method in the applet, you must create a Thread object and call its start() method. Notice that the start() method checks to make sure the thread member is null before creating and starting the thread. This is done to make sure that multiple threads aren't created by accident if the applet is restarted.

That's all it takes to create a multithreaded applet. Of course, writing meaningful code to go in the run() method is another issue!

Putting Threads to Sleep

To use threads as the timing mechanism for Java programs, you have to be able to put them to sleep. Typically, thread timing is useful when you want a program to perform a certain repetitive function at timed intervals. To carry this out, you must call the repetitive code and then put the thread to sleep. Placing all of this within an infinite loop results in a timed function. I know this might not immediately make sense, so let's look at an example. Following is the code for a run() method that sets up a timer for an applet:

```java
public void run() {
  while (Thread.currentThread() == thread) {
    // Repetitive code goes here
```

```
// Wait for one second
try {
  Thread.sleep(1000);
}
catch (InterruptedException e) {
  break;
}
    }
  }
}
```

This run() method establishes an infinite while loop in an unexpected way. Because it's possible for an applet to create multiple threads, you should always check the current thread in the run() method to make sure it is the correct one. Assuming there is only one thread in this applet, you can use the currentThread() method in the Thread class as the basis for an infinite loop. This approach is a little safer than just setting up an infinite loop with while(true) because it makes sure the appropriate thread is executing.

Inside the while loop I placed a comment to show where repetitive code should go. This code could increment or decrement a counter, update an animation, or perform any other timed function your heart desires. The actual timing mechanism comes into play with the call to the sleep() method. The sleep() method puts a thread to sleep for a given amount of time, specified in milliseconds.

You can think of a sleeping thread as a thread whose execution is paused for a specified amount of time, after which it wakes up and continues executing. In this example, the thread is put to sleep for one second, or 1000 milliseconds. This establishes a one-second timer, which executes any code above the sleep code once every second.

Applet: AdBanner

Although I could go on and on about the theoretical underpinnings of multithreaded programming, I have a hunch you would probably nod off and risk injury by falling out of your chair. So, I decided to skirt a legal entanglement and try to solidify your understanding of multithreaded Java programming with an example. Without further ado, please turn your attention to the following figure, which shows the AdBanner applet in action.

The AdBanner applet is a multithreaded applet that implements the Runnable interface to create a thread that performs a timing operation. The AdBanner applet uses this thread to cycle through the display of a series of advertisement banners; a new banner is displayed every eight seconds. Clicking on an ad banner takes you to the Web site it is advertising. In keeping with the spirit of the Searcher applet from the previous chapter, I decided to use search engine Web sites as examples in the AdBanner applet. You can of course modify the applet to include any banners you want.

The AdBanner applet.

In case you aren't too familiar with ad banners, they are the principal means of advertising on the Web. Although they can sometimes be an annoyance, ad banners serve the same economic function as commercials on television. Without paid advertising, some Web sites simply wouldn't be able to exist. For this reason, the AdBanner applet can serve a very practical role in your own Web pages. Now that I've sold you on the usefulness of the applet, let's take a look at its source code to see how it works:

```java
import java.applet.*;
import java.awt.*;
import java.awt.event.*;
import java.net.*;

public class AdBanner extends Applet implements Runnable {
  static String[] bannerNames = { "Excite.gif",
                                  "Lycos.gif",
                                  "Supernews.gif",
                                  "WebCrawler.gif" };
  static String[] bannerURLs = { "http://www.excite.com",
                                 "http://www.lycos.com",
                                 "http://www.supernews.com",
                                 "http://www.webcrawler.com" };
  Image[]       banners;
  int           bannerNum = 0;
  Thread        thread;
```

```
public void init() {
  // Register the mouse event handler
  addMouseListener(new MouseHandler());

  // Load the banner images
  banners = new Image[bannerNames.length];
  for (int i = 0; i < bannerNames.length; i++)
    banners[i] = getImage(getCodeBase(), bannerNames[i]);
}

public void start() {
  if (thread == null) {
    thread = new Thread(this);
    thread.start();
  }
}

public void run() {
  // Update everything
  while (Thread.currentThread() == thread) {
    // Display the next banner
    nextBanner();

    // Wait for 8 seconds
    try {
      Thread.sleep(8000);
    }
    catch (InterruptedException e) {
      break;
    }
  }
}

public void update(Graphics g) {
  // Eliminate flicker by not erasing the background
  paint(g);
}

public void paint(Graphics g) {
  // Draw the current slide image
  if (banners[bannerNum] != null)
    g.drawImage(banners[bannerNum], 0, 0, this);
}

class MouseHandler extends MouseAdapter {
  public void mouseClicked(MouseEvent evt) {
    // Obtain a URL for the selected banner
```

```
       URL url = null;
       try {
         url = new URL(bannerURLs[bannerNum]);
       }
       catch (MalformedURLException e) {
         System.out.println("Bad URL: " + url);
       }

       // Jump to the banner site
       getAppletContext().showDocument(url);
     }
   }

  private void nextBanner() {
    // Move to the next banner
    if (++bannerNum == banners.length)
      bannerNum = 0;
    repaint();
  }
}
```

The applet begins by defining some member variables required to support the multiple banners. The two static string arrays, bannerNames and bannerURLs, contain the banner image names and URLs for the different Web sites being advertised. The banners image array is used to store the actual banner images. The bannerNum member keeps track of the banner currently being displayed. Finally, the thread member represents the thread that controls the timing of the banner display.

The init() method isn't too groundbreaking. It registers a mouse handler so that it can process mouse click events. The init() method then proceeds to load the banner images.

The start() method is exactly the same as the version you saw a little earlier in the chapter; it creates a Thread object and calls the start() method to get the thread started.

The run() method is where all the threaded excitement takes place; it establishes an eight-second timer that cycles through the banners. The run() method results in the nextBanner() method being called every eight seconds, which means that the banner is changed every eight seconds. You learn about the nextBanner() method in just a moment. Of course, this timing is made possible thanks to the sleep() method, which you learned about a little earlier in the chapter.

Before examining how the banners are cycled, let's take a look at the update() method. The update() method is called to prepare the applet window before it is painted. More specifically, the default behavior of the update() method erases the applet's background and then calls the paint() method. Although this functionality works fine in most cases, it creates flicker in applets where painting is occurring rapidly. And because many banner images are animated, flicker is a realistic problem in the AdBanner applet. The easy solution in this case is to skip erasing the background in the update() method and just call paint().

The last method of interest in the AdBanner applet is the nextBanner() method, which cycles to the next banner in the list of banners. The nextBanner() method simply increments the bannerNum member and calls the repaint() method. If the bannerNum member moves past the last banner in the list, it just wraps around to the first one again. If you recall from Chapter 12, "Your Next Work of Art," the SlideShow applet used a very similar approach to move through a series of slide images.

The Least You Need to Know

Although they are somewhat specialized in the types of problems they solve, threads can come in very handy. You learned in this chapter that threads are extremely useful for establishing timing mechanisms in applets. This is a relatively simple application of threads, but one that is useful in a variety of different programming situations. Let's go over what you learned in this chapter:

➤ Multithreading is a feature of Java that enables a program to perform multiple tasks at once.

➤ A thread is a single sequence of code executing within a program.

➤ The Java API provides a Thread class in the default java.lang package that is used to represent threads.

➤ All you have to do to get a thread running is create a thread object and call its start() method.

➤ The Runnable interface provides a very simple approach to creating threads.

➤ The sleep() method puts a thread to sleep for a given amount of time, specified in milliseconds.

Java on a Saturday Morning

Java Can Do Cartoons

Do you ever yearn for the days of old when your problems consisted of struggling with the decision of which cartoon to watch on a Saturday morning? Okay, so maybe you didn't spend the greater part of your childhood watching cartoons. Truth be told, I didn't spend too much time in front of the television, but I did love lazy Saturday mornings watching *Captain Caveman*. And now the question you've asked yourself throughout the book at every one of my personal interludes: What can this possibly have to do with Java? Glad you asked!

Saturday morning cartoons are animations, and in many ways they aren't much different from video games and other types of animation such as Web pages that use animated images. In theory, animation is a pretty simple process. However, implementing animation on a computer can often be tricky. I've developed my fair share of computer games, so trust me on that one. Having said that, let me now say that Java offers perhaps the simplest environment I've ever encountered for building animations. You've already learned how to draw non-animated images back in Chapter 12, "Your Next Work of Art." Now it's time to put those images in motion!

With the classes I give you in this chapter, you'll be able to build animated applets, including games, with an amazingly small amount of work. Let's get started!

Animation Basics

Animation is defined as the illusion of movement. Just like a magician pulling a rabbit out of a hat, when you view an animation you are being tricked into believing something is really moving, when in fact it isn't. Perhaps the most surprising animated illusion is the one that caught our collective attention long before computers or the Internet—the television. When you watch television, you see all kinds of things moving around. But what you perceive as movement is really just a trick being played on your eyes. Television will never be the same again!

The Importance of Frame Rate

The number of frames per second displayed in an animation is referred to as the frame rate of the animation. Although 12 fps (frames per second) is technically enough to fool your eyes into perceiving animation, animations at speeds that low often appear jerky. For this reason, most professional animations use a higher frame rate. For example, television uses 30 fps and motion pictures rely on 24 fps. Computers don't have it so easy because higher frame rates demand significant memory and processing power. Consequently, computer animations typically shoot for the lowest possible frame rate, even settling on 12 fps in some cases.

In television animation, the illusion of movement is created by displaying a rapid series of images with slight changes in content between the images. The human eye perceives these changes as a flowing movement because of its low visual acuity, which means that our eyes are pretty easy to trick. More specifically, the human eye can be tricked into perceiving animated movement with as few as 12 frames of movement per second. This means that you would have to see at least 12 images displayed one after another in a second's time to perceive animation. Any less and it would just appear as a bunch of images flashing.

Understanding Sprites

Although there are other types of animation, sprite animation is undoubtedly the simplest form of animation used in computer games. Granted, you might have no desire to ever program a computer game, but games have lots to teach us when it comes to programming challenges. Besides, in many ways a computer game is just a big fancy animation of which the user has some sort of control. So, forgive me if I tend to use games as a basis for some of this discussion on sprite animation.

Getting back to the point, sprite animation consists of graphical objects that move around on top of a background. One interesting way to think of sprite animation is to liken it to a theatrical play: a play consists of props and actors appearing in front of a decorative backdrop. The actors and props can move around independent of the background and interact with each other. Sprites work exactly the same way, and you never have to worry about them forgetting their lines.

Each graphical object in a sprite animation is referred to as a sprite and can have a position that varies over time. More specifically, sprites have a velocity associated with them that determines how their positions change over time.

Stacking Sprites

Just as actors in a play can move in front of and behind each other, so do sprites overlap each other, one on top of another (or in front or back of another) on a screen. This means that sprites need to have a sense of the depth of the screen. Given that the width and height of the screen are the x-axis and y-axis, respectively, the "depth" of the screen is referred to as the z-axis. The sprite moves horizontally on the x-axis, vertically on the y-axis, and in back of or in front of another sprite on the z-axis. The screen depth of a sprite is called the Z-order of the sprite.

When Sprites Collide

No discussion of sprite animation would really be complete without touching on collision detection. Collision detection is the process of determining whether sprites have collided with each other. Although collision doesn't directly play a role in the illusion of movement, it does affect the realism of sprites and how they interact with each other. There are many different approaches available for detecting collisions between sprites. The simplest approach is to compare the rectangular dimensions of each sprite with all other sprites. If there is an overlap, then a collision occurred.

A Simple Suite of Sprite Classes

Now that you have an idea about how sprite animation works, let's take a look at a pair of classes that bring it to life. The sprite system you're going to learn about is centered on two classes, Sprite and SpriteVector. There are a few more support classes involved, but the Sprite and SpriteVector classes form the heart of the sprite system. Because the code that makes these classes work is a little beyond the scope of this book, I'm going to provide you with the finished classes and explain how to use them. You can think of the sprite classes as an extension to the Java API.

Finding the Sprite Classes on the Web

To find the sprite classes on the Web, enter the address `http://www.mcp.com/info` in the location box of your Web browser. Click the link called **Downloadable Code, Examples, and Info for book "Companion Sites."** In the space provided under the Book Information section, enter **0-7897-1804-9**, which is the 10-digit ISBN for this book. Click the **Search** button.

The *Sprite Class*

Before I introduce you to the nuts and bolts of the Sprite class, let's take a moment to examine it at a conceptual level. Based on what you've learned about sprites, with exactly what information should the Sprite class keep up? The following list contains the key information required of the Sprite class:

➤ Array of frame images
➤ Current frame
➤ x,y position
➤ Velocity
➤ Z-Order
➤ Boundary

The first piece of information, an array of frame images, is necessary for the sprite to support individual frame animation. In addition to being able to move, a sprite can provide multiple image frames that are displayed in succession. (An explosion is a good example of a sprite that would require multiple image frames.) It is perfectly acceptable for a sprite to use just one frame image and not take advantage of individual frame animation.

As mentioned earlier, the x,y position keeps up with the position of the sprite. You can move the sprite by simply altering this position, or you can change the velocity and allow the sprite to alter its own position accordingly. The Z-order stores the screen depth of the sprite in relation to other sprites. Ultimately, the Z-order of the sprite determines the sprite's drawing order.

The sprite's boundary is the bounded region in which the sprite can move. This region is typically set to the size of the applet window, but you can limit it if necessary. The sprite's boundary is important because it determines the limits of the sprite's movement.

Perhaps the most important parts of the Sprite class for your purposes are the constructors. There are two constructors for the Sprite class. The first constructor creates a Sprite object without frame animations, which means that the sprite only uses a single image:

```
public Sprite(Component comp, Image img, Point pos, Point vel, int z,
➥int ba)
```

The parameters to this constructor include a component for helping load the sprite image, along with the position, velocity, Z-order, and bounds action of the sprite. The second constructor fully supports frame-animated sprites and has a few extra parameters for defining the starting frame, frame increment, and frame delay:

```
public Sprite(Component comp, Image[] img, int f, int fi, int fd,
➥Point pos,
  Point vel, int z, int ba)
```

The last parameter to both constructors is a bounds action, which you use to indicate how a sprite is to act when it encounters a boundary. Following are the bounds actions supported by the Sprite class:

➤ BA_STOP   causes a sprite to stop when it encounters a boundary.

➤ BA_WRAP   causes a sprite to wrap around to the other side of the boundary.

➤ BA_BOUNCE   causes a sprite to reverse its velocity in the direction it encountered the boundary, thereby appearing to bounce off of the boundary.

➤ BA_DIE   causes a sprite to die when it encounters a boundary.

The Sprite class defines accessor methods for getting and setting all of the members that are intended to be publicly accessible. The Sprite class also defines other useful methods such as the isPointInside() method, which returns whether or not a point lies within a sprite. This method is useful in situations where you are using the mouse to interact with sprites. For example, a chess game might use this method to detect when the user clicks on a piece to move it.

The real workhorse method in the Sprite class is the update() method, which takes on the chore of updating the animation frame and position of the sprite. An applet that uses the Sprite class would need to call the update() method at regular intervals to establish a frame rate for the animation. You learn how to do this a little later when you build an animated applet.

The last method of interest in the Sprite class is the draw() method, which draws the sprite. The draw() method takes into consideration the current frame of the sprite if it is frame animated and then draws the frame image to the graphics context provided. An animated applet could call the draw() method in its own paint() method to draw a sprite. However, you learn next that a class named SpriteVector takes on the chore of updating and drawing individual sprites.

The SpriteVector Class

You now have a Sprite class with lots of bells and whistles, but you have no way of managing more than one sprite. A true sprite animation system requires a means of managing multiple sprites. This is where the SpriteVector class comes into play. The SpriteVector class manages a list of sprites and handles all the details of coordinating interactions between them.

The SpriteVector class declares only one member variable, background, which stores the background for the sprites. You learn about the Background class a little later in the chapter. The background member is set in the constructor for SpriteVector, which takes a Background object as its only parameter:

```
public SpriteVector(Background back)
```

The SpriteVector class provides accessor methods for the background, getBackground() and setBackground(), which are useful in situations where you want to change the background of an animation.

The SpriteVector class also offers a getEmptyPosition() method, which is used to help position new sprites. When I talk about positioning new sprites, I'm referring to the physical position on the background. This method would be extremely useful if you were randomly placing sprites and you wanted to make sure that they weren't placed on top of each other.

There is also an isPointInside() method that is similar to the version of the method defined in the Sprite class, except that this one goes through the entire sprite list, looking for a match.

Finally, the SpriteVector class provides update() and draw() methods that are used to update and draw the entire list of sprites as a group. These two methods alone are all an applet needs to effectively control a sprite animation consisting of multiple sprites.

That concludes the SpriteVector class, which is the second of the two major classes comprising the sprite system. You now have a powerful Sprite class and a SpriteVector class to manage it with. However, there are a few support classes about which you still need to learn. I promise I'll keep the discussion short and sweet, as I know you're getting eager to see this stuff in action.

The Background Classes

When examining the SpriteVector class, you might recall the use of a Background class. The Background class provides the necessary overhead for managing a background on top of which the sprites appear. The Background class offers a single constructor that accepts a parent component as its only parameter:

```
public Background(Component comp)
```

The parent component is used to determine the initial size of the background along with the fill color. The Background class also defines a couple of members used to keep track of the parent component and the size of the background. This class provides a very basic background suitable for the most simple of sprite animations.

For a more interesting animation, you might want to consider using the ColorBackground class. The ColorBackground class extends Background and provides support for a different colored background. The background color is provided in the constructor for `ColorBackground`:

```
public ColorBackground(Component comp, Color c)
```

Other than the addition of the background color, the `ColorBackground` class is very similar to the `Background` class.

If you really want to jazz things up, how about using an image as a background? The `ImageBackground` class enables you to specify an image as a background for sprite animations. The `ImageBackground` class accepts an `Image` object in its constructor and then draws the image as the background:

```
public ImageBackground(Component comp, Image img)
```

As you'll soon see, the `ImageBackground` class can significantly improve the appearance of sprite animations.

Applet: Flying Saucer

Okay, you've suffered just about enough. I know you're probably sick of reading about animation. The good news is that you now have a complete sprite system ready to unleash on any applet you choose. To give you an idea as to how easy the sprite classes are to use, let's work through a simple example applet that puts them to work.

If you're like me and you weren't fortunate enough to be in Roswell, New Mexico, back when all of the UFOs landed, then you're probably feeling a bit cheated. I thought I would try to remedy this situation by giving you a chance to pilot you're very own UFO over the New Mexico desert. The following figure shows the FlyingSaucer applet, which uses the sprite classes to enable you to control a flying saucer sprite. I also threw in some frame-animated blob-like aliens just to make the applet more interesting!

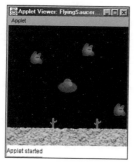

The FlyingSaucer applet.

Finding the FlyingSaucer Applet Example on the Web

To find the FlyingSaucer applet example source code on the Web, enter the address `http://www.mcp.com/info` in the location box of your Web browser. Click the link called **Downloadable Code, Examples, and Info for book "Companion Sites."** In the space provided under the Book Information section, enter **0-7897-1804-9**, which is the 10-digit ISBN for this book. Click the **Search** button.

The code for the FlyingSaucer applet demonstrates how to use the sprite classes for simple sprite animation:

```java
import java.applet.*;
import java.awt.*;
import java.awt.event.*;
import java.util.*;

public class FlyingSaucer extends Applet implements Runnable {
  Image        offImage, back, saucer;
  Image[]      blob = new Image[8];
  Dimension    saucerSize;
  Graphics     offGrfx;
  Thread       animate;
  SpriteVector sv;
  Sprite       theSaucer;
  int          lastKey;
  int          delay = 83; // 12 fps
  Random       rand = new Random(System.currentTimeMillis());

  public void init() {
    // Load the images
    back = getImage(getCodeBase(), "Back.gif");
    saucer = getImage(getCodeBase(), "Saucer.gif");
    for (int i = 0; i < 8; i++)
      blob[i] = getImage(getCodeBase(), "Blob" + i + ".gif");

    // Register the mouse and keyboard event handlers
    addMouseListener(new MouseHandler());
    addMouseMotionListener(new MouseMotionHandler());
```

```
      addKeyListener(new KeyHandler());
  }

  public void start() {
    if (animate == null) {
      animate = new Thread(this);
      animate.start();
    }
  }

  public void run() {
    // Create the sprite vector and add the saucer sprite
    sv = new SpriteVector(new ImageBackground(this, back));
    saucerSize = new Dimension(saucer.getWidth(this),
      saucer.getHeight(this));
    theSaucer = new Sprite(this, saucer, new Point((getSize().width -
      saucerSize.width) / 2, (getSize().height - saucerSize.height) /
      2), new Point(0, 0), 0, Sprite.BA_STOP);
    sv.add(theSaucer);

    // Create and add the blob sprites
    Dimension blobDim = new Dimension(blob[0].getWidth(this),
      blob[0].getHeight(this));
    for (int i = 0; i < 3; i++) {
      Sprite s = new Sprite(this, blob, 0, 1, 2,
      ➥sv.getEmptyPosition(blobDim),
        new Point(rand.nextInt() % 3, rand.nextInt() % 3), 0,
        Sprite.BA_BOUNCE);
      sv.add(s);
    }

    // Update everything
    long t = System.currentTimeMillis();
    while (Thread.currentThread() == animate) {
      sv.update();
      repaint();
      try {
        t += delay;
        Thread.sleep(Math.max(0, t - System.currentTimeMillis()));
      }
      catch (InterruptedException e) {
        break;
      }
    }
  }

  public void update(Graphics g) {
    // Create the offscreen graphics context
```

```
      if (offGrfx == null) {
        offImage = createImage(getSize().width, getSize().height);
        offGrfx = offImage.getGraphics();
      }

      // Draw the sprites
      sv.draw(offGrfx);

      // Draw the image onto the screen
      g.drawImage(offImage, 0, 0, null);
    }

    public void paint(Graphics g) {
      // Draw the offscreen image
      if (offImage != null) {
        g.drawImage(offImage, 0, 0, null);
      }
    }

    class KeyHandler extends KeyAdapter {
      public void keyPressed(KeyEvent e) {
        // Change the saucer velocity based on the key pressed
        Point vel = theSaucer.getVelocity();
        switch (e.getKeyCode()) {
        case KeyEvent.VK_LEFT:
          vel.x = -4;
          if (lastKey == KeyEvent.VK_LEFT)
            vel.y = 0;
          break;
        case KeyEvent.VK_RIGHT:
          vel.x = 4;
          if (lastKey == KeyEvent.VK_RIGHT)
            vel.y = 0;
          break;
        case KeyEvent.VK_UP:
          vel.y = -4;
          if (lastKey == KeyEvent.VK_UP)
            vel.x = 0;
          break;
        case KeyEvent.VK_DOWN:
          vel.y = 4;
          if (lastKey == KeyEvent.VK_DOWN)
            vel.x = 0;
          break;
        default:
          vel.x = vel.y = 0;
        }
        theSaucer.setVelocity(vel);
```

```
        lastKey = e.getKeyCode();
    }
}

class MouseHandler extends MouseAdapter {
  public void mousePressed(MouseEvent e) {
    theSaucer.setPosition(new Point(e.getX() - (saucerSize.width /
    ➡2),
      e.getY() - (saucerSize.height / 2)));
  }
}

class MouseMotionHandler extends MouseMotionAdapter {
  public void mouseDragged(MouseEvent e) {
    theSaucer.setPosition(new Point(e.getX() - (saucerSize.width /
    ➡2),
      e.getY() - (saucerSize.height / 2)));
  }
}
}
```

The `FlyingSaucer` applet class relies on three `Image` member variables: an offscreen image, a background image, and a flying saucer image, along with an `Image` array for holding the blob images. The offscreen image is used as a workspace for drawing the sprites before they actually appear on the screen. Drawing to an offscreen image prior to drawing to the screen helps to reduce the flicker commonly associated with animation. Without taking any special precautions, drawing in a Java applet at frequent intervals would create flicker because an applet typically erases its background each time before it is painted. Flicker causes the area being painted in an applet to appear to flash, which is a bad thing. The offscreen image gets rid of flicker because it is drawn to the screen at once without ever erasing the screen. This approach to eliminating flicker is called double buffering.

The `Applet` class also declares member variables for storing the flying saucer's size, along with a graphics context used to draw to the offscreen image. Additionally, there is a `Thread` member for controlling the animation thread.

You also probably noticed the `SpriteVector` member variable, which is extremely important. There is also one `Sprite` member, `theSaucer`, which represents the flying saucer.

The `lastKey` member is used to keep track of the last key pressed on the keyboard, which is used in determining how to set the velocity of the saucer. Finally, the frame rate of the animation is established using a delay in the animation thread. A delay value of 83 milliseconds results in a frame rate of 12 fps, which is the minimum for animation. I'm using the minimum frame rate because it's hard to tell how fast of a frame rate a typical user's computer will support. If I cranked up the frame rate really high, some computers wouldn't be able to keep up with the animation. So, it's generally safer to use the minimum frame rate possible.

241

The init() method loads the images for background, flying saucer, and blobs, and then registers the mouse and keyboard event handlers. The run() method takes on the responsibility of creating the sprite vector with an image background, along with creating the saucer sprite and adding it to the sprite vector. The run() method also creates three frame-animated blob sprites. The run() method then enters a loop where it continually updates the sprite vector, repaints the applet, and waits for the delayed amount of 83 milliseconds.

The update() method creates the offscreen image and graphics context, draws the sprites to the offscreen image, and then draws this image to the screen. Similarly, the paint() method just draws the offscreen image to the screen. The structure of the update() method is ultimately responsible for eliminating flicker in the animation.

The remainder of the code in the applet deals with responding to user input via the keyboard and mouse. Keyboard and mouse input are used as the basis for calling the setVelocity() and setPosition() methods on the saucer sprite to move it around on the desert background.

I encourage you to take some time to try out the applet and notice how the saucer sprite moves in response to user input. You might also want to pay attention to how the blob sprites react when you run into them with the saucer.

The Least You Need to Know

Animation is an exciting and challenging area of Java programming that really isn't done justice with a single chapter. You might be feeling like I rushed some of the material in this chapter, in which case you're partially right. Sprite animation is something that requires a certain base amount of source code that's hard to get around. However, the classes to which you were introduced in this chapter are extremely extensible and should serve you well in all kinds of different animation situations. I encourage you to experiment with the classes on your own and explore different ways you can put them to use. Let's go over what you learned in this chapter:

➤ Animation is defined as the illusion of movement.

➤ The human eye can be tricked into perceiving animated movement with as few as 12 frames of movement per second.

➤ Sprite animation involves graphical objects that move around on top of a background.

➤ Z-order determines the screen depth of a sprite in relation to other sprites.

➤ Collision detection is the process of determining whether sprites have collided with each other.

➤ The SpriteVector class serves as a container for holding and managing multiple Sprite objects.

➤ The Background class serves as a basic background upon which sprites can move around and do their thing.

Java on a Saturday Night

Digital Audio Primer

I have to confess that I was hooked the first time I learned how to make noise with a computer. It goes all the way back to my second computer, a Commodore 64; a Texas Instruments 99/4A was my first computer, but that's an experience I'd rather not talk about! Anyway, the first time I was able to write a program that generated musical notes on the computer I felt empowered. Granted, it took some programming effort to make it happen, but the Commodore 64 was a surprisingly powerful audio computer for its time.

Returning to the present, it is now possible not only to generate musical notes, but also to play digital audio recorded directly from a microphone attached to your computer. You can also record music straight from a CD and play it back in a Java program. You could create your own Web-based night club and spin tunes using a Java applet! Before we get into how Java makes all of this possible, let's take a moment to clarify exactly what digital audio is.

The Physics of Sound

You might be surprised to learn that the nature of digital audio can be traced back to elementary physics. When I talk about audio, I'm really talking about sound, and sound travels as waves of compressed air. A sound wave is actually the result of the pressure of air expanding and contracting. You hear sound because the traveling sound wave eventually gets to your ears, where the pressure changes are processed and interpreted by your eardrums.

When a sound wave is converted to an electrical signal (by a microphone, for example), an electrical voltage represents the height, or *amplitude*, of the wave. The amplitude of the voltage corresponds directly to the amplitude of the physical sound wave. As the amplitude of the wave varies over time, so does the corresponding voltage.

The voltage signal obtained by a microphone is an analog signal, which means it forms a continuous curve when graphed (see the following figure). Because computers are digital machines, it is necessary to convert this analog signal to a digital signal. Analog-to-digital (A/D) converters handle the task of converting analog signals to digital signals. This is also referred to as sampling. Have you ever played with a keyboard that has a sample button? Countless hours of pleasure can be derived from sampling words and playing them back on one of these keyboards. Try it sometime!

The analog nature of sound.

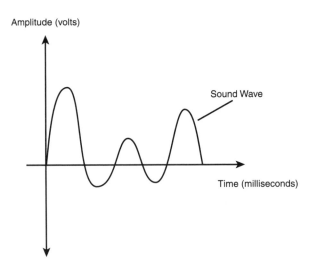

The process of converting an analog signal to a digital signal doesn't always yield exact results. How closely a digital signal matches its analog counterpart is determined by the frequency at which it is sampled, as well as the amount of information stored at each sample. To sample a sound, you just grab the amplitude of the sound wave at regular intervals. The following figure shows an analog sound wave and its digital representation.

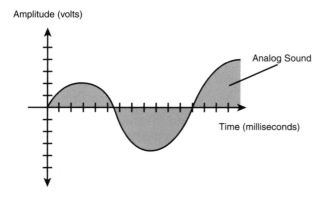

An analog sound wave and its digital representation.

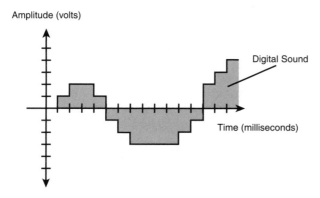

Notice in the figure that the digital representation of the analog sound wave is not really a very good one. Taking samples at more frequent intervals causes the digital signal to more closely approximate the analog signal, and therefore sound more like the analog signal when played back.

Digital Sound Quality

Okay, so I've impressed you with my incredible insight into the physics of sound, even though it has absolutely nothing to do with Java. What gives? Well, the reason I've spent the past couple of pages playing Mr. Wizard is because I want you to understand the basis for different sound qualities. By understanding the sound properties that affect quality, you can decide whether you want the audio in your applets to sound like a cheap cordless phone or like a high-end stereo system. Actually, this decision is largely taken out of your hands by the current bandwidth limitations of most Internet connections. In other words, you are likely to have to settle on a relatively low sound quality so users won't have to wait around all day for sounds to be downloaded.

When sampling a sound, the rate (frequency) at which the sound is sampled is very important, as well as how much data is stored for each sample. Let's first consider the frequency part of the sound quality equation. The unit of measure for frequency is Hertz (Hz), which specifies how many samples are taken per second. A higher frequency results in higher sound quality. For example, CD-quality audio is sampled at 44,000 Hz.

Early Java Sound

Prior to Java 2, the only supported Java sound format was the AU sound format, which allowed for sounds sampled at 8,000 Hz with 8 bits of data per sample. As you might guess, this resulted in relatively poor sound quality. However, considering the fact that sounds are often transferred over a Web connection with an applet, it makes sense to use a lower quality format to ensure that users aren't waiting around for hours while CD-quality sounds are loaded.

The other important ingredient in sound quality is the amount of data used to store each sample. This determines the number of discrete amplitudes that a digital signal can represent. Please refer back to the earlier figure if you aren't following. To put it in simpler terms, the more data used to store each sample, the better the quality of sound. This is due to the fact that more data per sample results in the digitized sound more closely approximating the original analog sound. As a baseline for quality, consider that CD-quality audio relies on 16 bits of data per sample.

Even though it might be tempting to use an incredibly high sound quality, keep in mind that high-quality sounds take up tons of memory and drive space, and therefore take a long time to transfer over most Internet connections. For applets, it's crucial that sound sizes be kept at a minimum, so you'll probably want to experiment with the tradeoff in sound quality versus size.

Making Noise with Java

If Java 2 represents your first foray into Java audio, you're in luck. Java 2 includes support for a much wider range of audio than prior versions of Java. More specifically, Java now supports the following four sound formats:

➤ AU

➤ AIFF

➤ WAVE

➤ MIDI

The first format, AU, was the only sound format supported in versions of Java prior to 2. The AIFF and WAVE formats are similar to the AU format in that they are used to represent digitized sounds. Unlike the AU format, WAVE formats offer a much wider range of sound qualities. The MIDI sound format is interesting because it is used specifically for music and is based on musical notes and instruments instead of digitized sound.

Playing sounds in Java is as simple as loading a sound and calling a method to play it. You load a sound in Java by calling the `newAudioClip()` method, which is provided as part of the `Applet` class. The `newAudioClip()` method is a static method, which means that you don't have to rely on an instance of the `Applet` class to call the method. This is important because it allows graphical Java applications to load sounds. Prior to Java 2, only applets could play sounds.

Creating Sounds

There are many audio utilities available for creating sounds. Most audio utilities are geared toward creating either digitized sounds or MIDI songs. Perhaps the simplest sound creation utility is the Sound Recorder application that comes standard with Windows 95/98. There is also a wide variety of professional quality applications for sampling and editing digitized sounds and composing and arranging MIDI songs.

Following is an example of loading an audio clip with the `newAudioClip()` method:

```
AudioClip audio =
Applet.newAudioClip(new
URL(getCodeBase(), "Sound.au"));
```

This code loads a new audio clip by first creating a URL containing the applet's code base (source directory) along with the name of the sound file. The sound stored in the file `Sound.au` is loaded and stored in an `AudioClip` object, which models a sound in Java. The `AudioClip` interface is where you actually control the playback of Java audio. Audio clips loaded using the `newAudioClip()` method conform to the `AudioClip` interface, which defines the following methods:

➤ `play()`

➤ `stop()`

➤ `loop()`

The `play()` method plays an audio clip once. You can call it repeatedly to play an audio clip multiple times. The `stop()` method stops an audio clip that is already playing. Finally, the `loop()` method plays an audio clip over and over continuously until you call the `stop()` method or the applet terminates. The `loop()` method can be useful in situations where you want a sampled sound effect or musical melody to repeat continuously. The problem with the `loop()` method is that there isn't a good way to control exactly how many times it loops a clip. So, it's usually better to use the `play()` method if you want to repeat a sound with some control over the repetitions.

Static Cling

Unlike the static cling that causes two socks to act as one when they come out of the dryer, static members in Java are beneficial. A static class member, be it a variable or a method, is associated with a class, not an instance of a class. What this means is that you can access a static member without creating an instance of a class (an object). When doing so, you use the class name where you would typically use a specific object name for non-static members. For example, the static `newAudioClip()` method of the `Applet` class is called as `Applet.newAudioClip()`.

You might be glad to find out that none of the methods defined in the `AudioClip` interface require parameters. For this reason, there isn't much of a learning curve when it comes to using audio clips. By simply understanding the `play()`, `stop()`, and `loop()` methods you are practically already a Java sound expert! Following is an example of using the `play()` method to play a sound in Java:

```
audio.play();
```

Likewise, to stop the clip while it is being played you call the `stop()` method:

```
audio.stop();
```

Like I said, Java audio is one of the easiest areas of Java programming; and in a lot of ways it is one of the most rewarding.

Setting the Mood with Music

A little later in the chapter I lead you through the development of a pretty interesting sound effects applet. However, I didn't want to completely overlook the importance of music, especially MIDI music. So, let's take a look at a simple music applet that plays a MIDI song. By the way, this is a great applet to incorporate into your own Web pages. The following figure shows the MusicPlayer applet busily cranking out a tune. You'll have to trust me on this one because it's difficult to simulate music with text!

The MusicPlayer applet.

As you can see, the MusicPlayer applet consists solely of a check box with the option Music Enabled. This check box controls whether or not music is played. Although the check box might not seem like a big deal, you have to consider the fact that not everyone is into hearing music while surfing Web pages. I, for one, am sometimes annoyed if I'm working late at night and music blares when I visit a Web page. Including an option for disabling a musical clip is a nice touch that users will appreciate.

Another cool thing about the MusicPlayer applet is that it accepts the name of the music clip as an applet parameter. This enables you to play different clips by simply modifying the HTML source code for the Web page containing the applet. Speaking of HTML source code, following is the code for the MusicPlayer.html Web page:

Finding the MusicPlayer Applet Example on the Web

To find the MusicPlayer applet example source code on the Web, enter the address **http://www.mcp.com/info** in the location box of your Web browser. Click the link called **Downloadable Code, Examples, and Info for book "Companion Sites."** In the space provided under the Book Information section, enter **0-7897-1804-9**, which is the 10-digit ISBN for this book. Click the **Search** button.

```
<HTML>
<HEAD>
<TITLE>MusicPlayer Applet
➥Example</TITLE>
</HEAD>
<BODY>
<H1>MusicPlayer Applet</H1>
<HR>
<APPLET CODE="MusicPlayer.class"
➥WIDTH=150 HEIGHT=50>
<PARAM NAME=clip
➥VALUE="BankHard.mid">
</APPLET>
<P>
Above is the Java MusicPlayer
➥applet, which demonstrates how to play musical audio clips.
</P>
</BODY>
</HTML>
```

The music clip parameter is named `clip`, and in this case its value is set to `BankHard.mid`, which is the name of a MIDI sound file. That's all it takes to specify a music clip and play it in a Web page using the MusicPlayer applet.

Following is the source code for the MusicPlayer applet:

```
import java.applet.*;
import java.awt.*;
import java.awt.event.*;
import java.net.*;

public class MusicPlayer extends Applet implements ItemListener {
  AudioClip clip;
  Checkbox  cb;

  public void init() {
    // Load the audio clip
    String s = getParameter("clip");
```

```
        if (null != s) {
          try {
            clip = Applet.newAudioClip(new URL(getCodeBase(), s));
            clip.loop();
          }
          catch (MalformedURLException e) {
            System.out.println("Bad URL.");
          }
        }

        // Create the checkbox and register the applet as an item listener
        cb = new Checkbox("Music enabled", true);
        add(cb);
        cb.addItemListener(this);
      }

      public void itemStateChanged(ItemEvent e) {
        if (e.getStateChange() == ItemEvent.DESELECTED)
          clip.stop();
        else
          clip.loop();
      }
    }
```

As you might notice, the MusicPlayer applet really wasn't designed solely to play musical audio clips. You can actually use it to play any audio clip as long as you intend to loop the clip repeatedly. Musical clips tend to make more sense looping than most other types of sounds, however.

The applet contains two member variables: clip and cb. The clip member is an AudioClip object used to store the music clip being played. The cb member is a Checkbox object used to control the playing of the music clip.

The init() method loads the music clip based on the clip applet parameter. Notice that the newAudioClip() method is used to load the music clip. The code for loading the music clip is probably a little strange looking due to the fact that the URL class's constructor is capable of throwing an exception if the URL is bad. Exceptions are used to gracefully handle unexpected errors that might occur in Java programs. You are required to handle an exception if a method is capable of throwing one. The last part of the init() method creates the check box, adds it as part of the applet's user interface, and registers the applet as an event listener for the check box.

The itemStateChanged() method is an event handler that is called whenever the user checks or unchecks the check box. The method simply looks at the state of the check box and stops or loops the music clip accordingly. And you probably thought it was hard to play music in Java!

Applet: WildAnimals

Although the MusicPlayer applet is certainly a practical applet for playing music clips, I want to show you a more interesting example of playing sounds in an applet. Have you ever been out in the wilderness at night and marveled at the range of animal sounds? Better yet, have you ever been scared of what might be out there when you hear a strange sound and see a pair of eyes staring at you out of the darkness? I thought it might be fun to simulate this experience in a Java applet. The following figure shows the WildAnimals applet, which simulates a "wilderness experience."

The WildAnimals applet.

In the figure you can't see the eyes occasionally blinking. In addition to making the applet more realistic, the eye movement also makes it a lot more fun to experience. The blinking eyes are made possible thanks to the Sprite classes you learned about in the previous chapter. Combined with a rich set of sound effects, the animation in the WildAnimals applet makes for pretty cheap entertainment!

The blinking eyes in the applet are modeled using the Eyes class, which derives from the Sprite class. The Eyes class supports two different size eyes, along with frame animations for each of them opening and closing. Following is the source code for the Eyes class:

```
import java.awt.*;
import java.applet.Applet;

public class Eyes extends Sprite {
```

Finding the WildAnimals Applet Example on the Web

To find the WildAnimals applet example source code on the Web, enter the address `http://www.mcp.com/info` in the location box of your Web browser. Click the link called **Downloadable Code, Examples, and Info for book "Companion Sites."** In the space provided under the Book Information section, enter **0-7897-1804-9**, which is the 10-digit ISBN for this book. Click the **Search** button.

```
static Image[][] image = new Image[2][4];
int             blinkDelay,
                blinkTrigger;

public Eyes(Component comp, Point pos, int i, int bd) {
  super(comp, image[i], 0, 1, 2, pos, new Point(0, 0), 0,
    Sprite.BA_WRAP);
  blinkTrigger = blinkDelay = bd;
}

public static void initResources(Applet app, int id) {
  for (int i = 0; i < 4; i++) {
    image[0][i] = app.getImage(app.getCodeBase(), "SmEye" + i +
    ➥".gif");
    image[1][i] = app.getImage(app.getCodeBase(), "LgEye" + i +
    ➥".gif");
  }
}

protected void incFrame() {
  if ((frameDelay > 0) && (--frameTrigger <= 0) &&
    (--blinkTrigger <= 0)) {
    // Reset the frame trigger
    frameTrigger = frameDelay;

    // Increment the frame
    frame += frameInc;
    if (frame >= 4) {
      frame = 3;
      frameInc = -1;
    }
    else if (frame <= 0) {
      frame = 0;
      frameInc = 1;
      blinkTrigger = blinkDelay;
    }
  }
}
```

The main function of the eyes in the applet is to blink, which requires a frame animation in the Eyes Sprite class. Consequently, the majority of the source code in the
Eyes class manages the frame animation so that the eyes look like they are actually
blinking. The Sprite class provides the framework for this functionality, but the Eyes
class must do some of the work itself because it actually moves back and forth
through the frame animations.

You are free to study the Eyes class more on your own, but I'm ready to move on to the WildAnimals applet class, which is where most of the real work takes place. Following is the source code for the WildAnimals applet class:

```java
import java.applet.*;
import java.awt.*;
import java.util.*;
import java.net.*;

public class WildAnimals extends Applet implements Runnable {
  Image          offImage;
  Graphics       offGrfx;
  Thread         animate;
  SpriteVector   sv;
  int            delay = 83; // 12 fps
  Random         rand = new Random(System.currentTimeMillis());
  AudioClip[]    clip = new AudioClip[5];

  public void init() {
    // Load the images
    Eyes.initResources(this, 0);

    // Load the audio clips
    try {
      clip[0] = Applet.newAudioClip(new URL(getCodeBase(),
      ➥"Crow.au"));
      clip[1] = Applet.newAudioClip(new URL(getCodeBase(),
      ➥"Hyena.au"));
      clip[2] = Applet.newAudioClip(new URL(getCodeBase(),
      ➥"Monkey.au"));
      clip[3] = Applet.newAudioClip(new URL(getCodeBase(),
      ➥"Tiger.au"));
      clip[4] = Applet.newAudioClip(new URL(getCodeBase(),
      ➥"Wolf.au"));
    }
    catch (MalformedURLException e) {
      System.out.println("Bad URL.");
    }
  }

  public void start() {
    if (animate == null) {
      animate = new Thread(this);
```

```
        animate.start();
    }
}

public void run() {
  // Create and add the sprites
  sv = new SpriteVector(new ColorBackground(this, Color.black));
  for (int i = 0; i < 8; i++) {
    sv.add(new Eyes(this, new Point(Math.abs(rand.nextInt() %
      getSize().width), Math.abs(rand.nextInt() % getSize().width)),
      i % 2, Math.abs(rand.nextInt() % 200)));
  }

  // Update everything
  long t = System.currentTimeMillis();
  while (Thread.currentThread() == animate) {
    // Update the animations
    sv.update();
    repaint();

    // Play an animal sound
    if ((rand.nextInt() % 15) == 0)
      clip[Math.abs(rand.nextInt() % 5)].play();

    try {
      t += delay;
      Thread.sleep(Math.max(0, t - System.currentTimeMillis()));
    }
    catch (InterruptedException e) {
      break;
    }
  }
}

public void update(Graphics g) {
  // Create the offscreen graphics context
  if (offGrfx == null) {
    offImage = createImage(getSize().width, getSize().height);
    offGrfx = offImage.getGraphics();
  }

  // Draw the sprites
  sv.draw(offGrfx);
```

```
      // Draw the image onto the screen
      g.drawImage(offImage, 0, 0, null);
    }

    public void paint(Graphics g) {
      // Draw the offscreen image
      if (offImage != null)
        g.drawImage(offImage, 0, 0, null);
    }
  }
```

A great deal of the code in the WildAnimals applet class should look familiar to you from the FlyingSaucer applet you built in the previous chapter. Both applets require much of the same code to support sprite animation. The main thing I want to focus on is the audio-related code, which is pretty straightforward.

The init() method first loads the audio clips for the sound effects using the newAudioClip() method. The sounds are then played in the run() method at irregular intervals thanks to the if branch that is based on a random number. The random number generated here is between 0 and 14, which means that there is a 1 in 15 chance of playing an audio clip each time through the animation loop. The animation loop is ticking along at 12 fps, which means that an audio clip is being played roughly once every second. However, the fact that the playback is random gives the sounds a more natural feel.

Also random is the actual selection of the sound to be played. A random number between 0 and 4 is generated and used as the basis for selecting one of the audio clips from the clip array of audio clips.

One last code detail worth pointing out is the creation of the Eyes sprite objects, which takes place in the beginning of the run() method. The eyes are positioned at random locations and with a random frame delay, which means that they each blink at a different rate. This helps to give the applet a more natural feel. A little randomness goes a long way when it comes to real world simulations!

The Least You Need to Know

Sound plays an incredibly important role in creating a mood or just livening things up—especially when a Java program stands to benefit from it. From a programming perspective, playing sound and music in Java couldn't be much easier. This is because the real work involved in playing sound and music is handled by Java itself. Along with teaching you the basics of digital audio and how to use the Java API to play sound and music, I hope you also learned something in this chapter about creating fun applets:

➤ The frequency at which the sound is sampled and the amount of information stored at each sample determine the quality of digital sound.

➤ CD-quality audio is sampled at 44,000 Hz with 16 bits of data per sample.

➤ High-quality sounds take up a great deal of memory and drive space and, therefore, take a long time to transfer over most Internet connections.

➤ The AU, AIFF, and WAVE sound formats are used to represent digitized sounds, while the MIDI format is used solely for music.

➤ You load a sound in Java by calling the `newAudioClip()` method, which is a static method of the `Applet` class.

➤ The `AudioClip` interface is used to control the playback of Java audio.

Part 5
Java as a Self-Help Technology

Just when I thought I had run out of ways to achieve a higher status in the minds of my fellow gearheads, along comes Java. By learning Java, you too can improve your position among fellow nerds and practically guarantee a local computer club speaking gig.

Okay, maybe I've painted too glamorous a picture of life after Java, but I do have to admit to a sense of confidence in knowing what the real scoop is when I hear people yammering on about Java. Maybe you won't be nominated Grand Poo-Bah of your local TRS-80 Fan Club, but you will be able to make family and friends uncomfortable at the dinner table: "Please iterate through a sprite vector and pass me the potatoes, please."

Chapter 20

How to Break the Chains of Idiocy

In This Chapter:

➤ Debugging Fundamentals

➤ Preventing Bugs

➤ Detecting Bugs

➤ Documenting Java Code

Debugging Basics

It has been said that computers give humans the capability to achieve perfection because digital machines are incapable of error. This assertion is false for a couple of reasons:

1. At a subatomic level, computers are in fact capable of making errors.
2. More importantly, humans that design and build computers are still very error prone.

A bug is simply a coding error that results in an unwanted action that takes place in a program. Unfortunately, bugs are a fact of life when it comes to programming.

Although all programmers strive for perfection, few are ever able to attain it. Those who do reach the nerd nirvana of a bug-free program typically find and fix a significant number of bugs along the way. The saving grace of these programmers is that they anticipate the occurrence of a certain number of bugs and actively set out to uncover these bugs as they develop a program.

This brings us to the first rule of debugging, which is to assume that your code has bugs and that it is your responsibility to hunt them down and fix them to the best of your ability. Following are three fundamental debugging techniques that are indispensable to finding and fixing bugs in Java programs:

➤ Single-stepping through code

➤ Watching variables

➤ Using breakpoints

Strolling Through Code

The most basic of all debugging approaches is single-stepping through code—the process of executing a program a line at a time, in single steps. Single-stepping provides you with a way to see exactly what code is being executed, which gives you insight into the flow of execution through a program. Typically, single-stepping through code isn't entirely useful by itself; you usually combine it with another debugging technique, known as watch variables, to keep an eye on what happens to variables as you step through the code.

Bug Detection Tools

Single-stepping through Java code requires a special program called a debugger. There is a command-line debugger provided with the JDK, but it is somewhat more difficult to use than graphical debuggers that are integrated with third-party Java development environments such as Symantec Café, Inprise's JBuilder, and Microsoft Visual J++. For more information on third-party Java development tools, please refer to Appendix B, "Java Tools & Technologies."

Keeping an Eye on Your Variables

Another commonly used debugging technique involves watch variables, which are variables whose contents you observe while Java code is executing in a debugger. By watching a variable in a debugger, you can quickly tell if the variable is being set to a value that doesn't jive with the rest of the program code. Of course, in the context of a program running at full speed, watch variables aren't very useful. But if you watch a variable as you are single-stepping through code, you can learn a lot about what is happening to the variable.

A Debugging Tutorial

Sun Microsystems has a good online tutorial for learning how to use the jdb debugger that comes standard with the JDK. You can access the tutorial from Sun's Java Web site at http://java.sun.com.

It is fairly common for a watch variable to reveal an unexpected value that doesn't make sense in the context of what you thought some code was supposed to be doing. For example, consider the following code:

```
String[] names = { "Big Ern", "Dignan", "Max", "Vernie" };
for (int i = 0; i <= 4; i++)
  System.out.println(names[i]);
```

Upon first inspection, the code probably appears to be fine to you. However, this code has a subtle bug that might not be immediately apparent without single-stepping and watching the i variable. I'll spare you the suspense and just tell you what's wrong with the code. Because all Java arrays are zero based, only the numbers 0 through 3 are valid indexes for the names array. However, the conditional part of the for loop (i <= 4) mistakenly causes the loop to iterate from 0 to 4 instead of 0 to 3. Consequently, the last time through the loop, the array is indexed with 4, which results in an exception being thrown. You learn more about exceptions a little later in the chapter.

This type of coding error is occasionally made by even the most experienced of Java programmers. Incidentally, the fix for the problem is simply to change the for loop conditional to i < 4.

Setting Up Code Roadblocks

The last of the big three debugging techniques is the breakpoint, which acts some-what like a roadblock for program execution. It works like this: You place a break-point on a line of code, and when the program runs and gets to that line of code it stops. It's called a breakpoint because the program effectively takes a break at that particular point in the code. Breakpoints are extremely useful in isolating certain parts of a program and analyzing them.

To understand the significance of breakpoints, imagine that you are interested in see-ing what happens in a program at a particular point in the code. You could obviously single-step through the code a line at a time until you arrive at the code in question.

261

However, some programs have long loops that perform a bunch of iterations, which would take a long time through which to single-step, not to mention putting you to sleep with the boredom of stepping through code for hours on end. Setting a breakpoint on the line of code solves this problem quite nicely. After setting the breakpoint, you run the program in the debugger until it hits the breakpoint, after which the program halts. You are then free to watch variables and even single-step through the code if you want.

Using Debugging Strategies

I mentioned earlier in the chapter that there are fancy graphical debuggers built into most professional Java development environments. Although these debuggers significantly improve the debugging process, keep in mind that they are only tools to help you find problems; they are not debugging strategies in themselves.

I can't emphasize enough how important it is to try to avoid creating bugs in the first place. Let's talk about a couple of strategies you can use for minimizing bugs: bug prevention and bug detection.

Bug Preventive Programming

It is commonly accepted that the most effective way to stay healthy is to practice preventive healthcare. This means that rather than taking medicine for an illness after you catch it, you try to avoid getting sick in the first place. Bug prevention in Java programming works in a similar way by trying initially to avoid introducing bugs into a program. As logical as bug prevention might sound, a surprising number of programmers don't employ enough bug prevention strategies in their code, and they pay for it later in the debugger. Just remember that bug detection is a much more difficult task than bug prevention, so try to focus on eliminating bugs as you develop code the first time around.

Getting back to the human health analogy, you can think of bug prevention as roughly parallel to getting an immunization shot versus treating a disease after you've contracted it. Certainly the short-term pain and expense of getting the shot are much easier to deal with than the long-term suffering and treatment associated with a full-blown disease. This analogy is dangerously on target when it comes to debugging because bugs can often act like diseases in your code; just when you think you've got a bug whipped, it rears its ugly head in a new way that you never anticipated.

Now that I've hopefully gotten you excited about preventing bugs, let's look at some practical ways of doing it.

Exception Handling

One useful bug prevention mechanism built into Java is exception handling, which is a programming technique involving the detection and resolution of unexpected events that take place while a program is running, such as running out of memory. To give you a better definition, an exception is something (usually bad) that occurs in your program that you weren't expecting.

To handle exceptions in Java code, you use a try-catch construct. The try part of the construct isolates a section of code as having the potential to cause trouble. The catch part of the construct contains special code that is executed if the try code indeed causes trouble. The code in the catch clause is referred to as an exception handler because it attempts to deal with (handle) the exception.

Is This Baseball or Java?

The try-catch construct is named the way it is because when an exception occurs, it is referred to as being "thrown." Consequently, the code that handles an exception is effectively "catching" the exception and dealing with it.

Following is some code you saw in the Countdown applet back in Chapter 9, "Feeling a Little Loopy":

```
try {
  // Repaint the applet window and wait a second
  repaint();
  thread.sleep(1000);
}
catch (InterruptedException e) {
  System.out.println("Something interrupted the count!");
}
```

In this code the sleep() method is capable of throwing an exception if the thread is interrupted while sleeping. Because interrupting the sleeping thread isn't a problem in the Countdown applet, you can just display a message to standard output in the exception handler code. If the exception actually has a negative impact on the applet, you could try to include some kind of recovery code in the exception handler.

Although I've presented exception handling as a bug prevention measure, it actually isn't an option. If a method is defined as being capable of throwing an exception, you have to either handle the exception via a try-catch construct, or you have to pass the exception along for another method to deal with it; there is no way to completely ignore exceptions. The bug prevention slant comes into play when you code the exception handler. The more likely a program is to recover gracefully from exceptions, the more robust and bug free it will be.

Parentheses and Precedence

Let's shift gears and take a look at a common programming area that is highly susceptible to bugs—operator precedence. To come clean, in a few situations operator precedence bugs have bitten me, at which point I got confused and assumed the wrong operator precedence in an expression. The following code demonstrates how this can happen:

```
int x = 37, y = 26;
int z = x % 3 + y / 7 ^ 8;
```

If you happen to remember the cute phrase involving Dear Aunt Sally from Chapter 8, "Expressing Yourself in Java," then you might be able to tell me the computed value of z. Although I remember the phrase perfectly well ("Picture My Dear Aunt Sally in England"), I've still bungled code like this before. So I consider this a risky coding practice because it's simply too easy to confuse the order of evaluation of the different operators. It's all too easy to write what you think is doing one thing, but is actually doing quite another.

What's the solution? Well, the solution is to explicitly group specific operations within parentheses to force their evaluation. Following is the same example code with parentheses added to clarify the order of evaluation:

```
int x = 37, y = 26;
int z = ((x % 3) + (y / 7)) ^ 8;
```

Notice how the use of parentheses clearly identifies the order of evaluation of this expression. Additionally, this code is impervious to operator precedence because the parentheses force the evaluation of each sub-expression.

Import Restrictions

Another very common bug in Java programming is that of forgetting to import a package or class. Fortunately, this is by far the easiest bug to track down and fix. If you receive a compiler error that claims to not recognize a standard Java API class (such as Font or Color), then you know you've forgotten to import the class. You can either import the single class or the entire package in which the class resides; my preference is to import the whole package because you might end up using other classes in the package later.

Confused Parentheses

While we're on the subject of parentheses, let's consider another problem that sometimes creeps into Java code: unmatched parentheses. Parentheses always come in pairs, and the specific pairing of parentheses determines many things about the structure of a Java program, such as the order of operation. If you use an open parenthesis (() without a close parenthesis ()), or vice-versa, you will experience some very interesting compiler errors. This same rule applies to curly braces ({}), which must also be paired appropriately.

If you aren't sure to what package a standard Java class belongs, then refer to the Java API documentation, which is freely available from Sun's Java Web site (`http://java.sun.com`). For classes you've seen in this book, use the book's index to look up the class, and then observe how I used the class. Following is an example of importing the `java.awt` package, which would solve the earlier example of a compiler error based on an unrecognized `Font` or `Color` class:

```
import java.awt.*;
```

The Equal Opportunity Bug

The next bug you need to try to avoid is so prevalent that there is a programming practice specifically designed to sidestep it. I'm referring to the accidental use of the assignment (=) operator instead of the comparison (==) operator. Take a look at the following code:

```
boolean isOn = false;
if (isOn = true)
   System.out.println("The light is on!");
```

At a glance, this code looks as if it is perfectly fine, but it hides an extremely insidious bug. It is fairly rare that you would perform an assignment within an `if` conditional, which means that the conditional was intended to use the comparison (==) operator. Because the code looks a lot like it's supposed to and the compiler doesn't generate an error, this kind of bug is very hard to detect. Fortunately, there is a very simple programming practice to help keep it from occurring. Check out the modified `if` conditional:

```
if (true = isOn)
```

Unlike the first example, this code generates a compiler error because it is illegal to assign something to a literal. Of course, this particular example can be further simplified by reducing the `if` conditional to this:

```
if (isOn)
```

Members in Hiding

Although bugs were certainly commonplace prior to object-oriented programming, OOP has created opportunities for new types of insect enemies. One really tricky OOP-related bug to avoid is the hidden member variable. A hidden member variable is a member that has become "hidden" due to a derived class implementing a new variable of the exact same name. The newer member effectively hides the first member because the class will automatically reference the newer member. Many times, this isn't the intention of the programmer.

To get a better idea as to what a hidden member variable looks like, check out the following code:

```
class Weapon {
  int power;
  int numShots;

  public Weapon() {
    power = 5;
    numShots = 10;
  }

  public void fire() {
    numShots--;
  }
}

class Bazooka extends Weapon {
  int numShots;

  public Bazooka() {
    super();
  }

  public blastEm() {
    power--;
    numShots -= 2;
  }
}
```

The Weapon class defines two member variables, power and numShots. The Bazooka class is derived from Weapon and also defines a member variable named numShots, which has the effect of hiding the original numShots member inherited from Weapon. The problem with this code is that when the Weapon constructor is called by Bazooka (via the call to super()), the hidden numShots variable defined in Weapon is initialized, not the one in Bazooka. Later, when the blastEm() method is called in Bazooka, the visible numShots variable in Bazooka is used, which has a default initialization value of 0. This code could cause serious confusion because you fully expect the numShots variable to be initialized to 10.

The solution to the hidden member problem is simply to make sure that you never hide variables. In reality, it's fairly rare that you would even consider naming a variable in a derived class the same as a variable in a parent class. Just keep in mind that if you ever do, you are likely to create some inconsistencies in the code that might be hard to trace.

Sleuthing for Bugs

Unfortunately, the dedicated application of bug prevention techniques isn't always enough. It's just a fact of life that even the most astute programmers make mistakes, and the sheer complexity of some programming projects often creates bugs that slip through the prevention cracks. A little self-affirmation at times like this is all it takes to deal with the fact that you're human, and bugs are an inevitable part of life as a programmer. With that knowledge in mind, let's now look at a few techniques for detecting and hunting down bugs.

Making the Most of Standard Output

The simplest technique for tracking down bugs is simply to print information to standard output at strategic points in a program. This technique might sound a little archaic—that's because it is—but if you want a quick look into what's going on in a program, it's not a bad start. This technique is especially useful if you aren't using a graphical Java debugger. In fact, I did my fair share of standard output debugging while developing the example programs in this book because, as of this writing, none of the fancy Java development environments supported Java 2.

Standard output debugging is implemented simply by placing calls to System.out.println() at appropriate locations in your code. You can use this technique for anything from looking at the value of variables to determining when or whether a method is being called. Just make sure to watch the command-line prompt or Java console for the printed messages when running an applet that prints to standard output.

Tracking Methods

A more advanced technique for tracking down bugs involves analyzing the list of methods that were called to arrive at a given point in a program. This list of methods is referred to as the method call stack and can be readily viewed in a debugger. The method call stack often sheds light on a problem involving a method being called inadvertently or at the wrong time.

You can print the call stack to standard output by calling the printStackTrace() method, which is a member of the Throwable class. Of course, this requires you to have an object of type Throwable lying around. Well you're in luck because all exceptions are derived from Throwable, which means you can easily print the call stack when an exception is thrown. The following code shows how this is done:

```
class Test {
  public static void main (String args[]) {
    printNames();
  }
```

```
public static void printNames() {
  try {
    String[] names = { "Big Ern", "Dignan", "Max", "Vernie" };
    for (int i = 0; i <= 4; i++)
      System.out.println(names[i]);
  }
  catch (ArrayIndexOutOfBoundsException e) {
    System.out.println("Exception thrown: " + e.getMessage());
    e.printStackTrace();
  }
 }
}
```

Does the code in the try clause of the printNames() method look at all familiar? This is the same code from earlier in the chapter that indexes past the last element in an array of strings. However, this time the code is wrapped by a try clause with an exception handler that prints a call stack. Following are the results of running this application:

```
Big Ern
Dignan
Max
Vernie
Exception thrown: null
java.lang.ArrayIndexOutOfBoundsException
        at Test.printNames(Compiled Code)
        at Test.main(Test.java:7)
```

Notice that the four names are printed and then the array is improperly indexed, resulting in the exception being thrown. After the exception is thrown, the call stack is printed. The call stack reflects the methods called in order to execute the offending code. The order in which the methods appear is the reverse order in which they were executed. So, you must read from the bottom up to trace the order of the method calls.

Understanding Code Documentation

Although it is not directly related to debugging, code documentation plays an important role in effective Java programming. You've seen documented code throughout the book thus far in all of the examples, but I haven't really established a basis for its importance. Code documentation is similar to debugging in that it requires an effort that is seemingly inconsequential at the time, but later proves to be well worth the trouble.

You see, beyond the code itself, you often have nothing to describe the inner workings of a program except code documentation. And, as good as your memory might be, it never hurts to create comments that remind you of how a section of code works, just in case you have to come back and change it at some point way off in the future. Additionally, it's quite possible that someone else will eventually inherit your code, in which case that person will need to be able to understand what is going on. Solid documentation on your part will save them a great deal of time learning how your code works.

Code documentation basically boils down to inserting descriptive comments throughout a program that highlight important parts of the program. These comments can include descriptions of code issues along with suggestions for future improvements. Think of the comments in your code as sort of a diary for a program.

It is important that you understand the different types of comments at your disposal so that you can effectively document your code. The following table shows the different types of comments supported in Java:

Types of Comments Supported by Java

Type	Usage
`// comment`	All characters after `//` and to the end of the line are ignored.
`/* comment */`	All characters between `/*` and `*/` are ignored.
`/** comment */`	All characters between `/**` and `*/` are ignored, and the comment has relevance to the `javadoc` code documentation tool.

I've tried to stick with the first type of comment (`//`) throughout this book to maintain consistency and keep the code as simple as possible. The only problem with it is that it can only be used with a single line of code at a time. The second type of comment (`/* */`) works across multiple lines of code and results in the Java compiler ignoring everything appearing between the comment markers (`/* */`). For example, consider the following code:

```
/* This
   is
   a
   multi-line
   comment. */
```

This code is perfectly legal in Java because everything between the comment markers (`/* */`) is ignored by the compiler.

The third type of comment (`/** */`) works just like the second, but has the added bonus of supporting the `javadoc` code documentation tool. The `javadoc` tool comes standard with the JDK, and it is used to generate code documentation in Web page form straight from Java source code comments. You only need to use a few special tags to identify the classes, methods, and variables in your code, and the `javadoc` tool does the rest.

Automatic API Documentation

The primary benefit of the javadoc tool is that it automates the process of documenting your code for future reference. To give you an idea about the power of javadoc, consider the fact that the entire Java API documentation was automatically generated from heavily commented Java source code.

The javadoc utility is really beyond the scope of this book, but it is something I encourage you to investigate on your own as you gain more experience with Java.

The Least You Need to Know

Although as humans we aren't perfect, we can certainly make up for our programming shortcomings with diligence and a little insight into the common Java programming pitfalls. Let's recap what you learned in the chapter:

➤ A bug is a coding error that results in some unwanted action that takes place in a program.

➤ Single-stepping is the process of executing a program a line at a time, in single steps.

➤ Watch variables are variables whose contents you observe while Java code is executing in a debugger.

➤ Breakpoints act like roadblocks for program execution because a program will run until it gets to a line of code containing a breakpoint.

➤ Bug detection is a much more difficult task than bug prevention.

➤ Exception handling is a programming technique that involves the detection and resolution of unexpected events that take place while a program is running, such as running out of memory.

➤ A hidden member variable is a member that has become "hidden" due to a derived class implementing a new variable of the exact same name.

➤ The simplest technique for tracking down bugs is simply to print information to standard output at strategic points in a program.

➤ Code documentation involves inserting descriptive comments that highlight important parts of the program throughout a program.

Chapter 21

How to Win Friends at Nerd Parties

In This Chapter

➤ Writing Appealing Code

➤ Java's Many Standards

Putting a Pretty Face on Your Code

Let's face it, there is really no way to come off as being a cool Java programmer. Programming is an inherently un-cool career choice; students please take note of this fact! As I write this I'm preparing for my 10ᵗʰ year high school reunion and for the life of me, I can't figure out a way to glamorize my career. There is just no way to cultivate a hip image when your job amounts to sitting at a desk in front of a computer trying your best to communicate with it. Sure, I thought about saying I'm a "cyber-technology prognosticator," an "information leader in the world of soft computer goods," or simply "the czar of Java," with hopes of someone confusing the programming language with the island. But alas, I'm just honest enough to tell the truth and admit to being a "computer geek."

As difficult as it might be for programmers to come off as being part of a stylish profession, it is possible for us to inject style into the code we write. In fact, the style of your code in many ways determines the usefulness of the code, at least from a programming perspective. Granted, the Java compiler could care less about how your code is lined up and arranged and whether your variables have descriptive names, but it makes a huge difference when it comes to you (and others) being able to understand the code. It also might help you become a more respected member of the Java community, or at least make you the life of a nerd party when everyone brags about your incredible sense of Java programming style.

To understand what I'm talking about when I refer to Java programming style, take a look at the following Java program, which will compile perfectly well:

```
import java.applet.*;import java.text.*;import java.util.*;
import java.awt.*;public class DateTime extends Applet {
public void paint(Graphics g){DateFormat df =
DateFormat.getDateTimeInstance(DateFormat.LONG,DateFormat.SHORT);
String str = df.format(new Date());FontMetrics fm =
g.getFontMetrics();g.drawString(str, (getSize().width -
fm.stringWidth(str)) / 2,((getSize().height - fm.getHeight()) /
2) + fm.getAscent());}}
```

In case you don't recognize it, this is the same DateTime applet you built back in Chapter 4, "Constructing Applets of Your Own," with the code strung out differently. Nothing syntactical has changed in this code from the code you learned about earlier in the book, meaning that the compiler sees it as exactly the same program. However, notice how much more understandable the original version is:

```
import java.applet.*;
import java.text.*;
import java.util.*;
import java.awt.*;

public class DateTime extends Applet {
  public void paint(Graphics g) {
    // Format the current date/time
    DateFormat df = DateFormat.getDateTimeInstance(DateFormat.LONG,
      DateFormat.SHORT);
    String str = df.format(new Date());

    // Draw the date/time
    FontMetrics fm = g.getFontMetrics();
    g.drawString(str, (getSize().width - fm.stringWidth(str)) / 2,
      ((getSize().height - fm.getHeight()) / 2) + fm.getAscent());
  }
}
```

This organization of the DateTime applet code is a reflection of Java style conventions, which dictate the manner in which code is organized in a program. Let's take a moment to analyze some of the major style conventions and why they are important. Following are the most important style conventions you should try to adhere to as an aspiring Java programmer:

➤ Code indentation

➤ Effective use of white space

➤ Concise comments

➤ Meaningful names

➤ Highlighted constants

Repent and Indent

As you already know, Java relies on curly braces ({}) to mark blocks of code. It is very important, at least from a stylistic perspective, that you indent blocks of code appropriately to indicate their relationship with the rest of a program. This makes it easy to see where a block starts and ends, along with how blocks are nested within each other.

Getting more specific, it's fairly standard Java practice to place the opening curly brace in a block of code just to the right of the code prior to the block, like this:

```
for (int count = 1; count <= 10; count++) {
  System.out.println("I'm thinking of a number...");
  System.out.println(count);
}
```

The closing curly brace appears just after the last line of code in the block and lines up with the code containing the opening curly brace. Also notice that the code within the block is indented so that it appears inside of the curly braces. This indentation is critical in making block code easy to read and understand.

How Much to Indent?

The question of how much to indent has been tossed around among programmers for years and there really is no correct answer. Most programmers tend to like four spaces per indention, but I have to admit to being in the minority on this one. I think four spaces spreads code out too much horizontally, so I prefer using two spaces.

While we're on the subject of indention spaces, allow me to suggest that you stay away from using tab stops in your code. Tab stops are sometimes open to interpretation by different Java development environments and can result in indented code not lining up properly. Using spaces eliminates this potential problem because there is only one way to interpret a space. It is worth noting that some Java development environments allow you to use the Tab key to insert a given number of spaces, which is a nice feature.

Indentation doesn't apply just to blocks of code, however. The following example shows a similar `for` loop with a single statement that is indented:

```
for (int count = 1; count <= 10; count++)
   System.out.println(count);
```

White Space Is Your Friend

Because the Java compiler ignores white space in Java code (except in strings), you are free to space your code however you see fit. I will warn you that too much white space can spread out code too much and make it hard to see enough on the screen at a time. My suggestion is to use white space primarily to break up functionally different sections of code. For example, the SlideShow applet from Chapter 8, "Expressing Yourself in Java," made use of white space in its `mouseClicked()` event handler method:

```
public void mouseClicked(MouseEvent e) {
   // Move to the next slide
   if (++slideNum == SLIDETOTAL)
     slideNum = 0;

   // Draw the next slide
   repaint();
}
```

The blank line between the two sections of code in this method helps to differentiate between the two tasks the method is undertaking; it first moves to the next slide, and then it draws the slide. Also notice that comments supplement the white space by describing exactly what the code is doing.

Short and Sweet Comments

Speaking of comments, you learned in the previous chapter that comments are extremely important for making sure your code is well documented. However, you needn't go crazy with long, wordy comments that describe in intimate detail how a line of code works. Comments should usually be quick, concise explanations about how a particular line or section of code works, or the code's function. The previous example code involving the `mouseClicked()` method shows a perfect example of how short, simple comments help clarify a section of code.

Make the Most of Names

It would be impossible to develop a useful Java applet without using identifiers in your code. If you recall, identifiers are names used to uniquely identify packages, classes, interfaces, variables, and methods in Java. Although technically you are free to use any naming convention you choose, I highly recommend you use the general guidelines I describe below. These guidelines mainly have to do with the case of the identifiers for each type of language construct.

For instance, package names are always in lowercase, class and interface names are always in lowercase, but with an uppercase first letter for each word in the name. Following are a few package names:

```
java.awt.event
java.net
my.stuff
```

The first two package names are for legitimate Java API packages, while the last one is hypothetical. Now take a look at some class and interface names:

```
AudioClip
Button
SpriteVector
```

Notice how these names all begin with an uppercase letter and also include uppercase letters at the beginning of each word if the name consists of more than one word. This is standard fare for interface and class names.

Let's now move on to variables and methods, which are named very similarly. Variables and methods both adhere to a naming convention that is similar to that for interfaces and classes, except for the fact that the first letter in the name is always in lowercase. However, words after the first word in multiple word names begin with an uppercase letter. Confused? Let's look at a few examples:

```
play()
getColor()
addMouseMotionListener()
score
hitPoints
```

The first three names identify methods and adhere to the rule of the first letter being in lowercase, and the first letter in any other words appearing in the name is uppercase. The same applies to the last two names, which identify variables. This naming stuff is pretty easy after you see a few examples. If these examples aren't enough, you have all of the example code in the book to examine because it follows these conventions.

One more thing regarding names and Java—please make a big effort to use names that are as meaningful as possible. Using abstract names like x, y, and z when a set of variables really represents distance, rate, and time just doesn't make sense; go ahead and name the variables distance, rate, and time. I know it's a little more typing, but so what? I'll trade typing effort for reduced mental anguish any day! The same thing applies to naming all other Java language constructs, because descriptive names ultimately serve to make a program more readable and understandable.

Highlight All Constants

Let's cover one final issue in regard to writing stylistically appealing Java code—highlighting constants. Because constants serve a special role in representing a value that cannot change, it is important for you to distinguish them from other variables. The commonly accepted way of doing this is to name constants using all capital letters. This might seem a little extreme, but it comes in quite handy because constants will practically jump out of the code at you when they are in all uppercase. As an example, consider the following code, which uses a constant defined in the Java API:

```
double radius = 6.0;
double circumference = 2 * Math.PI * radius;
```

The PI constant defined in the Math class is a perfect example of an uppercase constant that is easy to identify in a program. The entire Java API conforms to this standard of constant naming, and I encourage you to follow its lead.

Cultivating an Appreciation of Java

Although programming style goes a long way, being a popular Java programmer involves more than just coming up with catchy variable names. In fact, one skill required of Java programmers in this day and age is being able to appreciate the many benefits Java has to offer.

One of these benefits is Java's unrelenting support for technology standards. Many of the things Java has to offer as built-in features, such as networking support, are proprietary add-ons for most other programming languages.

Following are the major areas where Java steps up to the plate to support a standard technology or accepted programming construct:

➤ Graphical User Interfaces
➤ Networking
➤ Security
➤ Threads
➤ Exceptions
➤ SQL
➤ CORBA
➤ Component Software
➤ ZIP Files

Believe it or not, few other programming languages have made it a standard, built-in feature to support any of these programming constructs and technologies. Wait a minute, you know for a fact that people use C++ to build applications with graphical user interfaces. But C++, as a language, knows nothing about graphical user interfaces. As a matter of fact, C++ by itself knows little about any of the items listed above. Is C++ a bad programming language? Absolutely not, but it does require third-party add-on APIs to write professional applications with modern features. Java comes standard with these APIs.

Java has all the necessary support for building graphical user interfaces and connecting to networks via sockets, not to mention its intense approach to handling security. You also have the capability of building multithreaded programs and handling exceptions using standard Java API interfaces and classes. This level of built-in support for modern programming constructs is unprecedented in a programming language. In case you're wondering, I promise I'm not getting paid by Sun to say any of this. I'm just trying to get the point across that Java has done a great job of keeping up with the times and giving programmers what they need.

Taking a more applied look at Java, it uses SQL (Structured Query Language) to communicate with databases and CORBA (Common Object Request Broker Architecture) to manipulate objects in distributed environments. SQL and CORBA are both very established technologies that serve as industry standards.

The last two standards Java addresses are component software and ZIP files, which are seemingly unrelated. JavaBeans, which is a part of the Java API, defines a standard for creating and using Java objects as independent software components. JavaBeans components can be integrated with visual Java development environments and used as graphical building blocks in application development. Java's support for ZIP files, also known as JAR files, enables you to compress and package a group of files into a single file for organization and efficiency. JAR files and JavaBeans cross paths because it is extremely helpful to package the classes and resources comprising a JavaBeans component into a JAR file for distribution.

ZIP? JAR? What's the Difference?

Although Java archive (JAR) files are based on the ZIP file standard, they are a little different from ZIP files. The difference is that a JAR file includes a special text file that lists information about the files contained in the archive. You can open and manipulate a JAR file in a program that supports ZIP files, but you are better off using the jar utility that comes with the JDK.

The Least You Need to Know

Being the life of a nerd party involves more than just establishing yourself as an expert in the Java language. Not only should you follow guidelines that result in more readable code, but you should also cultivate an appreciation for what Java has to offer and the standards it supports. Let's go over what you learned in this chapter:

➤ It is important to indent blocks of code appropriately to indicate their relationship with the rest of a program.

➤ Because the Java compiler ignores white space in Java code (except in strings), you can use it to break up functionally different sections of code.

➤ Comments should usually be quick, concise explanations about how a particular line or section of code works, or the code's function.

➤ The commonly accepted way of highlighting constants is to name them using all capital letters.

➤ Java's level of built-in support for modern programming constructs is unprecedented in a programming language.

Chapter 22

How to Stay On Top of Java

In This Chapter

➤ Keeping Up with Java

➤ Java Resources

Java Isn't for Slackers

Although the term has been around for some time, the 1991 movie *Slacker* made the term "slacker" a part of everyday language. In case you missed out on the movie and aren't familiar with the term, a slacker is someone who just kind of goes with the flow and isn't in any hurry to do much with their life. Although referring to someone as a slacker is certainly denigrating in most cases, it can also take on a humorous tone when referring to someone as being a little lazy. Because most of us are prone to laziness from time to time, I think most people qualify as at least part-time slackers.

Having said that, I don't encourage slackery when it comes to your new status as a Java programmer. And it's not because I'm some kind of blowhard who thinks everyone should be a Java expert. If that were the case, I'd be in the wrong profession! Anyway, the reality is that Java is an extremely fast-moving technology, and, realistically, it is impossible to keep up with it without some serious effort. Granted, you might not be concerned about the latest techno-gadget that is now Java enabled, but it helps to keep track of where Java is headed.

For example, a couple of years ago Java was useful only for building cute applets that made Web pages more interesting. I don't think too many people expected Java to become a serious contender as a professional programming language beyond the realm of the Web. Java is now making serious inroads into embedded hardware systems such as cell phones and personal digital assistants. These applications ultimately affect the future of Java and how it will evolve as a technology.

If all you ever intend to do is use Java to build applets, then it's not a big deal whether or not you keep up with every new feature Sun announces. However, there is still a wide range of technologies that will affect Java's relationship with the Web. For one, the Java Wallet stands to change the way we handle money on the Web. If you run an online store that uses Java applets, this is a very real technology you might want to consider using at some point. The point is that you should make at least a minimal effort to keep up with what's going on with Java and how future Java technologies might affect your own Java projects.

Java Resources Abound

Because we've now established that you're going to do your best to not be a Java slacker, let's turn our attention to some specific Java resources. Following are the types of resources available for learning more about Java:

➤ Web sites

➤ Books

➤ Magazines

➤ Newsgroups

I find it fun to think of my Java education as an ongoing quest for information. If you adopt this frame of mind, then you can think of the following resources as stepping stones on the path toward Java enlightenment. I know I'm being a little melodramatic here, but what the heck, learning is supposed to be fulfilling!

JavaSoft's Web Site

JavaSoft is the name of the division of Sun Microsystems that is responsible for Java. JavaSoft maintains a very comprehensive Java Web site that contains all kinds of useful information, not to mention freely available downloads of the JDK and other Java development tools and technologies. The JavaSoft Web site is located at `http://java.sun.com`. While visiting the JavaSoft Web site, I encourage you to take a look at their Java Tutorial, which serves as a great learning tool for supplementing the knowledge you've gained from this book. The Java Tutorial is located at `http://java.sun.com/docs/books/tutorial`.

The Java Developer Connection

For Java developers who are looking for more nuts and bolts about the Java programming language and API, JavaSoft has the Java Developer Connection (JDC) Web site. The JDC Web site is also the place to go to find out about upcoming Java technologies and early releases of Java software. For example, a beta version of Java 2 was available on the JDC Web site long before the final version was released on the main Java Web site. If you really want to keep up with Java, joining the JDC Web site is a must. It's free to join, but you do have to register and enter a username and password. The JDC Web site is located at `http://java.sun.com/jdc`.

Developer.com

Developer.com is a Web site devoted to all things related to software development. There is a Java section of Developer.com that is by far the most comprehensive information source for Java. Granted, JavaSoft's Web site is the official place to go for Java news, documentation, and software downloads, but Developer.com is invaluable as a means of seeing the many ways Java is being used. There are sections of Developer.com devoted to different applications of Java, so you're sure to find something of interest. It's also a great place to look for programming examples, because many of the applets referenced there include source code. The Java section of the Developer.com Web site is located at `http://java.developer.com`.

Shameless Self Promotion

You might notice that the following list of Java resources is void of any references to Java books. Because you're reading this book, I'm making the judgement that you have the ability to successfully select other books on Java. I have written some other books on Java, but I'd prefer to let you make an unbiased decision when you make a book purchase. I'd rather not have to subject you to a shameless plug for one of my books. On the other hand, if you happen to just be flipping through this book in a bookstore, then please ignore what I just said and immediately purchase this book!

Java World *Magazine*

If you're in the mood for a more journalistic Java resource, then look no further than *Java World. Java World* is an online Java magazine chock full of useful commentaries on Java, not to mention a healthy dose of programming examples. I highly recommend *Java World* as yet another means of keeping tabs on Java, along with being a great information source for sharpening your Java programming skills. *Java World* is located at `http://www.javaworld.com`.

Java Report *Magazine*

If a print magazine is more up your alley, then *Java Report* successfully fills the bill. *Java Report* is a Java magazine that is similar in some ways to *Java World*. I sometimes like the convenience of the printed page over having to peer through a Web browser, in which case I usually refer to *Java Report*. *Java Report* also has an online counterpart called *Java Report Online*, so you have the option of reading *Java Report* as a print or Web-based magazine. *Java Report Online* is located at http://www.javareport.com. The print version of *Java Report* is available at most bookstores.

Java Developer's Journal *Magazine*

OK, so maybe you're a speed reader and one print magazine just isn't enough. Thankfully, there is also *Java Developer's Journal*, which certainly has plenty to interest the aspiring Java guru. You can either pick up a print copy at a bookstore or opt for the online version, which is located at http://www.sys-con.com/java/index2.html.

The Java Newsgroups

The main newsgroup for Java discussion is comp.lang.java, but there are many more specific groups underneath this one. There is also a Web site containing a Frequently Asked Questions (FAQ) page for comp.lang.java newsgroup postings. This Web site is located at http://sunsite.unc.edu/javafaq/.

Java Applet Rating Service

After you've perused some of the aforementioned references and built a world class applet of your own, you might want to consider visiting the Java Applet Review Service, or JARS. JARS is a Web site devoted to reviewing Java applets and issuing applet ratings. You can submit your own applets for review and also review applets developed by others. This makes a good screening process if you're considering purchasing applets from others. The JARS Web site is located at http://www.jars.com.

The Least You Need to Know

It is imperative for any Java programmer to keep up with the progress of the Java technology because in many ways it is a moving target. Fortunately, there are lots of good resources out there to help you stay on top of Java and improve your Java knowledge. Let's recap what you learned in this chapter:

➤ A slacker is someone who just kind of goes with the flow and isn't in any hurry to do much with their life; lest you think I'm being judgmental, I readily admit to being a slacker from time to time.

➤ You should make at least a minimal effort to keep up with Java and how future Java technologies might affect your own Java projects.

➤ JavaSoft, the Java division of Sun Microsystems, maintains a very comprehensive Web site at `http://java.sun.com` that contains all kinds of useful information on Java.

➤ *Java World*, located at `http://www.javaworld.com`, is an online Java magazine chock full of useful commentaries and Java example code.

➤ To be fair, *Java Report* is another good Java magazine that is available in both print and online (`http://www.javareport.com`) formats.

➤ Because I'm an equal opportunity media hound, I'll also recommend *Java Developer's Journal*, yet another good Java magazine that is available in both print and online (`http://www.sys-con.com/java/index2.html`) formats.

Glossary—Speak Like a Geek

abstract class A class that contains unimplemented methods, which means you must derive from the class and implement the methods to create an instance of the class.

Abstract Windowing Toolkit (AWT) A set of classes and interfaces devoted to building graphics into Java applets and applications.

accessor method A method that gets or sets the value of a member variable.

ActiveX A family of technologies developed by Microsoft that combines computing capabilities with Internet connectivity.

Application Programming Interface (API) The set of Java packages and classes included in the Java Development Kit (JDK) that programmers use to create Java programs.

applet A graphical Java program that executes within a Web page.

applet viewer A utility included with the Java Development Kit that enables you to test applets without using a Web browser.

application A Java program that executes through a Java interpreter, independent of a Web browser.

array A special construct in Java that enables you to store a list of items of the same data type.

attribute A property of an HTML element, specified in the opening tag of the element.

block   The Java code between a pair of matching curly braces { and }.

Boolean   A data type that has a value of `true` or `false`.

JavaBeans   A Java-based technology that enables you to create self-contained, reusable software components.

bytecode   The executable form of Java code, which is capable of being executed in the Java runtime system.

canvas   A basic drawing surface on which you can perform drawing operations.

class   A template that defines the implementation of an object, effectively acting as a blueprint for the object; a class defines data and methods and is a unit of organization in a Java program.

command-line applications   Java programs that are run from a command-line such as the MS-DOS prompt in Windows; all Java programs that aren't applets are considered command-line applications.

command-line arguments   Information passed into a command-line application that controls the way the application runs.

compiler   A software program that translates human-readable source code into machine-readable code.

component   An object that performs a function within a graphical user interface.

console window   A special window in Web browsers that serves as the standard output "device" for applets; whenever an applet prints information to standard output, it appears in the console window.

constructor   A special method used to create objects of a given class.

container   A component that serves as a context for grouping together other components.

cross-platform   A term indicating that a piece of software can execute on multiple operating systems (platforms).

digital signature   A security technique that consists of attaching a code to a piece of software that identifies the vendor of the software.

double buffering   A solution to getting rid of animation flicker that involves first drawing to an offscreen image and then drawing the offscreen image to the screen without erasing the background.

encapsulation   The packaging of data together with procedures.

event   Something that happens within an object that an application or other object might want to know about and to which it might possibly react.

event adapter   A "convenience class" used to make the handling of events much cleaner.

event listener   An applet, application, or object capable of responding to events.

event source   An object capable of generating events.

event response method   A method defined in an event listener that is used to respond to event notifications sent by an event source.

event state object   An object used to store information associated with an event.

expression   A programming equation that usually involves an equal sign (=) and somehow manipulates one or more variables or values.

File Transfer Protocol (FTP)   A set of rules that governs the transfer of files between networked computers; it is the standard form of file transfer on the Internet.

flicker   A problem associated with rapid painting in an applet where the area being painted appears to flash.

garbage collection   The process by which memory allocated for objects in a program is reclaimed; Java automatically performs this process.

getter method   An accessor method that reads, or gets, the value of a member variable.

Graphics Interchange Format (GIF)   An image format that is useful for storing non-photographic images; illustrations and diagrams are great for the GIF image format.

graphical user interface (GUI)   The program elements involved in communicating with the user through visual cues, typically utilizing both the keyboard and mouse.

HotJava   A Web browser designed to execute applets written in the Java programming language.

hyperlink   A special word, phrase, or image in a Web page that jumps to another location or Web page when clicked.

Hypertext Markup Language (HTML)   The formatting language used to create Web pages.

Hypertext Transfer Protocol (HTTP)   A set of rules that governs the exchange of Web page information between a Web host and a Web client (browser).

inheritance   The ability of a class to be derived from another class, thereby forming a parent-child relationship.

inner classes   Java classes that are defined within the scope of another class; this feature is often used to make event handling easier.

interface   A group of public methods that can be implemented and then used as the basis for interacting with an object.

interpreter   A program that translates Java bytecode into native code that can execute on a given computing platform.

IP address   A number used to uniquely identify computers connected to the Internet.

Java   An object-oriented programming language that is useful for creating distributed, executable applets and applications.

Java-enabled browser   A Web browser that can execute and display Java applets.

Java Development Kit (JDK)   A standard suite of tools, utilities, and related resources used to build Java applets and applications.

Joint Photographic Experts Group (JPEG)   An image format that is useful for storing photographic images.

koi   An ornamental Japanese carp (fish) that can have very unusual color patterns and grow to nearly three feet in length.

koi pond   A pond specially designed as a home for koi; usually constructed at least three feet deep. Also serves as a great distraction for overworked Java programmers, the author included.

language-independent   A term used to indicate that a piece of software can be developed in any programming language.

layout manager   A container property that describes the way components are positioned relative to each other.

link   See *hyperlink*.

low-level event   An event fired in response to a low-level input or visual user interface interaction.

`main()` **method**   The method within a Java application that is called by the Java interpreter to run the application.

method   An isolated section of code in an object that performs a particular function.

multimedia   The general term used to describe information that we observe using more than one of our five senses, namely vision and sound.

multithreading   The capability of a program to have multiple paths of execution.

network protocol   A set of rules and standards that governs how network communication works.

object   A collection of data and the procedures (methods) that act on that data.

Object class   The class that forms the root of the Java class hierarchy, which means that it serves as the basis for all Java classes, including the classes in the Java API.

object-oriented   A term that specifies that a piece of software is composed of objects—self-contained modules that contain both data and procedures that act on the data.

object-oriented programming (OOP)   The implementation of a program using objects.

operator   A programming construct that performs an evaluation or computation on a data object or objects.

overload   To use the same name for several items in the same scope; Java methods can be overloaded.

package   A collection of reusable classes and interfaces.

parameter   A name and value pair identified by the name and value attributes of the PARAM element used inside an APPLET element. Also see *parameter list* for the definition of *parameter* as it applies to Java methods.

parameter list   The set of values passed to a method; the definition of the method describes how these values are manipulated.

pixel   The smallest graphical unit within an image; each pixel in an image is square in shape and is assigned a color.

random access file   A file structured as an array of bytes that you can read from or write to at any location within the file.

semantic event   An event fired when an action occurs that is based on the semantics of a particular object.

setter method   An accessor method that writes, or sets, the value of a member variable.

sprite   A graphical object that moves around on top of a background.

sprite animation   A simple form of animation that consists of graphical objects (sprites) that move around on top of a background.

socket   A "fitting" used to connect a stream of network data to a program.

software component   A piece of software isolated into a discrete, easily reusable structure.

standard input   A Java object used to retrieve information from the standard input device, usually the keyboard.

standard output   A Java object used to send information to the standard output device, usually a command-line prompt (applications) or a console window (applets).

string   A series of characters.

tag   The HTML code used to define part of an HTML element.

token   The smallest code element in a program that is meaningful to the compiler.

thread   The basic unit of program execution; a program can have several threads running concurrently, each performing a different task.

thread synchronization   The structuring of threads so that they never interrupt each other at inopportune times.

Transmission Control Protocol/Internet Protocol (TCP/IP)   The set of protocols used for network communication on the Internet.

uniform resource locator (URL)   A text address used to identify sites on the Internet.

visual component   A type of software component with a visual representation that requires physical space on the display surface of a parent container.

Z-order   The screen depth of a sprite, which is used to determine how sprites overlap each other.

Installing the Java Development Kit (JDK)

The Java Development Kit, or JDK, is currently available directly from Sun Microsystems in versions for Windows and Solaris. Ported versions of the JDK are available for other platforms such as Macintosh, but they aren't supported by Sun. The following Web site contains information about these ports of the JDK along with how to download them:

```
http://java.sun.com/cgi-bin/java-ports.cgi
```

To obtain the Windows or Solaris version of the JDK, you can simply visit Sun's JDK Web site:

```
http://java.sun.com/products/jdk
```

Sun's JDK Web site contains versions of the JDK that you can download and install. Both the Windows and Solaris versions of the JDK are distributed as self-installing applications. However, there are a few environment settings necessary to properly configure the JDK tools. Namely, there are two environment variables, PATH and CLASSPATH, that determine how the JDK tools are accessed and used.

The PATH environment variable is referenced by your operating system to determine where to look for executable applications. The bin directory within the JDK installation should be added to the PATH variable so that all of the JDK tools can be executed from any directory.

The CLASSPATH environment variable is used to notify JDK tools and some other Java programs where they can find support classes. If you're using any classes that aren't in the directory of a dependent class you're compiling, then you'll need to include the directory where the classes are located in the CLASSPATH variable. If you don't have any support classes of your own that you are referencing from another directory, then you don't need to worry about setting the CLASSPATH variable.

If You Don't Set CLASSPATH...

If you don't set the CLASSPATH environment variable, the JDK will assume all user classes are located in the current directory. Standard Java API classes will still be correctly found, though. In fact, these classes are always found regardless of the CLASSPATH setting.

The remainder of this appendix focuses on installing the JDK on the Windows and Solaris platforms.

Installing the JDK on a Windows Computer

After you've downloaded the Windows JDK from Sun's Java Web site, all you need to do is execute the downloaded file to install the JDK. So, if the name of the downloaded file is jdk12-win32.exe, for example, then you just double-click the file in Explorer or enter the following at the MS-DOS command line:

```
jdk12-beta4-win32
```

The JDK installation will then continue, prompting you a few times to clarify options such as the installation directory. You can accept all of the default settings for installing the JDK. After the JDK finishes installing, you need to set the PATH and CLASSPATH variables as mentioned earlier in the appendix. There are three ways to do this in Windows:

1. Use the set command from an MS-DOS command line.
2. Use the set command in the autoexec.bat file.
3. Edit the environment variables using the Environment tab in the System control panel (Windows NT).

I recommend the second approach if you're using Windows 95/98, or the third approach if you're using Windows NT. The first approach is temporary and won't serve you too well in the long run. Following is the line in my autoexec.bat file that sets the PATH environment variable:

```
set PATH=%PATH%;c:\jdk1.2beta4\bin
```

This code actually results in the JDK's bin directory being appended to my existing PATH variable. Just be sure to change the JDK directory to reflect the version of the JDK you have installed; my example PATH setting is based on the beta 4 release of Java 2.

Installing the JDK on a Solaris Computer

The Solaris installation instructions parallel those for the Windows installation. After downloading the Solaris JDK from Sun's Java Web site, you must execute the downloaded file to install the JDK. You can do this by entering the filename at a command line. The JDK installation will then begin, prompting you a few times to clarify options such as the installation directory. You can accept all of the default settings for installing the JDK.

After the JDK finishes installing, you need to set the PATH and CLASSPATH variables as mentioned earlier in this appendix. There are two ways to do this in Solaris:

1. Use the setenv command from a command line.
2. Use the setenv command in your shell startup file.

I recommend the second approach because the first approach is temporary and probably won't serve your purposes in the long run.

Setting PATH and CLASSPATH Is Different in the sh and ksh Shells

Use PATH=/usr/local/bin;export PATH

Java Tools & Technologies

Visual Development Tools

If the JDK just isn't a high-caliber enough development tool for you, then you might want to consider trying a visual development tool. There are a variety of different visual development tools available for Java, all of which share reasonably similar features. Visual development tools typically have a modern visual user interface and a complete integration of Java compiler, debugger, and so on. Below is a list of the most popular Java development tools, along with their respective Web sites:

> ➤ Symantec's Visual Café—http://www.symantec.com/domain/cafe/vc4java.html
> ➤ Metrowerks Code Warrior Gold—http://www.metrowerks.com/
> ➤ Kawa—http://www.tek-tools.com/
> ➤ Supercede—http://www.supercede.com/
> ➤ Sun's Java Workshop and Java Studio—http://shop.sun.com/
> ➤ Microsoft's Visual J++—http://msdn.microsoft.com/visualj/
> ➤ INPRISE's JBuilder—http://www.inprise.com/jbuilder/

Some of the Web sites listed above contain evaluation versions of the development environments, which gives you an opportunity to try out the tool before you buy it. This can be very useful in comparing the tools with each other and making a more informed purchase decision.

Clash of the Java Titans

It's worth pointing out that as of this writing, Microsoft's Visual J++ product is in the middle of a lawsuit between Microsoft and Sun. Sun claims Microsoft's implementation of Java doesn't adhere to the Java licensing agreement. At the root of the lawsuit is a set of Windows-specific Java extensions that are part of Microsoft's Java implementation. Sun is suing Microsoft in an attempt to force them to ship a 100 percent pure Java product with no specific ties to Windows. Tune in to *JavaWorld* magazine's Net News Central Web site at `http://www.javaworld.com/javaworld/netnews/netnews.index.html` for late breaking news on this and other Java happenings.

Java Technologies

In addition to visual development tools, you might also be interested in learning about some Java technologies that you are likely to encounter sooner or later. Following is a list of some of the most popular Java-related technologies, along with Web sites where you can go to find out more information:

➤ JavaBeans—`http://java.sun.com/beans/`

➤ JavaScript—`http://www.webdeveloper.com/categories/javascript/`

➤ Java Foundation Classes—`http://java.sun.com/products/jfc/`

➤ Microsoft SDK for Java—`http://www.microsoft.com/java/sdk/`

➤ Java Electronic Commerce—`http://java.sun.com/products/commerce/`

➤ HotJava Browser—`http://java.sun.com/products/hotjava/`

➤ JavaOS—`http://www.sun.com/javaos/`

➤ Jini—`http://java.sun.com/products/jini/`

Index

X-Y-Z

Using Java 1.2

Michael Morgan

Using Java 1.2 is a task-based reference that uses clear organization, step-by-step tasks, abundant code samples, and new cross-indexing techniques to teach Java 1.2. This book covers the Java 1.2 language, APIs, class libraries, and programming tools. It also explains how to upgrade from earlier releases of Java. *Using Java 1.2* accomplishes these goals by anticipating the needs of the user and providing strong navigation and accessibility to the content. Java 1.2 is a major upgrade for the Java programming language, and this book serves as the definitive reference to get the user to the next programming level. It also helps inexperienced readers quickly become skilled Java programmers. A hands-on, practical approach and well-documented code examples ensure that readers understand and learn Java programming techniques. *Using Java 1.2* is written by a professional Java programmer and trainer who has used his classroom experience to write the best introduction to Java available.

$29.99 US/$42.95 CDN
0-7897-1627-5 Que

Internet-Programming: Beginner - Intermediate
864 pp.

Using Visual J++ 6.0

Scott Mulloy

Using Visual J++ 6.0 is a task-based reference that uses clear organization, step-by-step tasks, abundant code samples, and new cross-indexing techniques to teach Visual J++. This book covers all aspects of using Visual J++ to build a wide range of Java applets and applications, ActiveX objects, COM/DCOM objects, and more. The book also covers some of the more advanced features of the Java 1.2 language. *Using Visual J++ 6.0* accomplishes these goals by anticipating the needs of the user, providing strong navigation and accessibility to the content, and helping inexperienced readers quickly learn Visual J++. The hands-on, practical approach and well-documented code examples ensure that readers understand and learn Java programming techniques.

$29.99 US/$42.95 CDN
0-7897-1400-0 Que

Web Site Programming: Beginner - Intermediate
800 pp.

Sams Teach Yourself Visual J++ 6 in 21 Days

Rick Leinecker

Sams Teach Yourself Visual J++ 6 is an easy-to-use tutorial that breaks down the tasks of learning Visual J++ into 21 focused lessons. Readers learn through clear explanations of concepts, structured step-by-step tasks, and abundant code samples. This book covers all aspects of using Visual J++ to build a wide range of Java applets and applications, ActiveX objects, COM/DCOM objects, and more. The hands-on, practical approach and well-documented code examples ensure that readers understand and learn Visual J++ programming techniques. This book is an excellent companion to the #1 Java tutorial *Sams Teach Yourself Java in 21 Days*.

$29.99 US/$42.95 CDN
0-672-31351-0 Sams

Web Site Programming: Beginner - Intermediate
600 pp.

Special Edition Using Java 2 Platform

Joe Weber

This book is the programmer's tutorial/reference on Java 2 and contains detailed descriptions of Sun's Java 2 standards, APIs, class libraries, and programming tools. *Special Edition Using Java 2 Platform* covers major third-party products like Microsoft's Java SDK 2.0, AFC, and RNI products, which are rapidly gaining popularity. This book contains step-by-step instructions for developers on how to create channels that broadcast sound and video and how to charge users for accessing them. It covers other relevant Sun, Microsoft, and OMG technologies for Java and ActiveX, including CORBA, Java IDL, Joe, JavaBeans, and Enterprise JavaBeans. *Special Edition Using Java 2 Platform* also provides Web developers with tools to make information on their sites easily accessible to users, and tips to make the tools more efficient. This book contains more than 20,000 lines of documented Java code that show programmers the details of building sophisticated Java applications. It also contains all the tools necessary to get started, including a CD-ROM of JavaScript code, Java applets, style sheets, and templates. This book also contains complete tutorials and references for experienced users as well as a wealth of professional programming techniques and work-arounds. Netscape Netcaster is a new component of the Communicator package that implements "passive browsing" by collecting information from the Web and making it available immediately to the user.

$49.99 US/$71.95 CDN
0-7897-2018-3 Que

Internet-Programming: Accomplished - Expert
1200 pp.

Sams Teach Yourself JBuilder 2 in 21 Days

Don Doherty

Sams Teach Yourself JBuilder 2 in 21 Days is a tutorial in the format of the other bestselling *Sams Teach Yourself* books. Because JBuilder's programming language is Java, *Sams Teach Yourself JBuilder 2 in 21 Days* also teaches the reader how to program with Java within the JBuilder development environment, touching on the Java fundamentals and the object-oriented approach, and does not assume the reader already knows Java. JBuilder 2 is Borland International's updated graphical development environment that uses the Java programming language and is compatible with Sun's JDK 1.2. JBuilder has built an excellent reputation in the Java development market in the tradition of Delphi and C++ Builder. With its updated capabilities and release timed with Sun's JDK 1.2, it should gain even more ground in version 2.

$39.99 US/$57.95 CDN
0-672-31318-9 Sams

Internet-Programming
700 pp.

Add to Your Sams Library Today with the Best Books for Programming, Operating Systems, and New Technologies

To order, visit our Web site at www.mcp.com or fax us at

1-800-835-3202

ISBN	Quantity	Description of Item	Unit Cost	Total Cost
0-7897-1627-5		Using Java 1.2	$29.99	
0-7897-1400-0		Using Visual J++ 6.0	$29.99	
0-672-31351-0		Sams Teach Yourself Visual J++ 6 in 21 Days	$29.99	
0-7897-2018-3		Special Edition Using Java 2 Platform	$49.99	
0-672-31318-9		Sams Teach Yourself JBuilder in 21 Days	$39.99	
		Shipping and Handling: See information below.		
		TOTAL		

Shipping and Handling

Standard	$5.00
2nd Day	$10.00
Next Day	$17.50
International	$40.00

201 W. 103rd Street, Indianapolis, Indiana 46290   1-800-835-3202 — FAX

Book ISBN 0-7897-2131-7